borrowedtime

borrowed time

Two Centuries of Booms, Busts, and Bailouts at Citi

James Freeman and
Vern McKinley

HARPER
BUSINESS

An Imprint of HarperCollins*Publishers*

For Nona, Ruben, Catherine, Will, Neal, Jane, and Jack.

HarperCollins books may be purchased for educational, business, or sales promotional use. For information, please email the Special Markets Department at SPsales@harpercollins.com.

FIRST EDITION

Designed by Fritz Metsch

Library of Congress Cataloging-in-Publication Data

Names: Freeman, James (Journalist), author. | McKinley, Vern, author.
Title: Borrowed time: Citi, moral hazard, and the too-big-to-fail myth / James Freeman and Vern McKinley.
Description: First edition. | New York, NY: HarperCollins, [2018] | Includes bibliographical references and index.
Identifiers: LCCN 2018009514 (print) | LCCN 2018011256 (ebook) | ISBN 9780062669889 (ebk) | ISBN 9780062669872 (hc: alk. paper)
Subjects: LCSH: Citigroup (Firm) | Banks and banking—United States. | Bank failures—United States—Prevention. | Bailouts (Government policy)—United States. | Financial crises—United States.
Classification: LCC HG2613.N54 (ebook) | LCC HG2613.N54 C72245 2018 (print) | DDC 332.10973—dc23
LC record available at https://lccn.loc.gov/2018009514

18 19 20 21 22   LSC   10 9 8 7 6 5 4 3 2 1

Contents

Introduction

D"on't let it fail," said President George W. Bush. It was a cold and cloudy day in Washington on November 19, 2008. But the climate was even worse in New York's financial markets, where investors were increasingly betting that one of the world's best-known companies wasn't going to make it. Shares of Citigroup, a $2 trillion financial behemoth, plunged 23 percent that day, and were down a full 88 percent since May 2007. An American president who had seemed to understand the value of competition wasn't willing to let a Wall Street giant lose. "Just don't let Citi fail," he told Treasury Secretary Hank Paulson.

Mr. Paulson tells this story in his memoir of the financial crisis. But it's a story that has unfolded time and again in the century since the federal government began standing behind Citi. The bank's rescuers have included politicians and regulators of both parties. A striking number of them didn't believe that Citi deserved its bailouts and doubted whether it could be reformed after taxpayers helped it back from the financial ledge. Some even doubted whether the rescues were necessary. But what they all had in common was that they just couldn't manage to say no.

A few short months after President Bush's Oval Office directive to save the bank, Citigroup CEO Vikram Pandit was back in front of regulators seeking yet another bailout. "Don't give up on us," he pleaded with a senior federal official.[1] The government never does.

For obvious reasons, Citi's serial bailouts can be infuriating to taxpayers. But what may not be fully appreciated by the public or the press is how destructive the bailout culture connecting Wall Street and Washington can be for the economy and even for the institutions that directly benefit from it. This last point may seem a stretch, given that the company we now call Citigroup is more than two hundred years old and remains one of the largest financial institutions in the world. But our study of Citi's two centuries reveals that the bank was in many ways healthier and more stable during the century when it was independent than it has been during the roughly one hundred years in which it has been helped and guided by the federal government.

During the bank's era of serial bailouts, Citi has often been presented as the victim of events beyond its control—a broader financial panic, unforeseen economic disruptions overseas, or perhaps a perfect storm of credit expansion, private greed, and public incompetence. But through much of its history, Citi not only didn't fall victim to business cycles or financial crises, it actually thrived when others faltered. It became a banking giant precisely because it had the strength to seize opportunities—and new customers—in periods of panic.

As for the economic benefits of bailouts, which are after all undertaken in the name of saving the economy, to this day it remains impossible to prove that the nation's financial system couldn't live without Citi or the other financial giants. On the contrary, a sober look back at the financial panic of 2008, informed by eyewitness accounts, turns up new reasons to question the favored status of the banks labeled too big to fail. Can anyone name a single Citi service that couldn't be provided by other companies? And what price are we paying in terms of lost economic growth and innovation by keeping deeply flawed incumbents atop the financial world?

These questions, and in fact any kind of thorough inquiry about Citi, are most unwelcome to the nation's regulatory establishment. We've lately had as much trouble trying to pry records about government assistance to Citi in the 1920s out of the Federal Reserve as many reporters did trying to obtain key information about 2008. The history of instability and government support at Citi is not a story Washington wants to tell—or help others tell. This may be why not a single book has focused on Citi and its serial crises, even as multiple books have covered smaller institutions that received far less federal help. The fact that Citi has not received comparable attention may seem especially odd, given the frantic response of its rescuers to its impending doom in late 2008. Treasury Secretary Paulson declared that Citi must not be allowed to fail because, in his view, "If Citi isn't systemic, I don't know what is." Citigroup received the most generous government assistance of any bank during the crisis, with capital injections of $45 billion as well as hundreds of billions of dollars of additional help in the form of commercial paper sales, asset guarantees, debt guarantees, and liquidity assistance.

The story of Citi simply does not fit Washington's explanation of the crisis. Financial regulators and the Wall Street megabanks they oversee like to say the crisis was concentrated in the so-called shadow banking system, the gray area occupied by nonbank financial institutions that were outside the more heavily regulated commercial banking sector. Much of the attention and debate regarding troubled institutions has focused on the failures or near-failures of the nonbank troika of Bear Stearns, Lehman Brothers, and AIG. The 2010 Dodd-Frank Act was sold as a way to give regulators important powers they didn't previously have, to oversee such large, risky firms outside of commercial banking.

But because Citigroup was a federally regulated bank holding company containing a federally insured bank, it was already subject to the full range of supervisory authorities. It had not one but multiple federal banking agencies already overseeing its activities. And perhaps most embarrassing of all to the regulatory establishment, it was specifically overseen by the Federal Reserve Bank of New York and its chief Timothy Geithner, a principal architect of financial crisis policies during both the Bush and Obama administrations. It was for President Obama that Mr. Geithner served as Treasury secretary, and when he stepped down, he was replaced by a former Citi employee named Jack Lew. Don't count on him to expose the full dimensions of this disaster.

THE FINANCIAL markets can be a rough place, so one could argue that any business lasting so long must be doing something right. And the bank certainly did a lot right in its first one hundred years, although at its origin in 1812, Citi was more like the politically connected operation we see today than the market success it would become for much of the nineteenth century. Created just two days before the start of the War of 1812 and a year after the closing of the First Bank of the United States, City Bank of New York was conceived to serve the needs of both Washington and Wall Street.

Of course, back then Wall Street looked a lot more like Main Street. Before lower Manhattan became the world's financial center, it was a center for merchants and traders who wanted credit. Without the First Bank of the United States, both New York's merchant class and the relatively young national government saw the need for a new provider of financial services. The New Yorkers in particular wanted Gotham to compete with Baltimore, Boston, and Philadelphia as a banking center.

At its start, the bank we now call Citi was no obscure garage start-up. Many of the bank's initial stockholders had owned stock in the First Bank of the United States. Citi's first president, Samuel Osgood, had been a member of the Continental Congress and America's first postmaster general. The bank's creation was intensely political as rival factions in the New York state assembly— each aligned with factions in the federal government—competed in a lobbying battle for a state charter. Legislators eventually struck a compromise whereby the faction aligned with President James Madison and the rival group affiliated with Vice President George Clinton each secured a number of board seats in the new enterprise. Though Clinton died two months before the birth of the bank, rival politicos were able to come together in the pursuit of personal, civic, and sovereign advantage.

Just as today, Citi at its inception was deeply intertwined with the national government—with benefits for both parties. Early investors sought to profit from their alliance with Washington, while City Bank provided critically needed financing for the government to mount a national defense, as well as depository services. This meant the bank was significantly wounded by the founding of the Second Bank of the United States just a few years after City's founding. A private investor allowed it to survive into the 1820s.

Unlike in our current era of too-big-to-fail banks, when the Panic of 1837 proved too much for City to bear, there was no taxpayer bailout. John Jacob Astor, perhaps the country's richest person at the time, bought a piece of the bank and provided desperately needed capital. As important, he installed his protégé Moses Taylor on City Bank's board. Taylor would eventually lead the bank beginning in the 1850s through decades of stability and success. In striking contrast to the government-backed modern Citi, which has careened through long periods of serial crises, the nineteenth-century version of the bank seems to have absorbed the lessons of its 1837 near-collapse and did not repeat the mistakes that required a private rescue.

Astor the rescuer was New York City's preeminent real estate magnate. Unlike later Manhattan real estate titans like Donald Trump, the frugal Astor carried little debt and had the ready cash in a crisis to buy a controlling stake in the bank. Astor's man Taylor was similarly focused on earning steady profits rather than headlines. In 1919, financial historian John Moody wrote that Taylor's "cash reserve was his pride" and said of the bank that "with every panic it grew stronger." Unlike some more recent members of the Citi executive team, Taylor didn't seem to suffer from Potomac Fever. According to Anna Robeson Brown Burr, Taylor turned down the job of Treasury secretary during Reconstruction.

Taylor held to the view that he "must not spend a dollar unless absolutely necessary." To modern taxpayers, he might appear reassuringly boring. And that describes much of the nineteenth century at the bank. In contrast to the modern politicized Citi, which tends to falter during times of financial stress, the old bank thrived even as the US suffered numerous financial panics after the Civil War. The firm that would become Citibank grew its assets, its loans, and its profits—not too quickly, but reliably.

Taylor was not simply a banker but an activist investor and a sort of amiable corporate raider who would lend money and acquire stock in struggling industrial companies and then over time exercise control and install his own management team. "The friendly tone of many of the letters to Taylor suggest that he may have been less voracious than other New York financiers of the period," according to the New York Public Library, which houses Taylor's papers.

Upon Taylor's death, control passed to his son-in-law Percy Pyne, a low-key and cautious executive. In the era before taxpayers were standing behind the company, risk-taking was not very appealing.

Pyne's successor, James Stillman, was the Rockefeller family's favorite banker. Swelling deposits from Standard Oil and other customers who moved their money out of weaker banks helped make City Bank the country's largest savings institution. The bank also moved much closer to Washington as it helped finance the Spanish-American War. The good times at City wouldn't last. In the twentieth century, with increasing support and direction from the federal government, the good times would be replaced by great times and terrible times, a recurring cycle of exciting booms and horrific busts.

The bank's risk-taking in the 1920s inspired Senator Carter Glass to blame City Bank CEO "Sunshine Charlie" Mitchell "more than any fifty men" for the stock market crash of 1929. Ironically—or perhaps not—a future chairman of the Executive Committee at Citi, Robert Rubin, would lead the effort seventy years later to rewrite the senator's signature Glass-Steagall Act, which sought among other things to limit risk-taking at federally insured banks. In the late 1990s, Citi was actually in violation of Glass-Steagall until Rubin, then the US Treasury secretary, helped engineer a new law that made Citi compliant. Between the time the legislation was originally introduced and its enactment, Citi hired him to serve as a highly compensated executive with "no line responsibilities." He went on to advise the executives who *did* have responsibilities to ramp up the firm's risks in the years leading up to the financial crisis.

Citi needed serial government bailouts in 2008 and 2009 to stay afloat. This was nothing new at Citi, and sometimes the governments doing the rescuing haven't even been ours. Saudi prince Al-waleed bin Talal in the 1990s and an Abu Dhabi sovereign wealth fund in 2007 also provided life rafts to the bank. Prior to the 1990s, it was usually Uncle Sugar that helped out whenever Citi ran into trouble, especially after Walter Wriston ascended to the top of City Bank in the 1960s. But he had his own issues with foreign governments. Among the most influential bankers of his or any era, he is perhaps most famous for wildly overestimating the creditworthiness of developing countries.

During the financial panic of 2008 and in the years since, financial reporters, bank executives, and politicians liked to discuss the unprecedented nature of that crisis. But as you'll see in the pages to come, disasters have been relatively frequent during the century of government-protected banking—especially at Citi.

borrowedtime

A Bank for the Treasury Secretary

J ust as the financial crisis was beginning to flare in 2008, Citigroup hired Sanjiv Das to be CEO of the giant bank's $300 billion mortgage unit. More than a few people asked him why he had agreed to accept such an assignment. He may have been wondering the same thing as he took a cab to Citi's headquarters, then located at 399 Park Avenue in New York City.

It was to be his very first day on the job, and Das was enjoying a pleasant conversation with the taxi driver, a fellow immigrant from India. Das began to describe his new role at the bank. "Just my luck," the taxi driver interjected. "I have some keys I need to give you." The driver then produced two house keys and handed them to Citi's new mortgage boss. "Your guys sold me the loans to flip these houses." The cabbie then politely elaborated that with the market cratering, he was unable to sell the homes and, since he could not possibly afford to pay the mortgages, he would simply hand the properties back to Citi.

Das was incredulous that his new employer had given two mortgages to the cheerful speculator behind the wheel of the taxi. But the story got worse. The driver helpfully explained that while he only had two mortgages from Citi, he also had three other mortgages from rival financial institutions. Perhaps he was hoping to meet other bank CEOs—and return more keys—as he ferried executives around Manhattan.

With the keys jangling in his pocket, Das arrived for his first meeting with Citigroup's board of directors. He recalls walking into the room and seeing arrayed around the conference room "all the glitterati that had led them off the cliff." Das reports that director Robert Rubin never looked up from the BlackBerry device in his hands while asking, "How the f— do we get out of this problem?"

Das says that he walked over to Rubin and handed him the keys he had just received from the cabbie with five mortgages. Das then promised to propose a solution to Citi's mortgage problem "if you tell me how the f— you got in it."

The explanation will take a while.

Our story begins more than two centuries ago. Even more than in 2008—when Citi was led by politically connected directors like former US Treasury secretary Rubin—the bank at its founding was a creature of politics. It was quite literally a creation of government.

But Citi could only come into being after another government creation was allowed to die. Ironically, although Citi is a classic example of a bank considered too big to fail by Washington politicians and regulators, Citi exists only because lawmakers of the early nineteenth century decided to close a bank with a much larger role in the nation's financial system. In 1811, Congress decided not to renew the expiring charter of the First Bank of the United States, and the reasons had a lot to do with unresolved questions about its founding twenty years earlier.

Back in 1791, America's first secretary of the Treasury, Alexander Hamilton, had won the political argument for a national bank. But he had not necessarily won the intellectual argument. And the legal argument would not be won until fifteen years after his death with the unanimous decision of the Supreme Court in *McCulloch v. Maryland*.

Hamilton did manage to persuade Congress and President Washington that creating a national bank largely owned by private investors would help facilitate both public and private finance. What was more difficult was clearly demonstrating that the new federal government had the authority to do so. Where in America's new governing document did the feds enjoy the power to create a financial firm—or any other kind of corporation for that matter? Bank advocates argued that the power to create the bank was implicit in the new Constitution, and usually pointed to several phrases in Article I, Section 8 in making their case:

> The Congress shall have Power To lay and collect Taxes, Duties, Imposts and Excises, to pay the Debts and provide for the common Defence and general Welfare of the United States . . .
> To borrow Money on the credit of the United States;
> To regulate Commerce with foreign Nations, and among the several States . . .
> To coin Money . . .
> To make all Laws which shall be necessary and proper for carrying into Execution the foregoing Powers, and all other Powers vested by this Constitution in the Government of the United States . . .

Bank opponents, who included Representative James Madison, argued that while a government-created national bank might make it easier to exercise many of these powers, it wasn't necessary. They also saw an invitation to future mischief in the argument that a federal government of limited and enumerated powers also enjoyed other powers that weren't enumerated.

Secretary of State Thomas Jefferson warned of a banking monopoly and pointed out that authorization to create corporations and specifically banks had been debated and rejected during the drafting of the Constitution, so this authority could hardly be implicit. The issue was certainly not a new one. In 1781, long before the Constitution was drafted, the Congress operating under the Articles of Confederation had created a Bank of North America. But as with the First Bank of the United States, it seems that legislators had been more eager to solve financial problems than convinced of their authority to fix them. (Historians have debated whether one or the other or perhaps neither of these early institutions should be considered America's first central bank.)[1]

Ten years later, before President Washington signed the bill to create the First Bank of the United States, he separately asked Jefferson and Attorney General Edmund Randolph for their opinions. Jefferson warned:

> I consider the foundation of the Constitution as laid on this ground: That "all powers not delegated to the United States, by the Constitution, nor prohibited by it to the States, are reserved to the States or to the people." . . . To take a single step beyond the boundaries thus specially drawn around the powers of Congress, is to take possession of a boundless field of power, no longer susceptible of any definition.

Jefferson elaborated on the danger of perverting the "necessary and proper" clause into a vehicle to get around the Constitution's limits on federal power:

> . . . the Constitution allows only the means which are "necessary," not those which are merely "convenient" for effecting the enumerated powers. If such a latitude of construction be allowed to this phrase as to give any non-enumerated power, it will go to everyone, for there is not one which ingenuity may not torture into a convenience in some instance or other, to some one

of so long a list of enumerated powers. It would swallow up all the delegated powers . . . Therefore it was that the Constitution restrained them to the necessary means, that is to say, to those means without which the grant of power would be nugatory.[2]

Jefferson was a longtime philosophical rival of Hamilton and a reliable opponent of a strong central government. He was also generally suspicious of bankers, so his opposition was unsurprising. But Attorney General Randolph, who often straddled the philosophical divide between Jefferson and Hamilton, also concluded that the bank was unconstitutional. Since Randolph was the senior legal expert in the executive branch, his opinion on the legality of Hamilton's plan might have been expected to carry great weight. It certainly could not have been easy to ignore the clear logic in Randolph's letter to Washington:

"The phrase, 'and proper,' if it has any meaning, does not enlarge the powers of Congress, but rather restricts them . . ."[3]

Washington signed the bill anyway. Like most members of Congress, he wanted an institution to issue paper money, provide a safe place to keep public funds, collect the government's tax revenue, and provide commercial banking services for the burgeoning American economy. Hamilton largely modeled his creation on the Bank of England. While the elected lawmakers of the United States approved the idea, they perhaps wondered if the critics were right and gave the new Bank of the United States an expiration date. The bank would need to cease operations in twenty years if another law wasn't enacted to extend its charter.

It was a victory for Hamilton but also a threat to his wealth. His original design had been for a national bank based in Philadelphia and without branches in other cities. When lawmakers instead drafted the bill to include various branches he unsuccessfully argued against the idea. Publicly he expressed concern that mis-management of a single branch could hurt the reputation of the entire system, but he had a strong private incentive to hold this position. Hamilton was the founder of the Bank of New York and likely hoped that his bank would be the exclusive fiscal agent of the federal government in New York City.[4] Once it was clear that the new national bank would be handling that assignment with a new branch in Manhattan, perhaps he began to wonder if Jeffer-son was right about a new financial monopoly. Bank opponents had warned that a competitor created by the national government would threaten the three existing state-chartered banks as well as other state banks chartered in the future.[5]

On the day it opened for business in Philadelphia, Decem-ber 12, 1791, the First Bank of the United States did not just in-stantly become the country's largest bank. It was also by far the largest corporation of any kind. It enjoyed a capitalization of $10 million, "more than four times as much as that of the three existing banks combined and far more than the amount of all the gold and silver in the country."[6]

It's wrong for the government to pick winners and losers. But there's an old saying that when the government picks a winner—bet on it. Private investors did, supplying 80 percent of the bank's initial capital. The government bought the other 20 percent of the bank by issuing $2 million in federal bonds. The board of the new First Bank of the United States consisted of private directors rather than government appointees. While Hamilton preferred a strong central government, he didn't trust it to safeguard the young na-tion's currency. This is why he didn't want to leave the printing of money up to Congress or to his own Treasury department. "Hamilton saw the requirement that the Bank of the United States be a profit-making institution as a way to control the govern-ment's temptation to issue notes not backed by gold and silver," writes Thomas K. McCraw,[7] who adds that the "tendency to print money had run amok during the Revolution."

Hamilton wanted self-interested bankers rather than political actors looking after the issuance of paper, which he said was "an operation so much easier than the laying of taxes that a government, in the practice of paper emissions, would rarely fail in any such emergency to indulge itself too far."[8] The US government in our own time has certainly indulged itself when it comes to paper emissions. As we write, the Federal Reserve is presiding over a balance sheet of more than $4 trillion, which in turn helps the Treasury to operate with $20 trillion in debt—and that's just the debt that Uncle Sam formally acknowledges, never mind all the unfunded promises stretching far into the future. A question posed by Hamilton remains just as hard to answer more than two centuries later, as it was in his time: "What nation was ever blessed with a constant succession of upright and wise Administrators?"[9]

But in curing one problem, did Hamilton create others? In our own time, and specifically during the 2008 financial crisis, Americans saw the destruction that can occur when government anoints particular profit-seeking firms to carry out public missions like financing home purchases or evaluating credit risks. Back in Hamilton's day, the questions from critics largely focused on whether the government should advantage one institution instead of allowing an open market. The private investors who bought stakes in the First Bank of the United States enjoyed a wealth of advantages over existing and potential competitors, and not just because their new bank carried the imprimatur of the national government. It was the only bank that had a federal charter, and in short order it held most of the federal government's deposits. Its notes, based on commercial credit, were circulated as legal tender throughout the country. Paper from state-chartered banks wasn't as widely accepted.

Also, while the new national bank could open offices in different cities, the state-chartered competitors were "unit banks"—single locations without additional branches. The new national bank didn't have the explicit regulatory authority or responsibility for conducting monetary policy enjoyed by modern central banks like the Federal Reserve. But Jefferson argued that the new bank had de facto regulatory power because it could set standards regardless of what state laws said. And states were prohibited from taxing the First Bank of the United States.[10]

The new institution functioned both as a private commercial bank and as the fiscal agent for the Treasury. It was both a creditor and a debtor of the government, holding federal debt as well as federal deposits. The First Bank of the United States was also an emergency lender, but for the government, not for private financial institutions as the Fed is today.[11]

The model worked for investors as the bank immediately assumed a dominant position in American finance. By 1800 the bank's headquarters office was the "most imposing building in Philadelphia"[12] (and still stands today). In addition to this impressive flagship, "there were four branches of the bank (in Boston, New York, Baltimore and Charleston), and four more were about to be created (in Norfolk, Savannah, Washington and New Orleans)."[13] After Philadelphia, the outpost in New York was by far the largest.[14]

The private owners of the First Bank of the United States certainly didn't want this game to end. As early as 1808 they were asking Congress to extend its charter beyond the scheduled expiration in 1811. This request was forwarded to Treasury Secretary Albert Gallatin, who favored extending the charter and increasing the bank's capital from $10 million to $30 million. But Gallatin served under President Jefferson, who still objected to the bank on principle. When Jefferson left office in early 1809, the clock was still ticking down toward the scheduled sunset.

In January 1811, both chambers engaged in debate on the bank's charter. The House voted down a renewal, and the Senate requested that Gallatin, who remained Treasury secretary under President James Madison, draft another report. He again supported renewal, but the Senate voted it down, with Vice President George Clinton casting the tiebreaking vote. By this time, Hamilton had passed away and state-chartered banks had become a more potent lobbying force. It seems that the new colossus of American banking had not been quite as dominant as some feared, because numerous state-chartered banks had sprung up in the years of its existence. Perhaps ironically, it seems there was now a larger and more effective group of competitors able to make the case that the bank was impeding competition. Without a charter extension, the First Bank of the United States died.[15]

While the death of a financial giant seems unthinkable to many modern regulators, the young US economy seems to have taken it in stride. At the time the bank shut down, its New York branch was the largest bank in the city of New York. Unlike some of the sick giants of 2008, the branch was in good financial condition, and it was rather easily liquidated. This was not true everywhere. Litigation related to claims on some First Bank of the United States branches would continue for years, but the end of the big bank didn't trigger a panic.[16]

Still, just because there was no crisis when the bank closed, that doesn't mean the closure didn't leave a competitive vacuum. Public and private customers still wanted financial services, and a particular group of investors had an idea on how to serve them. The story of the business we now call Citigroup was about to begin.

When Failure Was Allowed (Because Government Wasn't Big Enough to Help)

f New York merchants were immediately missing the city's largest bank, federal officials were even more concerned about the closure of the country's most significant financial firm. The First Bank of the United States shut its doors just as the US government was preparing to borrow huge sums to finance a war. Treasury Secretary Gallatin had been hoping the bank would be a major source for these funds. The Napoleonic Wars in Europe had disrupted international trade, denting the young US economy. British ships were raiding American cargoes, kidnapping American sailors, and forcing them into service against the French—and in some cases forcing them to fight against fellow Americans. Several months after the closure of the bank, US troops fought British-backed Native Americans at the Battle of Tippecanoe in November of 1811. In Washington, members of Congress were discussing plans for a massive increase in land and naval forces to defend the young republic. And on top of all that, the Treasury still owed debt left over from the Revolutionary War, debt that Gallatin had hoped to retire by 1817.[1]

A new lender would soon emerge in New York. Just as Congress had been preparing to reject renewal of the First Bank of the United States in early 1811, a group of investors had petitioned the New York state assembly to grant a charter for a new financial institution to be based in Manhattan. Many of the investors were keenly aware of the opportunities about to be created by the national bank's closure because of their firsthand experience. According to a history Citigroup published to celebrate its two hundredth anniversary, "Shareholders in the Bank of the United States went on to provide more than 50 percent of the startup capital for a new institution, City Bank of New York. The new bank can be seen as a direct descendant of the United States' first central bank and went on to have a far greater impact on the nation's development."[2]

Especially after the bailouts of 2008, big politically connected financial firms like Citi are usually embarrassed to acknowledge their government ties. But in this case the institution proudly asserts the paternity of the first corporation created by Washington. And the new City Bank of New York even moved into its financial father's old building, buying the onetime New York branch of the First Bank of the United States at 52 Wall Street.[3]

Right from the start, the new outfit could hardly have been more political. This was no Silicon Valley start-up with bright, ambitious nobodies tinkering in a garage. The bank was born in a legislative compromise among some of New York's most powerful people. And since 1812 was an election year, crafting such a compromise was particularly difficult.

To be clear, back then Wall Street in particular and New York City in general were not yet the financial centers they would become. But commerce was booming, and the closure of the national bank had left just five single-unit banks[4] in a growing city with nearly one hundred thousand people. By way of comparison, in 2014 there were twenty-nine bank offices or branches for every one hundred thousand Americans.[5] The country's a lot richer now, but on the other hand, New Yorkers in 1811 had no online banking options.

In any case, between the needs of one hundred thousand New Yorkers and one national government, investors saw opportunity. But first they had to do some serious lobbying. Initially, the effort was led by a group of Democratic-Republican merchants aligned with President James Madison who wanted to make New York banking competitive with that of Philadelphia, Boston, and Baltimore. But Madison's allies didn't have enough votes in the New York legislature, partly because Madison's coalition was splintering. While he would still be reelected in the fall, it would be by a smaller margin than in his 1808 victory, and his party would lose seats in various levels of government.

New York City mayor DeWitt Clinton, a former member of Madison's party and the nephew of Madison's vice president, commanded a rival faction. The Clinton faction helped kill the petition to create City Bank in March of 1812. But after the death of Vice President George Clinton in April, New York legislators eventually managed to reach a deal in which director seats would be split between Madison and Clinton partisans. Leading the bank as its first president would be a pillar of the political and financial establishment: Harvard-educated Samuel Osgood had been a member of the Continental Congress, a New York Treasury commissioner, director of the Bank of North America, and the first postmaster general of the United States. The charter application was approved and City Bank was born on June 16, just two days before the start of the War of 1812.

The latter event certainly did create an opportunity for purveyors of financial services, because Washington was going to need to spend a lot of money, much of it borrowed. And this required finding lenders willing to bet on the debt of a developing country.

The US government in those days could hardly fund itself, never mind trying to bail out private companies as it has done in our more recent history.

In 1812, perhaps the most pressing issue was the need for a much larger army. That year, just eighty-nine men graduated from the ten-year-old United States Military Academy at West Point. As for the experienced officers who had fought in the Revolutionary War and were still around, they were "too old to be of any use," according to University of Virginia historian J. C. A. Stagg.[6] The president perhaps reached the same conclusion, and by the end of 1812, "Madison had offered commissions to more than 1,100 officers, 15 percent of whom declined to accept them."[7]

Paying for the ones who did accept was a constant challenge. Beginning in February of 1812, Congress had approved the first of a series of increases in various taxes and duties, but they would only come into effect after war had been declared. In the meantime, Congress also approved new federal borrowing and specifically authorized the government to take out a loan of $11 million at an interest rate of 6 percent. But this didn't mean any lenders had agreed to such terms. Gallatin figured that the lawmakers were being too optimistic, and he was proven right. When he sought to borrow the money in April, lenders subscribed for only a little more than $6 million of the debt offering.

To borrow money today, the US Treasury conducts hundreds of auctions each year of its bills, notes, and bonds. People and institutions wishing to loan funds to the US government can submit bids. Held by investors worldwide, US Treasury bonds trade in the world's largest and most liquid capital market.

It wasn't quite the same in the era of Madison. The process often involved the Treasury secretary asking wealthy men like Stephen Girard and John Jacob Astor for most of the money. Girard was a financier who in 1811 had bought various assets of the expiring

First Bank of the United States, including its grand headquarters in Philadelphia, and opened his own bank there. Astor was amassing a fortune in fur trading, New York real estate, and other ventures. Like Madison, Astor was a Democratic-Republican. He was also a friend of Gallatin's and was willing to fund the young republic—if the price was right. If Astor was a patriot, he wasn't a fanatic about it. When the US imposed restrictions on trade with British territories during the war, Astor "used various ruses to import furs from Canada," according to historian Donald R. Hickey.[8] Astor would eventually play a significant role in the history of City Bank.

What was also very different in Madison's time was a president's conception of his powers and responsibilities. On June 1, 1812, President Madison sent a message to Congress explaining all the reasons why the United States should declare war on Britain. He cited a "series of acts, hostile to the United States, as an Independent and neutral nation," including the appalling impressment of Americans by the British navy. Madison's "war message" said that "British cruisers have been in the continued practice of violating the American flag on the great highway of nations, and of seizing and carrying off persons sailing under it." He added that thousands of American citizens "have been torn from their country and from everything dear to them; have been dragged on board ships of war of a foreign nation and exposed, under the severities of their discipline, to be exiled to the most distant and deadly climes, to risk their lives in the battles of their oppressors, and to be the melancholy instruments of taking away those of their own brethren." Madison further reported:

> British cruisers have been in the practice also of violating the rights and the peace of our coasts. They hover over and harass our entering and departing commerce. To the most insulting pretensions they have added the most lawless proceedings in our

very harbors, and have wantonly spilt American blood within the sanctuary of our territorial jurisdiction.

In our own time, this would be more than enough cause for a president to request a declaration of war from Congress or even initiate military action without one to defend the country. But President Madison, who had been the principal drafter of the Constitution, thought it was not his job to start or even to ask for permission to start attacking another country.[9] So Madison's famous war message didn't actually ask for a war, but simply referred the matter to Congress:

Whether the United States shall continue passive under these progressive usurpations and these accumulating wrongs, or, opposing force to force in defense of their national rights, shall commit a just cause into the hands of the Almighty Disposer of Events . . . is a solemn question which the Constitution wisely confides to the legislative department of the government. In recommending it to their early deliberations I am happy in the assurance that the decision will be worthy the enlightened and patriotic councils of a virtuous, a free, and a powerful nation.

Congress declared war on the United Kingdom seventeen days later, which triggered the new taxes that Congress had already approved. But as has so often been the case in more recent American history, tax increases didn't solve the government's fiscal challenges, despite the hopes of advocates for such legislation. Even after the formal declaration of war, the federal financial picture didn't get much brighter. Stagg notes that "by the end of June 1812, when Gallatin finally estimated that government expenditures for the year would total $26 million, the Treasury could calculate on having only just over $16.6 million on hand."[10] But whether or not Gallatin had the money to finance it, the war was on. American

troops were already preparing to invade British-controlled Canada. This series of costly excursions proved to be less successful
than Washington expected, although American success against the
great British navy exceeded expectations.

By the end of 1812, "the army had enlisted nearly fourteen thousand new troops, which, when combined with the men recruited
before 1812, made for a force totaling nineteen thousand men—
considerably less than the preparedness legislation had called for."[11]
Gallatin is perhaps lucky that recruiting was not as successful as
hoped, because all these new recruits expected to get paid. When
they signed up, they were promised "a bounty of $16, a full set of
clothes, pay of $5 per month, and 160 acres of land upon discharge."[12]
But Gallatin's Treasury could not reliably deliver the funds, even
though army pay was hardly generous and in many cases less than
what farm workers were making. According to Stagg:

> Throughout 1812, army officers constantly complained that
> shortages of money and clothing gave many recruits a sense of
> grievance, which, once it was widely known, became an obsta-
> cle to continuing enlistments. The spectacle of ragged, barefoot,
> and otherwise poorly clad and seemingly destitute troops often
> brought the army, the government, and ultimately the war itself
> into public disrepute.[13]

By the early months of 1813, it was clear that the United States
couldn't afford to fight much longer. On March 5, Gallatin wrote
to Madison with a straightforward message:

> Dear Sir,—We have hardly enough money to last till the end of
> the month.[14]

Just in time, Astor, Girard, and Philadelphia financier David
Parish provided $9.1 million of a total $16 million raised by the

government via an April syndicated loan.[15] Soon after, President Madison dispatched Gallatin and other wise men to Europe to negotiate a peace deal. Gallatin's departure didn't make it any easier to sell Treasury bonds. As Hamilton had feared, politicians were finding it increasingly difficult to resist the urge to indulge in "paper emissions." McCraw notes:

> In desperation, Congress authorized the printing of federal currency notes—the first since the ratification of the Constitution. There were five separate issues from 1812 to 1815, totaling $36.7 million. This step amounted to fighting the war with printed money backed by nothing, much as the Continental Congress had done during the Revolution.[16]

Gallatin's diplomacy helped to bring about an eventual peace with the signing of the Treaty of Ghent in December of 1814—although news traveled too slowly to reach the United States before Andrew Jackson's victory over the British at the Battle of New Orleans. The conclusion of hostilities in early 1815 must have been as much of a relief to Gallatin as to the rest of America. But he may have already given up hope of a sound federal fisc when he formally quit his job running the Treasury a year earlier. Today his brief biography on the Department of the Treasury's website sums up his departure this way: "Having failed to convince Congress to recharter the First Bank of the United States in 1811, and foreseeing financial disaster, he resigned in 1814." Then, as now, it was hard to be optimistic that Washington would get its budgetary house in order. Government debt skyrocketed from $45 million in 1812 to over $127 million in 1816.[17]

But all wasn't lost. Along with the richest of the one-percenters like Astor and Girard, the new government could also increasingly count on New York's new bank. City Bank subscribed to Washington's war bond issuance in 1813 and the following year helped facilitate another government bond issue by lending the underwriter $500,000. The bank assisted Washington again in late 1814 when it lent the federal government $200,000 so the United States could make payments on its debt. City Bank also became a significant holder of government deposits. It was home to one-third of government balances held in New York.[18]

Also during the war, one of City's founding directors, Samuel Tooker, personally helped fund a fourteen-gun brig to serve as a privateer, on the hunt for British cargo ships to plunder. "Tooker was the principal shareholder in the $65,000 private military venture,"[19] according to the official history Citigroup published to celebrate its bicentennial in 2012. "With a crew of 120 men, the ship set sail one dark night, avoiding British warships blockading the harbor . . . Tooker's vessel, which was uninsured, was never seen again."[20]

Decades later, a bank examiner for the Office of the Comptroller of the Currency may have been a little too impressed with the firm he was supposed to be regulating when he described the bank's early days:

> Incorporated June 16, 1812 under the management of the first mercantile men of that day, the pioneers and innovators of a class now fondly styled as 'Merchant Princes.' Devoted from its birth to the best interests of our common country, we find this bank, during the War of 1812 lending its entire capital to the support of the General government during that dark hour.[21]

Still, it's clear that the institution was providing useful services to the Treasury. Perhaps City could have been even more helpful to the Treasury and to all the bank's other clients if City's directors hadn't been so busy serving themselves. "The directors were better politicians than businessmen," according to the bank's official history.[22] They certainly were good at politics. William Few, who would succeed Osgood as president of the bank after the latter's death in 1813, held a variety of public-sector positions and over the course of his career served in the state assemblies of both Georgia and New York. Abraham Bloodgood was also a politician as well as a leather merchant. Isaac Pierson was a doctor who would eventually become a New Jersey congressman.

As for what kind of businessmen they were, it seems they were better at looking after their own personal business than the business of the institution they were supposed to be overseeing. At a healthy bank, the owners put up substantial capital, risking their money to serve as a cushion in case the bank's assets turn out to be worth less than expected—for example if some loans to customers of the bank are not repaid. But when City Bank was being created, the bank's capital was something of a mirage, and the customers were often the directors themselves.

According to the official history, "shareholders generally had to pay cash for 5 percent of the par value of the shares, followed by two installments of 5 percent and 10 percent later in the year. Additional cash payments were not required for Bank of the United States shareholders. The founding directors exempted themselves from putting up any cash at all. Instead, they could take out indefinite loans from the bank by using their shares as collateral."[23]

When a bank's equity investors don't put up a large capital cushion, it means depositors—or in more recent history, taxpayers—are at risk if loans aren't repaid. When the owners not only fail to put up much capital but also lend bank funds to themselves, it creates risks on both sides of the balance sheet. The thin capital cushion leaves little room for error. And error is more likely when loan underwriting consists of self-dealing rather than a sober consideration of the creditworthiness of each potential borrower.

To top it off, there is the added danger when risks are not diversified. As of February 1814, a quarter of the bank's lending commitments were tied up with just 12 of the bank's 750 customers.[24]

City Bank in its early days was like a lot of banks in developing markets—business is concentrated among insiders and there is chronic "evergreening" of weak credits. In other words, when loans come due they are continually renewed, whether or not the borrower is likely to repay.

Suffice it to say that City Bank was not ideally suited to face formidable new competition. But it was coming nonetheless. In 1816, Congress chartered the Second Bank of the United States. Just as easily as the stable government deposits and fees from government lending had come to City, they generally left to find a new home in the national bank. The Second Bank of the United States was like the first one, except much bigger and with more authority. The second national bank had $35 million in capital instead of its predecessor's $10 million. Its charter was again set to run for twenty years.[25] Version 2.0 of this Washington-created institution was more like a modern central bank, expected to implement a rudimentary monetary policy. The bank would also eventually engage in limited circumstances as a lender of last resort—but doesn't seem to have done much for City.[26]

The 1820s brought more competition to the New York market, especially with the chartering of Chemical Bank in 1824. City meanwhile had been suffering a decline in both its earnings and its credit quality and had continued to allow "excessive borrowing by its directors."[27] City's stock price plummeted to below its par value. But this was not an age of government bailouts. With the bank's stock price depressed, a merchant named Charles Lawton purchased a majority of the shares.[28] It seems that Lawton and the other shareholders found the management of the bank to be less than entirely focused on the health of the institution. According to the bank's official history:

Peter Stagg and his brother were members of a private club renowned for bacchanalian parties where members bet cases of champagne as they played the children's game Follow the Leader on the streets of New York at night. As president of City Bank of New York, Stagg was ousted by the bank's owners in 1825 . . .

Lawton replaced the well-fed and well-connected directors with what appeared at least initially to be a more serious and competent crew. After struggling as a highly political organization created by the leaders of the government's first national banking venture, City was for the moment on a sounder footing as a more purely commercial organization. But the problem of bank directors looking out for themselves wasn't over, and neither was the problem of unintended consequences of government action. Not for the last time, the bank would embrace too much risk in both its assets and liabilities. Before long, a new financial crisis would test even the most principled and prudent of bankers.

3

City of Instability

I t seems unlikely that City Bank's new management would have been running around Manhattan at night betting cases of champagne as the firm's former president had done. But improved oversight of the bank didn't mean the oversight was good enough. Whereas City Bank's politically connected founders had almost run it off the cliff during the 1820s, in the next decade mistakes by the bank's leadership left it vulnerable to political actors outside the bank who were making even bigger mistakes.

The leaders of the new regime at City continued at least one bad habit of their predecessors and also developed a few new ones. Self-dealing is never a sign of a healthy institution. Loans to the bank's own directors were excessive compared to such loans at City's competitors.[1] Also, City's deposits increasingly came from banks in other cities—rather than from City's owners or other local customers. This was a problem because deposits from out-of-town banks tended to be less stable, with a greater likelihood of sudden large withdrawals. City was also funding itself by issuing a large volume of banknotes, which could create further strain on the bank if lots of note holders suddenly decided they wanted to redeem them for gold or silver. This was particularly dangerous for City because it had low reserves of the precious metals compared to other New York City banks.[2]

The bank also had relatively little capital to absorb losses, and its owners were reluctant to put up more. City even turned down a chance to become a federal depository because it didn't want to raise the additional capital required to support a larger business. So the administration of President Andrew Jackson ended up choosing other New York firms to be his "pet banks." Jackson was moving money out of the Second Bank of the United States in preparation for allowing its charter to expire in 1836 and was depositing the money in a host of state banks. It might seem like the height of incompetence for City to decide it didn't want the US government as a customer, and perhaps it's not surprising what happened next.

But incompetence could be found in both the private and public sectors. On the eve of the closing of the second national bank, City had allowed itself to become a thinly capitalized, unstable also-ran. With $2.6 million in assets in 1835, it held just a 3 percent share of the New York banking market. City was in no position to capitalize on the closing of a giant competitor, and in fact it had just turned down what for many banks would be the most prized customer imaginable. The bank's asset level was about to decline further, but the economic calamity that struck the United States and much of the world could hardly be blamed on City.

For more than a century after Andrew Jackson closed the Second Bank of the United States, historians often faulted him for the economic destruction that followed. A common theory was that by weakening and then eventually closing the national bank, he had removed the chief enforcer of monetary discipline. This theoretically encouraged state banks to be promiscuous in their note issuance, which caused an inflationary bubble, which eventually burst with catastrophic results. More recently this theory has given way to other explanations, but there is no question that the Panic of 1837 signaled the beginning of a global catastrophe.

Many of today's high school students have probably not even heard of it, yet the 1837 financial crisis and the economic downturn that followed have rightly been described as "America's First Great Depression."[3] The agony continued for years. Economists Milton Friedman and Anna Schwartz cited the contraction of 1839 to 1843 as the only period in our history "remotely comparable to the monetary collapse from 1929 to 1933."[4]

Visiting the United States for a lecture tour in early 1842—nearly five years after the initial panic—Charles Dickens found a humorless, "gloomy" people, a "melancholy air of business," and a landscape of shuttered enterprises and half-completed construction projects.[5] He had no desire to return. During the depression years, manufacturers laid off thousands of workers.[6] Americans witnessed not only food riots but even violent uprisings against landlords and various governmental authorities.

An economic disaster must have been just about the last thing most Americans expected before the Panic of 1837. Not only did the crisis follow a period of rising prosperity, but the federal government had just finished paying off the last of its debt in 1835. Jackson's Treasury secretary Levi Woodbury predicted that the United States would enjoy the "unprecedented spectacle" of being a nation that owed nothing.[7] Jackson became the only president in US history to preside over both a balanced budget and a debt-free Treasury. Unfortunately, many state governments were very far from debt-free on the eve of the country's first great economic contraction.

Many of the states had been borrowing heavily to construct canals and other transportation infrastructure. One could perhaps understand their enthusiasm for the economic benefits of allowing goods to more easily flow across the young country. By all accounts, business was booming. Although it's hard to tell exactly how fast the economy was growing in the years before the great panic because statistics were not collected and maintained as they are today, modern economists have made estimates based on the available records. According to a 2000 research paper from the Federal Reserve Bank of Minneapolis, gross national product was surging. "Between 1820 and 1836, real GNP grew at close to an 8 percent annual rate; between 1830 and 1836, at a 10 percent annual rate,"[8] write the authors.

Driving much of this growth was the swelling market for American cotton. While Eli Whitney's invention of the cotton gin famously enabled the efficient production of this commodity free of seeds, Alasdair Roberts points out that it was a series of British technological innovations in the production of textiles that created the massive demand for this crop. Only large-scale manufacturing of clothing could create large orders for American plantations. In the early decades of the nineteenth century, these orders were rising rapidly, and they were largely coming from northwest England. Manchester was known as the "Cottonopolis of the Universe," and nearby Liverpool was "the seaport through which passed almost all Anglo-American trade."[9] That included, according to Roberts, "almost one-third of a billion pounds of American cotton" in 1836.[10]

It isn't easy to grasp, as we enjoy the benefits of a diverse US economy today, the central role that cotton played in the US economy then—and how much it relied on trade with the United Kingdom. Today we sell agricultural products, aircraft, pharmaceuticals, movies, music, software, and services all over the world. Roberts explains that in the mid-1830s, "Almost half the total value of *all* U.S. exports in 1836—about fifty million dollars—was accounted for by the sale of cotton to Liverpool brokers."[11]

The cotton trade with the UK was five times as large as US tobacco exports, nearly nine times as large as US exports of manufactured goods, and more than ten times US exports of lumber

and wood products.[12] Over the course of four decades ending
in 1840, land in the American South devoted to cotton farming
would increase fifteenfold. America would become not only the
world's largest producer of cotton, but larger than all other countries combined.[13]

Of course, the cotton economy was built on America's original sin, the monstrous institution of slavery. And it wasn't just
Southern plantation owners who were sinning. Cotton production was capital intensive, and planters borrowing heavily used
both their land and the human beings they held captive as collateral. Financing was provided by US and British financiers and
merchants as well as lenders in other parts of Europe. The largest
slave trader in the US, Franklin and Armfield, frequently borrowed from the Second Bank of the United States. In the eight
years ending in 1832, loans from the bank to slave owners in
the Mississippi Valley increased sixteenfold.[14] With the retreat
and subsequent closure of the second national bank, state banks
popped up all over slave-holding regions to maintain the financing for King Cotton.

But there wasn't going to be enough financing for much of
anything, because of policy decisions in Washington and especially in London. These decisions were a particular shock to the
economy because they represented a complete policy reversal. In
the years before the panic a sharp rise in the money supply had
created *too much* financing, providing the fuel for a real estate investment mania. Prices for land and just about everything grown
and harvested on it had been surging. An index of key commodity
prices in New Orleans increased by more than 30 percent between
January 1835 and April 1836. In Cincinnati, commodity prices rose
by 60 percent.[15] Inflation wasn't rising quite as rapidly in eastern
cities, though it was still well into double digits.

The nationwide frenzy for land was even more dramatic. Towns
where government land offices were located were overrun with

eager potential buyers on auction days. When such towns ran out of space to house the visitors in hotels, saloons, and restaurants, speculators pitched tent cities to stay near the action.[16]

What was causing what appeared to be a runaway inflation in the price of real estate and its produce? Daniel Walker Howe notes that for a long time historians thought that Jackson's "pet banks" that replaced the Second Bank of the United States "had irresponsibly overextended their loans during the boom of 1836." But Howe writes that "now we know that, monitored by the Treasury, the state bankers showed appropriate caution," and that, with a few exceptions, "the pet banks were generally responsibly managed."[17] Students of more recent American history who are familiar with the way the Treasury's Office of Thrift Supervision monitored AIG in the years before the 2008 crisis may find this hard to believe. But there is evidence to argue that the surge of money that fueled skyrocketing prices was not the fault of Jackson's pet banks or Jackson's Treasury.

At the time, Britain was not just the principal customer for American exports but also the financial center of the Anglo-American economy. As important as Liverpool was to the flow of raw cotton and the subsequent manufacture of cotton fabrics, London was to the financing of this industry. Specifically, London was at the heart of the credit system that allowed merchants to buy cotton in America before they could sell it to the mills of Manchester—and allowed Manchester's mill owners to pay for the cotton before they had sold any shirts. Nearly two centuries later, much of this finance would be facilitated by banks like Citi, but in the mid-1830s the various brokers that participated in this trade understood there was one institution that dominated the market. The Bank of England decided whether and on what terms it would buy bills of exchange—written promises that the buyer of a load of cotton or shirts would pay for it several months later at his home bank. And the UK central bank used this market to

conduct monetary policy. According to Roberts, "The amount
by which the Bank of England discounted those bills—that is,
the difference between what it was prepared to pay for a bill and
its face value—was the main mechanism by which it influenced
prevailing interest rates."[18]

In the years before the panic, the bank was keeping interest
rates low, which not only meant easy money for businesspeople
up and down the cotton supply chain—it also meant that British
investors looking to earn a higher yield than they could get at
home in the UK started investing huge sums in the United States,
including in the bonds that many US states were issuing to build
all those canals. Back then, London financiers looked at American bonds the way that today's Wall Streeters look at debt issued
from a rapidly growing emerging market. Yes, there's risk, but the
creditor seems to have an increasing ability to make the payments.

A flood of capital into the US was driving up asset prices, and
of course the US economy was growing quickly, so one could argue that price increases were at least somewhat justified. But pol-
icymakers in both London and Washington were getting nervous
about the possibility of a credit bubble, and their roughly simul-
taneous responses would cause a sudden shortage of money across
the United States. The Jackson administration, never particularly
fond of paper money and finance in general—and wanting to rein
in what appeared to be a mania of real estate speculation—decreed
in the summer of 1836 that federal land could only be bought with
gold or silver.

Jackson was undermining faith in paper currency in America
even as he was creating more demand for gold and silver. This
made holders of banknotes increasingly want to trade them in
for precious metals, which reduced bank reserves of specie and
therefore limited banks' ability to lend. Meanwhile this so-called
Specie Circular from Jackson also inflamed a rising sentiment over
in London that the value of paper of all kinds issued in the US had

been dangerously inflated. The Bank of England realized that it had been holding interest rates too low for too long as its gold reserves started to decline. This is the traditional market signal that a central bank has printed too much paper—when people decide they would rather hold precious metal than currency. Mediocre harvests in Britain were also putting strain on the nation's economy and on the Bank of England's gold reserves, because more gold had to be shipped out of the country to pay for food imports.[19]

Just as Jackson was taking action in the US, the Bank of England sharply hiked rates and initiated a series of moves to limit London's financing of trade with the US. The strain on US banks became manifest the following spring. Researchers from the Minneapolis Fed describe the rolling crisis that began when US banks started refusing to allow customers to trade paper currency for gold or silver, known as suspension of specie payments:

> The Panic of 1837 began in the South with bank suspensions in Natchez, Mississippi, on May 4, followed by suspensions in Montgomery, Alabama, on May 9. Suspensions hit the North on May 10, when the banks in New York City suspended payments . . . then rapidly spread to other parts of the country . . . By the end of May, virtually all the banks in the country had suspended payments.[20]

Cotton prices had been plunging, which in turn put more strain on the banks because planters who had borrowed heavily to buy land, equipment, and slaves suddenly had less income with which to service their loans. It would be almost a year before any US banks resumed specie payments, and many would not resume their traditional practice until the fall of 1838. But while the panic had ended, another would occur in 1839, and a combination of misguided monetary policy and bad harvests in England combined to starve the US economy of credit for years.

Beyond the banks, a rolling crisis hit state governments, with a wave of bond defaults that also caused intense pain on both sides of the Atlantic. Unfortunately for Pennsylvania, it had the misfortune of not only defaulting on its debt but also counting various friends and relatives of the English poet William Wordsworth among its creditors.[21] They expressed their displeasure to Wordsworth, who in turn let the Keystone State have it in an 1845 poem. It may not be one of the great literary creations of all time or even one of Wordsworth's best. But it is without a doubt among the greatest poems ever written about a bond default:

TO THE PENNSYLVANIANS

Days undefiled by luxury or sloth,
Firm self-denial, manners grave and staid,
Rights equal, laws with cheerfulness obeyed,
Words that require no sanction from an oath,
And simple honesty a common growth—
This high repute, with bounteous Nature's aid,
Won confidence, now ruthlessly betrayed
At will, your power the measure of your troth!—
All who revere the memory of Penn
Grieve for the land on whose wild woods his name
Was fondly grafted with a virtuous aim,
Renounced, abandoned by degenerate Men
For state-dishonour black as ever came
To upper air from Mammon's loathsome den.

Speaking of Mammon's loathsome den, readers can imagine how well one of the worst-run banks in New York City fared during the worst financial crisis of the nineteenth century. City had already been losing ground to competitors when the panic began in 1837, and its deposits suffered a severe runoff. It would certainly have failed if it had not suspended specie payments that spring.[22] In fact, it would likely have failed even with the suspension if not for a rescue from one of its customers. Fortunately for City, he was the richest man in the United States.

4

Astor to the Rescue

John Jacob Astor was not the easiest client to maintain. For reasons that remain unclear, the First Bank of the United States had once closed his account and denied him additional credit even though he was on his way to becoming the richest man in the United States.[1] But at City Bank he ended up being both a customer and, the record suggests, the savior of the institution. Astor appears to have saved City in large part by placing on its board a young merchant who would help shape the institution and much of the American economy rising around it.

After spending its first twenty-five years as an unstable, underachieving political creation, City Bank in the next three-quarters of a century would become an island of stability even during the worst financial storms. While the bank had been founded by government action and would come to rely on federal help much later in its history, City in the nineteenth century became such a pillar of financial strength that not only consumers and businesses but even the government itself would look to the bank for assistance in times of crisis. New York City was now on its way to becoming a global financial center, and City was on its way to becoming the country's largest bank.

Not that the self-made Astor never used political influence. He seems to have used whatever was necessary to advance his financial interests. Looking back on the man a century and a half after his death, Cynthia Crossen observed that Astor "became America's richest man by working hard, taking risks and cheating, lying and bribing."[2] It would not be easy for anyone to defend his lucrative deal to illegally ship opium into China, and some modern readers may be offended by the fortune he made in the fur trade, shipping not just sea otter and beaver pelts but buffalo and muskrat skins by the tens of thousands annually to eastern cities and ultimately around the world. On the other hand, his furs did help people keep warm in an age before synthetic fabrics. Not insignificantly, Astor's business ventures helped develop the Pacific Northwest and claim it for the United States. Back east, Astor was among the investors in bonds that financed the construction of the Erie Canal, which would help make New York City a center of American and global commerce.

By the time that financial panic struck in 1837, Astor had already been divesting his assets in the fur trade, having noticed on a trip to England that silk hats were becoming more popular than those made of fur.[3] Throughout his career, Astor had been buying real estate in New York City, starting with his first purchase in 1789.[4] His exit from the fur trade only sharpened his focus on investing in raw land, and the crisis created lots of opportunities for Astor to buy at bargain prices. He presumably also picked up a stake in City Bank at a fire-sale price, but real property would be his primary investment. On his deathbed he is said to have remarked that he regretted not buying all of Manhattan.[5] He bought acres upon acres of it, and many of those acres would remain in the family for generations. His descendants would develop the properties, and they largely invented the luxury hotel in the United States. The fortune Astor built would also fund various philanthropic projects in the city he called home for more than a century after his death.

Like another famous New Yorker who assembled a Manhattan real estate empire that would eventually include luxury hotels, Astor was ill-mannered. Unlike Donald Trump, Astor seems to have also been bland and humorless. Astor shows up in most historical accounts as ruthless and single-minded in the pursuit of profit. But there's much to admire in the man that Astor appears to have installed on the fifteen-member board at City Bank, a man who has been largely ignored by history. Modern readers who remember the crisis of 2008 may particularly admire a man with such careful attention to the safety and soundness of his bank.

Moses Taylor is perhaps the greatest American businessman most Americans have never heard of. When he became a director of City Bank in June of 1837, America was in the midst of a financial panic and Taylor was just thirty-one years old. Detailed records from the period are limited, but we assume that Taylor bolstered the bank primarily with Astor's money but also with some of his own. Even before the panic, Taylor had been a City customer as well as a shareholder.[6] Though a young man, he had been running his own business for five years, and by the end of 1838 he would calculate his net worth at more than $200,000[7]—close to $5 million in today's currency.[8] Along with the money, Taylor brought along to City Bank his penchant for hard work and his prudence.

It may be hard for modern Wall Streeters to imagine a banker who doesn't like leverage, but the merchant Moses Taylor avoided taking on debt whenever possible. His business was the Caribbean trade, importing sugar from Cuba but also fruits and other commodities from wherever they were grown. Taylor seems to have been something of a fanatic about purchasing only the best, whether his firm was buying pineapples, limes, or coffee—but only when prices were low. Almost echoing Benjamin Franklin, he said that "a dollar saved is a dollar made," and he believed that he "must not spend a dollar unless absolutely necessary."[9] With such simple rules and a zealous attention to detail, Taylor figured that "profits would naturally follow," according to his biographer, Daniel Hodas.[10] They did.

Taylor had grown up in the city, and today's New Yorkers may be amused to learn that his childhood home near what is now Washington Square was considered "nearly out of town," as he walked south to school in lower Manhattan.[11] But he didn't have to walk to school for very long. In 1821, at age fifteen, he finished his formal education and started work as an apprentice clerk at the firm of J. D. Brown. He soon joined a more prestigious outfit— the import-export business of G. G. & S. S. Howland. Wherever he was, Taylor seems to have put in long hours inspecting cargoes on the docks and maintaining precise records of each transaction. He delighted in anticipating the needs of his employers and relished being able to respond to a request by saying, "It is already done, sir."[12] Rather than following his passion, Taylor seems to have been determined to allow the boss to follow his. And initially the boss wasn't even giving Taylor a salary.

"As was the custom, he served apprenticeship without pay," notes Hodas.[13] Even after he was promoted to junior clerk, Taylor was paid just $500 per year. But he was permitted to trade for his own account, in other words risking his own money in the purchase of goods and then trying to sell them at a profit. In this he seems to have done extremely well, building $15,000 in savings, which he used, along with a $35,000 loan from his father, to start his own firm.[14]

Before setting out on his own in business, Taylor first started something else. In 1831, he married Catherine Wilson, the daughter of a local grocer. They would be married for fifty years until his death in 1882 and had six children, the first of whom tragically died at just eighteen months. While the marital disappointments of some of Taylor's successors at City Bank would become public scandals, he seems to have been lucky at love. Decades into their marriage, Taylor couldn't stand to be apart from his wife.

But in 1832 it was time for Taylor to separate from the firm of G. G. & S. S. Howland. International trade had been growing, and Taylor had proved he had a keen eye for value and a formidable work ethic. Also, he had developed perhaps the most important relationship in the market for the largest agricultural import into the United States. Drake Brothers of Havana shipped most of the Cuban sugar bound for the US and the Drakes wanted Taylor to be their agent in New York.

Taylor would be at the center of the Cuban sugar trade for decades. In the twentieth century, the bank that Taylor helped rescue would have a less happy experience with Cuban sugar, but in the 1800s Taylor became much more than a merchant for the sweet commodity. His correspondence housed at the New York Public Library reveals that people frequently sought his advice on Cuba as well as introductions to key players in Havana and Matanzas, where many of the great plantations were located.

As for the planters and shippers in Cuba, Taylor became their investment adviser and facilitator of all kinds of business with US firms, including railroads and shipping lines that carried Cuban sugar. The Cuban clients thought so highly of Taylor that eventually they were handing over to him not just their sugar, but their children as well. It's not clear that Taylor ever visited Cuba, but Hodas recounts how important he became to many of its residents:

> Taylor often became responsible for the education and well-being of a planter's children while in the United States. Taylor placed these students in various schools or apprentice positions, paid their expenses, advanced them allowances, and served them *in loco parentis*. Sometimes Taylor was even called upon to obtain

confidential information on the character of prospective brides or grooms.[15]

If Taylor could be trusted to look after other people's children, he could certainly be trusted with other people's money—for example, if they were making a high-stakes wager on a matter of national importance. Years after he had joined the City board, letters in the autumn of 1844 would confirm that Taylor had been entrusted with $2,000, which he would deliver to "the winner of the bet." Specifically, one letter noted, "In the event of the election of Henry Clay, then the said $2,000 are to be handed to Andrew Foster Junior (or his agent or agents). In the event of the election of James K. Polk then the said $2,000 are to be handed to A.P. Stanton (or his agent or agents)."[16] One can only guess how vigorously Stanton celebrated the results of the presidential contest. In today's dollars, he won more than $50,000.

Seven years earlier, it's not clear whether the staff at City Bank was celebrating the arrival of Moses Taylor as a director, but he was eminently qualified. On top of that, he had a connection to City's savior. Taylor's father had been Astor's agent, overseeing the burgeoning real estate empire in New York, so Astor likely knew Taylor quite well before the bank rescue. And Taylor had used Astor as a reference when advertising the launch of his own merchant house in 1832.[17] The bank's bicentennial history notes one nineteenth-century account stating that Astor "always backed up Moses when he needed aid."[18] The families would remain close. Even after leaving Astor's employ, the elder Taylor would serve as a pallbearer at the business titan's funeral in 1848.

Qualified and connected, Moses Taylor also held assets that were highly liquid. During the Panic of 1837, one of the reasons that Taylor was in a position to help the bank was that, unlike his predecessors on City's board—or the directors who would one day steer the modern Citigroup into the financial storms of 2008—he had anticipated and prepared for a market panic. Believing that poor judgment by both bankers and government officials had created a speculative bubble, he had maintained a significant cash reserve. As a result his merchant house endured through the panic and the years-long economic downturn that followed.[19]

Reading the history of the period, one almost wonders if there was any disaster that could have possibly overwhelmed the careful and resilient merchant. Taylor operated his firm through the cholera epidemic of 1832. After the Great Fire of New York in 1835 burned through much of the business and financial district and entirely consumed his building, he opened for business the next morning out of the basement of his home.[20]

As a new director in 1837, Taylor was not yet running City Bank, but he became increasingly influential. Even at the start, he was deeply involved in the business. At that time, City was a small firm with just a handful of employees. The job of a director was not simply to oversee the management but in large measure to *be* the management, reviewing and deciding many of the day-to-day issues that today would be handled well below the level of the board. Also, within the board, it seems that Taylor quickly became not just the first among equals but an authority who was perhaps even bigger than the bank. On at least one occasion when the bank's senior managers were ill and a commitment had to be made on behalf of the institution, Taylor simply made it himself. In October of 1842, he sent a letter to Samuel and William Welsh of Philadelphia:

> I do not send a Cashier or President Certificate—both Cashier and President of our Bank / the City / are sick. For the time being I am the President. P.S. I think my name & word should pass without any further Certificate. If it is necessary I will send it.[21]

Taylor's name and word had been established as rock-solid in the New York merchant community and now they were becoming known and respected not just in banking but in a range of industries. In short order, he became one of the most important players in New York utilities. In 1841, he became a director of Manhattan Gas Light Company and later became the largest share-holder. By 1848, it was the nation's largest gas company, but just in case it lost its competitive edge, Taylor also acquired major stakes in competitors Metropolitan and New York Gas Light, and also joined the board of the latter. After a series of mergers, Taylor's descendants would one day own nearly half of what became the dominant utility in New York City, Consolidated Edison, known as Con Edison.[22] In a charitable view, Taylor helped to light up New York City. But consumers didn't always get the best deal. Owning stakes in a variety of companies and eager to cooperate with the firms he didn't own, Taylor often participated in efforts to fix prices and to divide the market into discrete neighborhood monopolies.[23]

Still, Taylor was in many ways becoming the man who made New York City go, especially with a series of acquisitions and expansions in the 1850s. His companies owned Pennsylvania coal fields and railroads that brought the coal into the city and ironworks that made the rails on which the coal cars traveled. He would soon be helping the whole national economy go. In 1853, he acquired a significant stake in Lackawanna Iron and Coal Company from the Scranton family of Pennsylvania. Lackawanna would often accept shares in railroad companies as payment for its iron, which allowed Taylor to own significant stakes in railroads across the South and the Midwest. He owned cargo ships pow-ered by both sails and steam and was an early telecommunications investor, backing a venture that would connect New York and London with a transatlantic cable in 1866.

Entrepreneurs in coal and iron country increasingly wrote to him seeking investments. They didn't necessarily relish having to go to a New York moneyman and hand over some level of ownership and control in exchange for funding, but many of them evidently thought it was a good trade. As a result, Taylor ended up funding a great deal of the industrialization that was enriching the country as it enabled enormous gains in productivity.

Given all the businesses Taylor was helping either to manage or to finance, perhaps the demands on his time were among the reasons why he tendered his resignation from City Bank's board in 1851. His board colleagues refused to accept it, and five years later elected him president of the bank. Appointed in April of 1856, Taylor would run City for twenty-six years and along the way acquire a controlling interest. City Bank, which had often been led by hacks and incompetents—and had more than once teetered on the edge of failure—was becoming the most respected bank in the country's most important business and financial center.[24]

After the Panic of 1837 and the ensuing default by the state of Pennsylvania that so upset Wordsworth's friends and relations, Philadelphia's hard-hit banking sector would never again challenge New York. Also, the new Erie Canal and the development of transatlantic shipping were making New York the country's premiere transportation hub for the movement of both goods and people. The telegraph was connecting New York's stock market with buyers and sellers across the country. Historian John Steele Gordon describes the special opportunity this presented to a Manhattan financier:

> New York City quickly became what the poet Oliver Wendell Holmes (the father of the Supreme Court justice) called "that tongue that is licking up the cream of commerce and finance of a continent." In 1800, 9% of the country's exports had passed through New York. By 1860 it was 62%. In 1820 New York had about 10% more people than Philadelphia. In 1860 it had twice as many.
>
> New York became the biggest boom town the world had

ever seen, roaring northwards up Manhattan Island at the rate of two blocks a year. Since Manhattan is about two miles wide, that meant that the city was developing about 10 miles of new street-front per year, year after year after year.[25]

Riding this wave of growth—and in many ways directing it as well—was the disciplined and opportunistic Moses Taylor. If progressive academics paid much attention to Taylor, they might dismiss him as a robber baron or at least a monopolist. Moreover, historical figures are bound to get rough treatment when they are judged by the standards of our own time—but not necessarily in this case. Shareholders and taxpayers could only dream that Citigroup in the mid-2000s had been run in the manner of Moses Taylor's bank. His natural caution and keen sense of the human instinct to get caught up in speculative manias persuaded him to create a rock of financial stability in lower Manhattan. An examination report from the Office of the Comptroller of the Currency during the Taylor era seems a bit over-the-top, but it does give a sense of the respect City's president carried, even among regulators:

> [O]n April 4th, 1856 the bank came under the management of its present President Moses Taylor, Esq. whose very name is the embodiment of integrity, energy, mercantile sagacity and patriotism and strongly reminds us of the Merchant Princes of Venice in the 12th Century who made that Commercial Emporium the seat of wealth, art, genius, luxury and power that has commanded the admiration of the civilized world.[26]

As we'll explore later in the bank's history, financial regulators have a sad history of being "captured" by the firms they are supposed to be overseeing. But when you look at the math of Taylor's City Bank, it's not hard to understand why bank examiners felt that this was one institution that wasn't going to be a problem. In fact, in the age of Taylor, City was routinely part of the solution to a financial crisis.

Taylor summed up his approach to business in general and banking in particular with one phrase: "ready money." Compared to modern megabanks, Taylor's bank was both more highly capitalized and more liquid. Put simply, he ensured that a lot more money was owed to City Bank than the bank owed to others, and he kept a lot of cash on hand in case of a panic. As an additional layer of protection, he sought out stable deposits—clients who were not likely to make huge, sudden withdrawals. Much of the money in the bank was his own, giving the bank not just a stable depositor but also a management that could not have been more deeply interested in the health of the institution. In contrast to the periods of instability in the bank's early years and also in the twentieth and twenty-first centuries, Taylor's arrival at the bank marked the beginning of roughly three-quarters of a century of strength and stability—without a government backstop.

Sixteen years after he joined the board, but before Taylor became president, City and other New York banks actually created a private system to backstop one another in times of crisis. While the idea for a clearinghouse had been suggested years earlier by a government official, Secretary of the Treasury Albert Gallatin, City and the fifty-nine other New York banks created a fully private system to regularly settle debts between them and, in times of crisis, to lend to member banks offering good collateral.

As for how Taylor ran his own bank, it wasn't rocket science. When making loans, he wanted to avoid people "disposed to overdo everything . . . and live by their wits."[27] Just in case the bank erred and ended up loaning money to such people, the goal was to have enough capital—the equity investment made by the bank's owners—to absorb the cost of bad loans so that the money deposited by customers was never in danger. Today, as in the 1800s, loans are counted as assets on a bank's balance sheet and a look at Taylor's balance sheet puts the modern megabanks to shame. At its lowest point in the Taylor era, City Bank's ratio of equity capital to assets stood at about 16 percent. The ratio at the modern Citigroup rarely rises near 10 percent. In our own time, banks and the government try to fool the public into believing banks are safer than they are by reporting higher ratios based on alternative measures that undercount certain assets claimed by regulators and bankers to be safe.

Taylor's accounting was more straightforward. His bank was always highly capitalized, though it did become less so over time. The equity capital ratio was more than 50 percent in 1841; 35 percent in 1849; just below 20 percent in 1862; and then remained around 16 percent from 1878 to 1891.[28] Compared to modern megabanks, even 16 percent represents a big capital cushion to withstand losses. And if City's capital ratio became smaller over time, that may have been because Taylor's deposits were also growing. During the 1870s, when the bank's deposits stood at $10 million, his personal deposits amounted to upward of 40 percent of this total.[29] Between the money he had contributed as an investor and the money he maintained there as a customer, City had resources to withstand just about any crisis.

In Taylor's time, the capital ratio at his bank was roughly in line with industry peers, but his bank was safer because it had more liquidity—meaning more cash and more assets that could be quickly sold for cash. The money was always ready. It would soon be put to work in the most important financing since the War of 1812, if not the American Revolution.

5

Taylor's Bank in an Age of Panics

ooking back, it's hard to find much fault with Moses Taylor as a banker, but there's plenty of room for argument over the rest of his life. One of the reasons he remains largely un-known is that he never launched major philanthropic efforts like those that continue to define other great industrialists of the age. But this doesn't mean he was entirely uncharitable. And as for the great moral question of his age, he was first an opponent and then an ally of Abraham Lincoln.

Like many New York businessmen in the years before the Civil War, Taylor was a Democrat who had extensive commercial rela-tionships in the South. Manhattan played a large role in financing the cotton and tobacco industries, and for much of the antebellum period Taylor favored compromises intended to prevent armed conflict. His position and that of other like-minded merchants was often portrayed as pro-slavery. Perhaps it was an expression of self-interest, motivated by a sense that war would be very bad for business. If so, this judgment would be proved wrong on eco-nomic as well as moral grounds. The explosion in federal debt to finance the war also created an explosion in Wall Street revenue.

"By the war's end New York was second only to London as a world financial center," writes Gordon.[1]

But prior to the war, there was widespread sympathy in the North's largest city for the Southern cause—or at least for the profits generated by commerce with the slave states. In January of 1861, New York City Mayor Fernando Wood proposed that the city secede from the Union and declare itself an independent republic open to trade with the South. This was months before the attack on South Carolina's Fort Sumter marked the beginning of the war. Wood's pronouncement also preceded secession declarations in a number of Southern states. The mayor was calling for New York City to leave the United States even before the creation of the Confederate government. Wood was taken seriously and supported by a significant segment of New York's business community—but not by Taylor.

Taylor had advocated against war and for the preservation of the Union. He had backed Stephen Douglas in the presidential election of 1860. But he had apparently meant what he said about preserving the Union. Once Lincoln was elected president and the South launched its rebellion, Taylor became a stalwart Lincoln ally and supported both the war effort and the president's reelection in 1864. The New York Public Library, which maintains Taylor's personal and business papers, notes that Taylor did not just become an advocate for Lincoln but was appointed chairman of the presidential reelection campaign committee of the Union Republican Party.

But long before Lincoln could make a case for reelection, the outbreak of war in 1861 created an immediate need for funds to raise and maintain an army. Taylor played a leading role in gathering private and municipal funds to equip and sustain Union troops and also in managing the issuance of federal debt to pay for the war. At the outbreak of hostilities Taylor helped organize a large rally for the Union cause and then called a meeting of an organization that would be named the Union Defense Committee. He served on its finance committee as the group collected private donations as well as appropriations from both the New York City and New York State governments. The committee paid for weapons and ammunition as well as transportation for volunteers heading to the front, and even supported the families of the troops.[2]

As for federal funding of the war, in July of 1861 Congress authorized the Treasury to borrow up to $150 million. A month later, Secretary of the Treasury Salmon Chase visited a group of New York bankers and told them he needed $50 million of it "at once." The bankers huddled, and then Taylor, speaking for the group, announced: "Mr. Secretary, we have decided to subscribe for fifty millions of the United States government's securities that you offer, and to place the amount at your disposal immediately so that you can begin to draw against it tomorrow."[3]

Taylor would continue to help the government finance the war and would eventually be asked to take a senior position in Lincoln's Treasury, which he declined. He also supported the Lincoln administration in enacting policy changes that would help defeat the Confederacy but also create enormous strain on the US financial system for decades afterward. Specifically, Washington was reorienting the nation's banking and currency systems to serve the funding needs of the federal government.

The official history of the Office of the Comptroller of the Currency, which was created during the Civil War as a new national bank regulator, says that the enabling legislation's "leading proponents—President Abraham Lincoln, Treasury Secretary Salmon P. Chase, and Ohio Senator John Sherman—saw the legislation not only as a way to tap the North's wealth and win the war but also as a means to assure the future greatness and permanence of the United States."[4] It certainly helped finance the Union army. Economic historians can debate whether it assured national greatness after the war. With a series of executive actions and laws, including the National Currency Act of 1863 and the National Bank Act of 1864, the feds suspended the gold standard (not to be resumed until 1879), changed the currency, and more or less forced American banks to buy US Treasury debt.

Ever since Andrew Jackson closed the Second Bank of the United States, much of the nation's currency had consisted of notes issued by state banks. But as financial historian George Selgin explains, the Civil War ushered in a 10 percent tax on all state banknotes outstanding, which essentially forced the state banks to stop issuing notes and apply to become national banks under a new federal charter. Going forward, the currency would consist only of notes issued by these new national banks, plus United States notes, or "greenbacks," issued by the US Treasury. The amount of greenbacks in circulation was fixed by statute, so the only growth in the money supply had to come from the national banks.

But there was a problem here, due to Washington's determination to force banks to lend money to the government. Under the new policy, national banks could issue only notes backed by US Treasury bonds. And until the law was changed again in 1900, banks had to keep $100 of Treasury bonds on deposit with the Comptroller of the Currency for every $90 of notes they had outstanding. Selgin explains that this requirement "caused the supply of national banknotes to vary, not with the public's changing currency needs, but with the availability and price of the requisite bonds." What would happen if suddenly there were fewer Treasury bonds in circulation? It was more than a hypothetical question. Selgin elaborates:

> During the last decades of the 19th century, the government, instead of being desperate for funds, ran frequent budget surpluses, which it chose to apply toward reducing the federal debt. As it did so, bonds bearing the banknote circulation privilege became increasingly scarce, and national banks, instead of trying to put

more notes into circulation as the economy grew, did just the opposite, retiring their notes so as to be able to sell and realize gains on the bonds that had been backing them. Between 1881 and 1890, a period of general business expansion and rapid population growth, the outstanding stock of national banknotes shrank from over $320 million to just under $123 million![5]

Taylor seems to have liked the policy as a check on inflation, and it certainly was. State banks could not promiscuously issue notes if state banks did not exist at all. And one can certainly understand why at that particular moment Taylor and lots of other people were concerned about inflation. The onset of war had brought surging demand for goods of all kinds, and prices had been skyrocketing. After zero inflation in 1860 and 1861, according to the Federal Reserve Bank of Minneapolis, inflation surged more than 11 percent in 1862 and more than 23 percent in each of the next two years.

But Washington's cure was, if not worse than the disease, certainly a radical change in monetary policy. Beginning in 1865, prices declined for four straight years, and inflation would not reappear in the US economy until the early twentieth century, with the single exception of a modest 3.6 percent increase in the year 1880.[6]

In short, the second half of the nineteenth century in the US was the era of the great deflation. There are worse things that can happen. Deflation rewards savers and shoppers tend to enjoy lower prices. But this Washington-made currency shortage, when combined with various regulations preventing branch banking— which further inhibited the ability of banks to access cash in a pinch—created a volatile era of finance. Despite a booming economy, driven by new technologies that were enabling a productivity revolution, financial panics were common. Perhaps the worst of them, the Panic of 1893, saw nearly six hundred banks fail or

suspend operations.[7] Much has been made of the financial instability of this so-called Gilded Age[8] of the late nineteenth century,
and the instability has often been cited to justify later government
interventions. Often forgotten are the Civil War–era interventions that helped create this age of panics. It should also be noted
that none of the Gilded Age crises resulted in nearly as many bank
failures as the thousands that occurred during the 1920s—when
five hundred banks failed nearly every year—or the early 1930s,
when nine thousand banks failed over the course of four years, all
after the opening of the Federal Reserve in 1914.

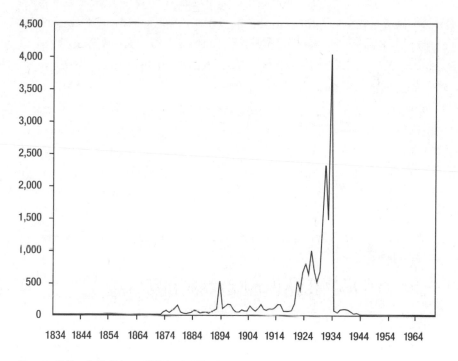

Figure 1: Bank Failures 1830s to 1960s

Source: John R. Walter, "Depression-Era Bank Failures: The Great Contagion or the Great
Shakeout," *Federal Bank of Richmond Economic Quarterly* 91, no. 1 (Winter 2005): 44.

Nevertheless, while the bank failures of the late 1800s never
approached the totals witnessed during the Great Depression, the

shocks were frequent and painful. Yet they never came close to taking down Taylor's institution, which was renamed National City Bank in 1865 to mark its conversion to a national charter. City, in fact, became a refuge for New York savers in times of crisis. When nervous customers ran to withdraw their savings from an institution perceived to be in trouble, increasingly they then ran the money over to Moses Taylor's financial fortress.

While the federal government was now overseeing banks and all but requiring them to lend it money, Taylor wasn't always eager to do so. Even though he was a key player helping to finance the war effort, he never liked keeping too many long-term government bonds on his books because he was worried about the interest-rate risk. He was always on the lookout for inflation, and the price spirals of 1862–1864 likely only strengthened his inclination to be wary of long-dated Treasuries. A long-term government bond paying a fixed amount of interest each year becomes less and less valuable as interest rates rise. On the other hand, a deflationary cycle makes such bonds even more valuable. Therefore, as successful as he was, he likely left a lot of money on the table by not holding more long-term Treasury bonds. Still, his concerns about inflation underscore his cautious approach to finance, which customers especially appreciated during times of market stress.

Taylor's "ready money" policy was embodied by a large cash reserve and stable funding sources. Stable funding meant that City did not hold large deposits from out-of-town banks. Especially if they were located in rural areas, such banks were bound to make big withdrawals whenever their customers needed to pay workers at harvest time, or when there was some localized financial turmoil. Instead, City tended to hold the deposits of successful sugar and coal companies and wealthy families like the Vanderbilts. Most of this money wasn't going anywhere fast. But just in case, Taylor made sure that there was sufficient money on the premises, or otherwise quickly obtainable, to see the bank through any emergency.[9]

In our own time, a "hands-on manager" is one who keeps in close contact with subordinates and is familiar with all the operating details of the business. The description could have been applied even more precisely to Moses Taylor. Bank examiner Charles A. Meigs once observed: "Taylor has always kept his own personal books by double entry with his <u>own hands</u>, and his business is much larger than that of his Bank in amount."[10] Taylor's ledgers still exist, with their orderly listing of debtors and creditors, of stocks and bonds, all noted in his neat cursive handwriting.

As for Charles Meigs, he was among the overseers working for the new Office of the Comptroller of the Currency. Many of these overseers had been state regulators who then signed on to become federal employees. For their labors, the examiners received $5 per day and $2 for every twenty-five miles they traveled to examine their assigned banks.[11] Over the years they would rarely find any fault with City. But as impressed as they generally were with Taylor's bank, they learned right away that it wasn't perfect.

The earliest recorded visit by examiners from the Comptroller's office occurred in the spring of 1868, five years after the creation of their new agency within the Department of the Treasury.

Examiner Charles Callender was inspecting a bank that had recently been victimized by an inside job, resulting in a substantial theft: "This institution has suffered heavily from the Leverich defalcation having charged off $352,392.46 as loss. Since that discovery they have been adopting the suggestions as to books, checks, etc. I recommended in June." This sum was quite a substantial portion of the $1.8 million in capital City had as of the examination date.[12] The *New York Herald* summarized the reasons James H. Leverich, a teller at the bank, was motivated to walk away with such a sum: "Leverich was a young man of twenty-five, and his crime is supposed to have been occasioned by unfortunate dabblings in Chicago, Rock Island and Pacific Railroad Stock."[13] Months later an investigation into Leverich's theft was undertaken, which concluded a number of his City colleagues were also defrauding the bank, according to a San Francisco newspaper:

> Then, as a fitting climax to the investigation, two or three of the guilty clerks, finding that there was no avenue of escape from the pit they had dug for themselves, confessed their complicity in the defalcation. So soon as the "combination" had been unveiled, and the fact made evident that James Leverich had not been the only guilty party, the Directors took strenuous measures to see to it that the bank should not be made a total loser by the defalcation.[14]

Callender, the federal examiner, highlighted the fact that Moses Taylor was a "successful business man and very wealthy," that the directors were "[a]ll men of position, wealth and influence," and that City occupied a "[n]ew office in Marble Building on Wall Street opposite Brown, Brothers and Co."[15] Taylor and the other directors may have been wealthy and successful, but they had clearly failed in vetting potential employees. But customers don't seem to have been worried. There was no run on City in response to the crime. It would be another fifty years before a federal examiner could report such an adverse event at the bank.

In the years ahead, the examiner Meigs seems to have had difficulty finding anything to say about the bank other than expressions of admiration. After an 1872 visit to City, he commented: "Such institutions are the pride of our nation, the bulwarks of our government and of our common civilization and should be held up to the admiring gaze of Americans and to all who value all that is noble and true. The purity of their record—in figures— will show your department that the Examiner here has nothing to explain."[16]

The balance sheets of New York banks during this period explain very clearly how much faith customers placed in City compared to its competitors. During each panic, City expanded its deposit base, while other New York banks generally suffered withdrawals. During the Panic of 1857, City Bank's deposits surged 42 percent while several of its competitors failed. A similar phenomenon occurred during each ensuing financial crisis of the late 1800s (see Table 1). A year after the Panic of 1893, City became the largest bank in the United States.[17]

John Moody explained the Taylor era and the days of crisis:

> The City Bank was always run on the formula, not of the ordinary commercial bank, but of the richest and most conservative old-time merchant, with a great holding of surplus cash . . . A panic is a time when everybody puts his money in the safest place he knows. It is the day of reckoning, the time of the survival of the fittest, in the world of business. Moses Taylor's bank was safe and strong; with every panic it grew stronger.[18]

The only "feature of note in their present condition is the fact that they have gone through the late panic absolutely unscathed," explained a federal bank examiner after the Panic of 1873. "It is a most remarkable specimen of profitable banking. They have dealt largely with Rail Roads but have made no bad debts with them."[19] A similar phenomenon was observed during the Panic of 1884. An exam report suggests that not only was City raking in deposits, it may also have been effectively supporting other banks via the New York Clearing House Association, which lent to member banks in need of cash:

> . . . this bank was creditor at the clearing house for <u>sixteen successive</u> days—the deposits nearly doubled—people poured their money into them for safekeeping. This when banks were suspending and rumor was attacking the soundest institutions.[20]

The clearinghouse eased some of the pressure during these panics by allowing banks to use their sound but temporarily illiquid assets as collateral for loans. In this way City was helping the weaker banks that didn't have much "ready money" meet their depositor withdrawals.[21]

Table 1: Banking in New York City in the Age of Panics (Change in Deposits)

	City Bank	All Other NYC Banks
Panic of 1857	42%	18%
Panic of 1873	32%	-17%
Panic of 1884	70%	-15%

Source: *Citibank 1812–1970*, Table 2.3, 30.

If any of today's taxpayers or Citigroup shareholders were to ask why the modern Citi has not been able to stand as tall as Taylor's City during times of crisis, perhaps one answer would be that Taylor was essentially running a "pocket bank," funded to a significant degree with his own savings and focused mainly on serving his own industrial companies.

It's true that it would be hard to design a modern compensation package with as much of an incentive as Taylor had to look after the long-term health of the institution. But this seems a worthy goal for any bank board. There could hardly be a higher priority than to protect taxpayers from having to fund future bailouts. Also, pocket banks can get in as much trouble as any other kind of bank if the management is not careful to diversify risks and avoid funding projects that are beloved by the owner but threatening to the bank's solvency. City Bank was not Taylor's primary source of income, and he used it to provide liquidity for himself and his firms.[22] But he also had the discipline to stick to a formula of high capital and "ready money." Moreover, contemporary bankers who argue that heavy leverage is necessary to generate robust earnings should consider the consistent profitability of Taylor's City, which routinely paid dividends of 10 percent, 15 percent, and sometimes even 20 percent per year.[23]

As we've seen, City's financial strength helped Taylor to assist the federal government when the survival of the United States itself hung in the balance. He also came to the aid of local governments. Hodas reports: "In 1865 the City Bank loaned New York City, then hard pressed for funds, $500,000, which enabled the city to meet its payroll. On another occasion, twelve years later, Taylor executed a secret confidential loan to the city of Savannah, Georgia, to enable it to meet its financial obligations."[24] It's not entirely clear that a government financing should have been kept secret, but the phenomenon of City helping to rescue government treasuries was as much a pattern of the late nineteenth century as the reverse would be in the twentieth and early twenty-first.

It may seem a very long time ago that the bank was the one helping the government. But in other ways, Taylor looks very contemporary. As we've noted, you can give just about any historical figure a fairly rough time by judging him under modern standards. But Taylor was ahead of his time in pursuing a kind of shareholder activism. In 1848, he became a trustee of the Ohio Life and Trust Company and quickly noted with displeasure that various of the other trustees were borrowing significant sums from the company. He urged them to repay the loans and focus on serving the shareholders they were supposed to be representing. Alas, his reform campaign does not appear to have been successful. He sold his stake in the company in 1852. It failed in 1857.[25]

In our own time, we also hear a great deal about striking the right balance between work and home life, and Taylor seems to have been an early adopter of this concept. Even as he was building his empire, he seems to have been a family man who occasionally attended large social events but otherwise enjoyed evenings at home. Hodas reports that Taylor particularly enjoyed setting the table and serving his children ice cream. Recollections and diary entries from the family suggest a happy household often filled with the sound of youngsters attempting to play music. Taylor was perhaps as down-to-earth as one can be while residing in a Fifth Avenue mansion and enjoying various vacation properties.

And while there is little evidence of any large charitable ventures, records show that he offered at least some support to various causes. Shortly before his death, Taylor gave money to create a hospital in Scranton to provide free health care for employees, and their families, of the Delaware, Lackawanna & Western Railroad and the Lackawanna Iron and Coal Company.[26]

Taylor's personal papers reflect other generosities. His sister Mary Hatfield wrote occasionally to thank him for gifts to one cause or another, often a church or religious organization. In June of 1859, she thanked him for a "very kind and liberal donation." She added, "It will make the hearts of very many of the poor children . . . glad, and greatly rejoice their teachers."[27] A couple of months later an F. W. Bogen wrote to thank Taylor for having "enjoyed for five years past your liberal patronage in behalf of my missionary labors among the German emigrants."[28]

But it seems that Taylor spent relatively little of the money he made on himself and even less on others. He was accumulating a fortune that would be estimated at more than $40 million at his death in 1882, more than $1 billion in today's dollars.[29]

Taylor also bequeathed to the other City shareholders a careful man to lead the bank. In 1836, back in Taylor's merchant days before joining City's board, he had hired a sixteen-year-old immigrant from the United Kingdom named Percy Pyne. Pyne became Taylor's "right-hand man"[30] and in 1855 also became his son-in-law by marrying Taylor's daughter Albertina.

Pyne seems to have been a careful banker and good neighbor but not much of a marketer, and certainly not an empire builder. He was in charge for nine years, but suffered from ill health for much of that time. The bank was in safe hands, but was hardly growing. Examiner Charles A. Meigs, in his inimitable fashion, shared his observations:

> Percy Pyne, Esq., a son-in-law of Moses Taylor, Esq., who is still living, but badly paralysed has been in sole charge of the Bank for the two years past—seems to have all the pride of his most remarkable father-in-law, in keeping the bank perfectly clean and entirely free from any and all "entangling alliances," of any kind whatever, at all times![31]

The bank saw a spike in deposits and assets during the Panic of 1884, but after the panic balances returned roughly to their pre-crisis levels. In 1891, another federal examiner, A. Barton Hepburn, found the expected, boringly reassuring story at City Bank:

> Reserve has not been short for many years . . . The Department need never have any anxiety on account of this Bank, so long as present management continues. The President is a very timid man. He pays no interest, carries the strongest reserve of any bank in the city and gets a large line of deposits from equally timid people who feel that their money is a little safer in this bank than it would be in Government Bonds.[32]

But there were not all that many such people. Pyne was carefully avoiding disasters but losing key customers and making little effort to win them back.

Fortunately for City shareholders, the next president would attract some of the greatest customers in the history of finance.

6

The Rockefeller Bank

I t wasn't much fun for employees when James Stillman showed up at City Bank, but the ones who didn't get fired were in for an amazing ride. A Texas cotton and railroad baron who joined the bank's board in 1890, Stillman would soon take over for the ailing Percy Pyne and transform City into the largest bank in the United States. Stillman managed this feat in part by maintaining a solid, safe haven for depositors in times of crisis. The Texan also lassoed the two greatest banking clients of that era, and perhaps any era: Standard Oil and the US government.

Stillman's achievement is all the more remarkable given that Standard Oil chairman John D. Rockefeller didn't like him.[1] Yet Standard Oil made so many deposits during this era that City became known as "the oil bank." And as for City's huge client in Washington, the bank appears to have won the business the same way it won the loyalty of commercial customers—with ready money available to lend. Later in its history, City would rely on the US government for rescues, but in the 1890s it was the reverse. Stillman's rock-solid bank came to Washington's aid even when the legendary J. P. Morgan was unable to stem investor flight from Treasury paper.

Stillman seems to have been destined to lead City from the start. His father did business with Moses Taylor and one of Stillman's first toys was a miniature bank, across the front of which he had printed, "City Bank." When his father fell ill, Stillman was thrown at age seventeen into a cotton business in which the oldest partner also had close connections with City.[2] Taylor himself would later ask the young Stillman to participate in many business ventures, including the reorganization of the Houston & Texas Central Railway Company.[3]

Taylor wasn't the only captain of finance and industry impressed with Stillman. Beginning in the 1880s Stillman served alongside William Rockefeller, John's brother and a Standard Oil cofounder, on the boards of a railroad and a bank. The two directors became close friends, and two of Stillman's daughters eventually married sons of William Rockefeller. The business side of the friendship would help turn City into a financial giant.

But the commanding heights of American finance were barely visible from City's modest New York offices when Stillman arrived as president in 1891. With a mere $22 million in assets, it ranked twelfth among New York City's commercial banks, far behind market leader Chemical. City held a tiny 0.3 percent share of the US banking market. It also ranked behind many of the large trust firms, like United States Trust Company, as well as savings banks like Bowery.[4] City had only a small number of officers and fewer than one hundred employees.[5] Writing nearly a century ago, financial historian John Moody observed that Stillman was hired as president in 1891 for two reasons: "[F]irst, there was no one else in sight; and second, he was a man of ability, sure to represent, to some extent, the traditions of the institution. He had been familiar, in both a personal and a business way, with the bank since his youth."[6]

That familiarity led him to accept a challenging assignment. A City executive reported that many years later, Stillman recalled an institution in decline:

> Mr. Stillman spoke of his early connection with the City Bank and said that as a kindness to his friend, Percy Pyne, who was paralyzed and had been sent to Europe, Mr. Stillman agreed to spend two hours a day at the City Bank looking after things in Mr. Pyne's absence. As soon as he got fairly into the affairs of the bank, he found a condition which made him wish for Mr. Pyne's early return; that it was only the big balances of the Moses Taylor estate and the friends of Moses Taylor that kept the bank going. Things did not improve and Mr. Pyne died abroad. His death and Mr. Stillman's active interest in the bank determined his future connection with it and started his career as a banker.[7]

Despite his long family history with the bank, Stillman was not sentimental about City's business practices or its personnel. Writing in the 1930s, John Winkler noted that some employees learned "to their sorrow" that Stillman was passionate about efficiency and organization. "With the thoroughness of a microbe hunter, he probed into details," wrote Winkler. "Every man was jacked up and snapped into place. Punctuality was rigidly enforced. The lunch hour was cut to thirty minutes, the work day lengthened. Even the most minute items of overhead, such as the cost and distribution of pads and pencils, were thoroughly scrutinized."

Stillman was not exactly a people person, and certainly not the type of nurturing mentor many of today's millennial employees are constantly demanding. Even in that era, some City workers "rebelled and were promptly fired. Others cooperated with the new management and their salaries were raised modest amounts. Yet not a single surviving veteran of those days recalls that President Stillman ever praised a job well done," added Winkler. "He ruled absolutely by fear and was thoroughly ruthless in his rebukes when a job was poorly done. The result was that, within an incredibly short time, his men were models of efficiency who would as soon have considered defying the devil as disobeying a Stillman regulation."[8]

Was Stillman in his day a more demanding boss than, say, Steve Jobs was in his? Like Jobs's Apple, Stillman's City Bank would achieve outstanding success, which surely must have made the workday more tolerable, interesting, and lucrative for many City employees. And long before Silicon Valley technology firms provided gourmet meals for their employees, City had a kitchen and dining room where lunch was provided free of charge to the staff, no doubt so they could stay close to their desks. A club room was made available for employees in the basement. There was also a suite of two bedrooms for officers of the bank in case they had to pull an all-nighter in response to a banking panic.[9]

As tough as Stillman was on employees, his scrutiny of bank loans was even more exacting, according to Winkler: "His all-seeing eye raked the portfolio. Notes long due were collected, bad debts wiped off or (more often) amortized, further credits were refused firms bearing honored names if even so much as a smudge were on their credit record, devilishly embarrassing personal questions had to be answered before the new president would consider a loan. Gradually the decade of decline ceased and the bank began to swing forward."[10] Modern shareholders and taxpayers could only dream that prior to the financial crisis of 2008 a Citigroup CEO had examined the bank's mortgage investments with such an energetic and skeptical eye. And even the shareholders and taxpayers of Stillman's own time would soon enough have reason to be grateful for his zealous defense of the bank's capital.

But of course they didn't have to live with him. Known on Wall Street as the "Man with the Iron Mask," he said little about

his business plans—or anything else. A former colleague remembered Stillman's "sharp and piercing eyes"[11] and his long silences.
And when he did speak he didn't necessarily tell people what they
wanted to hear. In his biography of John D. Rockefeller, Ron
Chernow reports that at one point Stillman "feuded with his wife
and banished her forever from the house, forbidding his five children from mentioning her name."[12]

Stillman's strained relations with John D. Rockefeller never
reached the level of a feud, because Rockefeller understood how
close his brother was to Stillman. But the oil baron didn't trust
Stillman, though the two men shared a reticent nature, a healthy
skepticism of the press, and a natural inclination not to seek public
attention. Both the Rockefellers and Stillman were also dedicated
to a relentless pursuit of business success, as well as the maintenance of well-capitalized firms with ample reserves of cash. They
were simply applying the same principle of "ready money" to different industries.

Finding crude oil, turning it into useful fuel, and then distributing it to customers has always been a capital-intensive business.
The Rockefellers sought to maintain deep wells of cash they could
tap at any time to seize opportunities or avoid calamities. William
Rockefeller was for decades in charge of the financial office of
the Standard Oil Company in New York, which was essentially a
large bank. "No living man knew better the use of ready money
as a tool, or what tremendous profits it would bring of its own
power against men who were on the verge of ruin for not having
it," writes Moody. While running the financial powerhouse inside Standard Oil, William Rockefeller also became a large stockholder in City.[13]

Why are empire builders driven to build their empires? In
a 1903 magazine profile, Edwin LeFevre wrote, "Mr. Stillman
dreams of a great national bank, and thinks that he can make one
of the City Bank. It is what he is trying to do, what occupies his

mind, and animates his actions. He is running his bank, not toward dividends, but toward an ideal. And he wishes to create such a bank, not for the personal aggrandizement of James Stillman, but because it is needed." Mr. Levfre added that such an institution "would be a great power for good" and was for Stillman "a duty more of patriotism than of profit."[14]

Whatever Stillman's motivations and aspirations for the bank, it would have been tempting to take shortcuts, chasing growth by embracing more risk rather than the harder job of building capital and acquiring profitable, creditworthy customers. But Stillman was building City for the long haul. "With the eyes and concern of a statesman he was looking always into the future, even beyond the unborn generation. The bank was not his, that was not at all the way he felt," recalled a colleague. Rather, the bank "was the institution we served."[15]

Bankers can easily become less cautious when times are good, and Stillman took over City during an economic and financial golden age. There were occasional crises, but in the late 1800s the US economy was booming, and Wall Street roared right along with it.

During the last three decades of the nineteenth century, the economy averaged more than 4 percent annual growth after inflation, the best of any industrialized nation in the world.[16] The New York Stock Exchange enjoyed its first million-share trading day in 1885.[17] The number of companies listed on the exchange increased rapidly during that era, and Main Street also thrived. In this second phase of the Industrial Revolution in the US, prices fell by 32 percent between 1873 and 1896, but real income soared 110 percent as expanded trade and technological innovation powered robust growth.[18] Politicians may have called the business titans of that time "robber barons," but for consumers and workers it was an era of lower prices and higher real wages.

Many government officials of our own time oddly view inflation as a prerequisite for prosperity. And too many politicians of the late 1800s suffered the same confusion. This led to a financial panic, and the government's first—but not last—need for a rescue by New York banks including City.

The seeds of the crisis had been planted right around the time Stillman was joining City's board of directors. The monetary deflation of that period was great for savers and consumers, and many businesses also liked the strong dollar and low production costs. But farmers wanted crop prices to rise, not fall, and so in 1890 they persuaded Washington to enact the Sherman Silver Purchase Act, which ordered the Treasury to print money to finance its purchase of 4.5 million ounces of silver each month at market prices.

The farmers got the weaker dollar they wanted, but there were consequences. With the 1890 law, the US had moved from a gold standard for its currency to a situation in which US Treasury paper could be exchanged for either gold or silver. This scared foreign investors, especially in London, where rival banks had recently had to organize a rescue of the storied Barings Bank due to soured investments in Argentina and Uruguay. To many old-school London financiers of that time, the US was still seen as a developing nation, not so different from the Latin American equity markets that had just imploded. In a pinch, investors would want gold, not silver, and many began to wonder if they needed to act quickly to ensure they could trade their US paper for the yellow metal instead of silver. Foreign investors began trading in their US notes for gold, which was soon flowing out of the country at an alarming rate. By December 1892, the US government's gold reserve had fallen by 40 percent to $114 million. By March of 1893, the reserve stood at barely more than $100 million and continued to fall.[19]

As always throughout recorded history, doubts about the value of a nation's currency triggered economic disruption and destruction. The young Dow Jones Industrial Average fell to a record low. In 1893, nearly a third of US railroads would go bankrupt.

President Grover Cleveland persuaded Congress to repeal the silver law, but Congress raised high tariffs on foreign goods even higher, adding another brake on economic growth. Unemployment surged. Years of depression followed, in which more than five hundred banks would fail, along with fifteen thousand other businesses.[20] Washington-created monetary chaos, combined with banking regulations that were a constant source of financial instability, put extreme pressure on banks nationwide.

Yet City, overseen by the exacting Stillman, remained an island of stability. "While other banks were drained of cash," wrote Winkler, there was never a day when Stillman "could not escort a favored or prospective customer to the cellar and display shining bars of gold. The psychological effect was enormous."[21] The financial effect was also enormous, as deposits flowed into one of the few institutions viewed as a safe haven. While many other financial firms were imploding, City's assets grew more than 26 percent in the panic year of 1893 and surged nearly 60 percent in 1894 (see Table 2).

Table 2: Building the First Billion-Dollar Bank
CITY'S GROWTH FROM 1891 TO 1920 (ASSETS AND LOANS IN MILLIONS OF DOLLARS)

	Assets		Loans	
1891	22.20	7.2%	10.80	2.9%
1892	23.50	5.9%	13.20	22.2%
1893	29.70	26.4%	13.30	0.8%
1894	47.40	59.6%	23.30	75.2%
1895	42.90	-9.5%	21.70	-6.9%
1896	37.10	-13.5%	19.80	-8.8%
1897	67.90	83.0%	40.10	102.5%
1898	113.80	67.6%	50.30	25.4%
1899	138.40	21.6%	70.90	41.0%
1900	188.60	36.3%	88.70	25.1%
1901	194.50	3.1%	90.50	2.0%

1902	202.80	4.3%	89.10	-1.5%
1903	197.60	-2.6%	105.70	18.6%
1904	290.40	47.0%	150.50	42.4%
1905	307.90	6.0%	178.10	18.3%
1906	242.40	-21.3%	126.00	-29.3%
1907	231.50	-4.5%	119.60	-5.1%
1908	334.10	44.3%	146.80	22.7%
1909	317.10	-5.1%	157.70	7.4%
1910	290.40	-8.4%	127.40	-19.2%
1911	307.00	5.7%	132.20	3.8%
1912	313.80	2.2%	163.50	23.7%
1913	276.10	-12.0%	132.00	-19.3%
1914	352.40	27.6%	179.00	35.6%
1915	441.10	25.2%	196.40	9.7%
1916	615.30	39.5%	330.00	68.0%
1917	902.10	46.6%	444.70	34.8%
1918	977.30	8.3%	531.60	19.5%
1919	1,039.40	6.4%	622.80	17.2%
1920	1,032.10	-0.7%	650.30	4.4%

Source: *Citibank 1812–1970*, 320, 321.

In our own time, celebrated investor Warren Buffett likes to say, "Be fearful when others are greedy and greedy when others are fearful." Having been fearful about potential customer defaults during the good times, Stillman didn't have to be so fearful during the downturn. Armed with swelling deposits, Stillman went bargain-hunting for quality investments at fire-sale prices. "To him the banker was not merely a man who loaned out money on good security at a nice rate of interest. He was a person who canvassed and looked into every possible profitable project or business opportunity and who took command in supplying the necessary finances," added Winkler.[22]

Among the fearful—and for good reason—was President Cleveland, who needed private help to maintain the Treasury's gold reserves. He turned to J. Pierpont Morgan, but even the great house of Morgan couldn't shoulder on its own the burden of maintaining the credibility of US currency. Fortunately for Morgan and for the United States, there was Stillman's basement. City had been buying additional gold from overseas as the financial winds began to howl. Bolstered further by its alliance with the cash-generating Standard Oil, City was ready to come to Washington's rescue—perhaps just in time.

In 1894, the Department of the Treasury made an emergency request to Morgan for a bond offering in which the subscribing banks would pay in gold. But Morgan couldn't squeeze enough orders out of his syndicate of banks—until he went to City. In telling the story many years later, Stillman may have exaggerated his tale about instantly summoning gold from abroad, but it illustrates how his also-ran bank was quickly becoming a titan of American finance:

> Morgan was upset and overcharged. He nearly wept crying: "They expect the impossible." So I calmed him down and told him to give me an hour; and by that time I cabled for ten millions from Europe for the Standard Oil and ten more from other resources and came back. I told him: "I have twenty millions." I told him the sources. He became perfectly bombastic and triumphant, as the Savior of his country. He took all the credit.[23]

By October of 1894, City was the largest bank in the United States.[24] It was about to get much larger thanks to another rescue of taxpayers.

Just as politicians in our own time find it hard to resist investments in high-speed rail projects, Gilded Age Washington had made a big losing bet on the Union Pacific Railway. The failing railroad had entered receivership in October of 1893. A battle of banks ensued over plans to recapitalize it, and much of the debate centered on how to treat the government's $45 million of claims. City, Stillman, and William Rockefeller provided money and management to help keep the trains running and begin a turn- around. Stillman was placed on a committee of five responsible for overseeing the bankruptcy and he used City to support the recapitalization, for which it earned fees and shares in the revived railroad. City also acted in part as an agent of the US Govern- ment.[25]

City profited from the deal and so did taxpayers. The govern- ment would soon receive $58 million in settlement money from the revived railroad, and in 1897 Washington deposited $24 mil- lion of it in City, making the bank the nation's largest government depository. City had only become a government depository in 1894, so it's not surprising that the bank's rapid ascent aroused the curiosity of the US Senate. Lawmakers issued a resolution di- recting the Treasury to provide it with copies of all letters, com- munications, agreements, papers, and documents between the Treasury and City regarding public funds, bonds, and revenues of the government. The Treasury responded that "no Treasury office is adapted" to house such a large sum. "It was necessary, therefore, to select a bank strong enough and with a volume of securities pledged for such deposits adequate to cover the transactions from day to day. The National City Bank of New York was the only bank that met this requirement, and it was therefore accordingly directed to assume the task."[26]

City would provide additional services to its Washington cli- ent. Stillman served as an adviser to President Cleveland and the bank actively supported the president's efforts to maintain the gold standard.[27] City later helped finance the Spanish-American War. This wasn't a new role for the bank, as it had supported such fund- ing efforts going back to the War of 1812. City also served as the agent of the US government in its transfer of $20 million in gold, which was paid to Spain for the Philippines.[28]

What *was* new—and uncharacteristic for Stillman—was a transaction in 1897 that suggested City's relationship with Washington was about to change. Through the 1890s, City was a model bank: careful, well capitalized, thriving, and perhaps even indispensable during moments of national financial crisis. Instead of looking to Washington for bailouts as it would do later in its corporate life, the bank was where Washington looked for help when politicians had gotten taxpayers into a jam. Whether the clients were government officials or commercial customers, City appeared to earn them by providing exemplary service while avoiding threats to its capital. The bank was growing quickly and organically, not relying on mergers with all their potential risks and complications.

The glaring exception was City's 1897 purchase of Third National Bank. It had strength in correspondent banking, essentially acting as a bankers' bank that provided a variety of services, typically for smaller banks outside New York City. This was a business line where Stillman recognized City was relatively weak. But Third National had struggled throughout the era of panic and was on the brink of failure as the merger was announced.[29] If this was simply another bargain that Stillman could collect during a time of market uncertainty, it was one that appears to have carried significant risk. Nearly a third the size of City, Third National was big enough to do real damage if its loan book turned out to be worse than expected. At the time, Stillman said he bought the bank to secure its business but also so that its president, Barton Hepburn, could be "associated with us in the management of our bank."[30]

Now why would Stillman want help managing City from the man who had just driven Third National to the edge of the cliff? Perhaps it was Hepburn's previous job that Stillman found most intriguing. Hepburn had served in Washington as the Comptroller of the Currency. And he was not the last political operator that Stillman would hire in the years ahead. In the Progressive Era, the man who built City into a financial powerhouse may have decided that a new set of skills would be needed to navigate a new world of banking.

7

A Political "Big Shot"

There were stories about Stillman—his eccentricities, his domineering ways, his tremendous power," recalled Frank Vanderlip, an assistant Treasury secretary who got the chance to observe Stillman up close. Vanderlip was invited to dine at Stillman's New York home, a brownstone on Fortieth Street just off Fifth Avenue. The year was 1900, and more than three decades later Vanderlip would call it "the most trying dinner I ever lived through."

How did Vanderlip end up spending such an uncomfortable evening in Manhattan? His boss, Secretary of the Treasury Lyman Gage, had recently visited Stillman in New York. City Bank's president mentioned Vanderlip and then pointed toward a corner of his office and said, "When you are through with that young man I want him to sit over there." Vanderlip would not only sit at the bank; one day he would run it.

But first Vanderlip had to sit at Stillman's dinner table, along with Stillman's daughter Elsie, who would later marry a Rockefeller, plus "a lady companion" and the great man himself. "Throughout the meal Mr. Stillman hardly spoke and I was obliged in spite of my distaste for small talk to carry on a conversation with the ladies, smothering as best I could my discomfort in the knowledge that Mr. Stillman was sitting there sizing me up."[1]

Stillman must have been satisfied with what he observed, because after dinner he had one of his lawyers come in to chat with Vanderlip about events in Washington. Then Stillman and his man withdrew for a private discussion, "leaving me to fuss with my tie, smooth my big brush of a black mustache, and to perspire deep into my mind," according to Vanderlip.[2] Stillman returned, spoke at length about New York banking, and then said to Vanderlip, "When you are through with the Treasury, and I understand Mr. Gage wants you to stay there for another year, we want you to come into the City Bank as vice-president."

Vanderlip said he needed time to consider it, but was secretly stunned and ecstatic. He had planned to accept even if Stillman had only offered him a job as a private secretary. "Upon my return to Washington and after a decent interval during which I was several times congratulated by my jubilant friend Mr. Gage, I wrote to Mr. Stillman accepting his offer."[3] Vanderlip continued at the Treasury before going to work for City in 1901.

It was a different time. Today, a top Treasury official probably wouldn't get away with remaining on the job for a year after accepting a job at a giant bank. The potential conflicts of interest would be too numerous to count. Even then, Vanderlip's plan relied on avoiding public disclosure. He admitted in his memoir, "None but Mr. Gage knew of the arrangement I had made to go to the City Bank; it would have been fatal to the arrangement if anyone had known about it."[4]

Perhaps things haven't changed all that much in the years since Vanderlip monetized his federal experience. In 2009, future Treasury secretary Jack Lew was paid by Citigroup for taking a job with the Obama administration. He was contractually due a bonus if he left Citi for a "high level position with the United States government or regulatory body."[5] Coming or going, it seems the bank has always found ways to compensate senior Washington officials.

Vanderlip certainly enjoyed being a Washington official. A farm boy from the Midwest, he was drawn at a young age to political power and prestige. Rural life had been difficult. While Vanderlip was a teenager, his father and brother died and the family farm was sold. Along with his mother and sister, Vanderlip moved in with a grandmother and two aunts and began working at a machine shop in Aurora, Illinois.

Vanderlip decided in 1881 to travel to Cleveland to witness the burial of President James Garfield. Garfield had finally died in September after being shot twice by an assassin in July. Vanderlip wrote in his memoir that he expected "it was going to be a thrilling and a dignifying adventure to travel on railroad trains from Aurora all the way to Cleveland to see the pageant of the Garfield obsequies."[6] Vanderlip, already a staunch Republican, was not disappointed. "The canopied and heavily draped catafalque in which the coffin was hauled through the streets was as large a platform and as carefully arranged as a Mardi Gras float; but not even the gloom of its blackness could spoil for me so rich a show." He added, "I saw former President Rutherford B. Hayes. I saw Arthur, the successor of the president who was in his coffin. I saw Blaine and Windom and the other members of the cabinet. These men were as deities to me."[7]

Vanderlip sought to be a person of influence in his own community. He saw an opportunity when he read in the *Aurora Evening Post* that the newspaper's city editor was leaving for another job in another city. Vanderlip asked the publisher for the job and was promptly hired. "Six dollars a week was the pay and quite often I had to go out and collect the amount from delinquent subscribers or advertisers, for rarely was there that much money in the till. The paper was housed in a one-story wooden building of two rooms, and which was the most gummy with a deposit of chewing tobacco it would be hard for me to say with accuracy," wrote Vanderlip. "The year was 1885 and I was twenty-one, but my soul was inches taller because I was now a personage."[8]

The future Treasury official and bank president enjoyed his new role in the affairs of the town. "I went to the police-station, I went to the city hall, and to the other sources of routine news and although the expression was not then in use I was, in Aurora, a big shot."[9] But he wanted a bigger town, and soon made his way to Chicago, where, after a few undistinguished years working in finance, Frank Vanderlip became a reporter for the *Chicago Tribune*.

More than a century before fake news involving Russia became a story in the 2016 presidential election, Vanderlip knew all about it. According to his memoirs, "a tradition of the time" held that it was "always open season for faking on the hotel beat." Chicago's newsmen would regale readers with invented tales of exotic characters allegedly staying in the Windy City's most luxurious hotels. A friend at a rival paper would sometimes share with Vanderlip the particulars of a fabricated story about an intriguing foreign visitor so that Vanderlip wouldn't get scooped on the made-up story. This also must have provided some protection to the inventor of the story because it would appear that the bogus account had been corroborated. It seems that the various reporters on the beat weren't the only ones in on the scam. Vanderlip wrote that if a curious or skeptical reader came to the hotel where, for example, a mysterious Russian guest was reported to be staying, the clerk at the front desk could be counted on to say, "Mr. Sonofagunsky has just left town."[10]

If Vanderlip was not a brilliant investor, he was certainly a tenacious one. Investing money that his father had left to his mother, he made an initially disastrous bet on the shares of a company called Central Market, which went into bankruptcy. This was not just a serious setback for his family's finances but also a professional embarrassment, since Vanderlip was by this time the financial editor at the *Tribune*. But all was not lost for the Vanderlip clan. The newsman dug into the issue and found what he believed to be a legal flaw in the process by which the company had distributed its shares. He showed up to press his case at a meeting of the company's creditors, which was presided over by First National Bank president Lyman Gage, who would become Vanderlip's boss at the Treasury.[11] Stubbornly confronting the lawyers representing creditors, Vanderlip demanded that he be made whole and succeeded in recovering "my mother's money and my self-respect."[12]

Whatever the legal merits, perhaps the creditors were inclined to resolve a dispute with the *Tribune*'s financial editor. In our own time, such an episode would certainly raise questions about conflicts of interest and journalistic ethics. But Vanderlip doesn't appear to have been burdened by such concerns. In his memoirs he wrote admiringly of a colleague who cut telegraph wires in order to prevent competing reporters from filing their stories.[13]

Instead of aiming for high professional standards, Vanderlip was focused on becoming "almost a daily stroke of apoplexy to a masterful financier of the city," Charles T. Yerkes, whom Vanderlip believed was "recklessly daring in his ambitions."[14] Vanderlip seems to have been bothered by Yerkes's control of various Chicago businesses. The future Treasury official was convinced that many companies of the day did not adequately disclose financial information to their investors. Vanderlip also admitted that he "resorted to some obnoxious methods" in uncovering the "scandal" that some railroads of the time gave discounts to large shippers that were not offered to retail customers.[15]

However "obnoxious" Vanderlip's methods were, they certainly helped him to obtain a rising profile among Chicago's movers and shakers. He joined the Union League after being proposed by "a banker friend" and became president of the Press Club.[16] He became a magazine editor, and it was around this time that there was "an alteration" in Vanderlip's "relations with financiers in Chicago."[17]

One night in 1896 he "was called out of bed to the telephone and asked to come to the house of P.D. Armour," the meat-packing baron. "I got there just before midnight and found the presidents of most of the banks and the governors of the stock exchange. There had been a financial collapse; Moore Brothers had failed. They were a couple of lawyers who had been running a big operation in Diamond Match Company stock. When it was discovered they would be unable to pay back their borrowings, a very dangerous situation was seen to exist. One of the bankers put the matter before me," wrote Vanderlip.[18]

The financier told Vanderlip they wanted him "to handle this story so as to minimize its effect. We have decided not to open the stock exchange tomorrow but unless the news is handled with discretion we will have runs on all the banks and savings institutions."

"I'll do it," said Vanderlip, "on one condition. Every man here must pledge himself not to see reporters or answer any questions tonight."[19] After gaining their ascent, Vanderlip then offered his exclusive to all the newspapers of the city on the condition that they would print the story exactly as he wrote it and allow him to inspect their headlines. All but one paper agreed, and Vanderlip managed to break the story while downplaying its significance, just as the bankers had hoped he would. "The end of my story was a curious sort of afterthought, a kind of—'by the way, The Stock Exchange will not open today.'"[20] Did Vanderlip bury the lede out of a public-spirited desire to prevent a financial panic—or because he managed in one stroke to gain a valuable exclusive while also ingratiating himself to Chicago's leading financiers and industrialists?

All we can say for sure is that Vanderlip's future lay in politics and finance, not journalism. A year later he went to work at the Treasury for Lyman Gage. While some might look back and question Gage's decision to hire Vanderlip—or his decision to let Vanderlip continue working at the Treasury even after he was committed to City Bank—it's hard to fault Gage for his management of the US dollar, which was his primary responsibility. Gage led the McKinley administration campaign to reestablish a currency backed solely by gold, an effort that culminated with the enactment of the Gold Standard Act of 1900.

Vanderlip for his part was planning his move to City Bank but decided that it would appear unseemly to go straight to the bank from his Treasury post. So he left the government in March of 1901 and spent four months traveling in Europe. Apparently, he was less concerned about appearances while overseas. With letters of introduction from City Bank, he met various leading bankers and finance ministers on the Continent. "It was the manner in which I was received in places of great power abroad which began to give me some glimmering of the new force with which I had become associated," he recalled.[21]

When he returned to the US, Vanderlip joined City as a vice president without portfolio—and without a clue. "I sat there on the busy platform on the first floor and I did not have the faintest idea what to do,"[22] he later recalled. Vanderlip knew little about banking, which, when combined with his experience as a Treasury official, allowed him to achieve remarkable success.

At the dawn of the twentieth century, banking was not a marketing culture. Bankers, especially those who worked at a giant New York institution like City, did not make cold calls. They did little in the way of advertising and were reluctant to solicit business even from people they knew well. The custom was to develop relationships and then respond when someone asked to become a client. Vanderlip hadn't grown up in this culture and didn't understand why the old-school bankers weren't asking people to open accounts. He also didn't understand the process of making loans or the intricacies of various financial instruments.

But as he sat there idle at an empty desk, largely ignorant of the work his busy colleagues were conducting right next to him, Vanderlip realized that he did possess some very special assets. "I knew a great number of bankers; the influential ones all over the country. As Assistant Secretary of the Treasury I had had charge of all the relationships between the Treasury and the National Banks." So he began writing these contacts and urging them to open accounts with City. This was called correspondent banking—serving as a bank for other banks. And beyond the contacts Vanderlip had developed while at the Treasury, there was another way in which the government helped him to develop this business. By restricting branch banking, regulators all but forced smaller banks to develop correspondent relationships with other banks, especially in New York, and regulators also passed judgment on which firms could serve as reserve banks and therefore appropriate depositories for the cash from rural banks outside of harvest season. The combination of Washington-created advantages and his own innovative marketing helped Vanderlip to grow City's deposits. By 1905, the bank's US correspondents had doubled.

Vanderlip also pushed the old-fashioned commercial bank into a significant role in Treasury bond trading and investment activities, for which taxpayers may have a difficult time forgiving him. Since he had overseen bond issuance while at the Treasury, he possessed unique insights into this market—and a well-placed source. "As Mr. Gage was still Secretary of the Treasury and my friend, I was easily able to keep myself well informed concerning changes of Government policy with respect to bond issues and retirements," noted Vanderlip. Lucky him. In an era when Washington was running a budget surplus, it must have been useful to know which bonds were going to be retired, as well as the course of future issuance. Vanderlip would later help arrange for Mr. Gage to leave the

Treasury to become president of United States Trust Company, so things seem to have worked out well for both men.

Drawing on his newspaper experience in Chicago, Vanderlip also published articles on the Treasury market and on issues of global finance and economics. This, too, had not been customary at City, but Stillman supported the effort and had copies printed for distribution to clients and potential clients. Vanderlip seems to have been revolutionizing the marketing of financial services, and City continued to thrive. Stillman for his part still wasn't talking much—except apparently to Vanderlip. City's president would frequently invite his younger colleague to dinner or for a Sunday drive, at which time the boss would offer all sorts of advice about the character of men with whom Vanderlip would have to deal, and about the operations of City. "Indeed, sometimes it seemed almost as if he were fearful that there would not be enough time to impart to me all that he felt I should know," recalled Vanderlip.[23]

"Caution was the thing he was trying to impress upon my character in all our talks and dealings," continued Vanderlip. "These were his earnest precepts, that a man is never so rich he can afford to have an enemy; enemies must be placated; competition must never become so keen as to wound the dignity of a rival man or institution; and, above all, I was to avoid having too many banking eggs in one basket."[1]

Yet despite preaching caution, Stillman seems to have appreciated Vanderlip's ambition and the growth in City's role as the go-to bank for other banks.

Vanderlip soon had his own office upstairs at the bank, as well as an expanding staff. He favored expensive cravats—often gifts from Stillman obtained on trips to Europe. Vanderlip developed a cigar habit, became a member of New York's Metropolitan Club, and eventually presided over a country estate.

While his fortunes were on the rise, the nation's financial system was headed toward a reckoning. As usual, Stillman was well prepared. According to one of his employees at the time, Stillman saw signs that the economy was "working toward a crash and indeed that he expected it as early as 1906."[25] His guess was a year early, but City was ready to play its now-familiar role as an island of stability in a financial storm.

As was often the case in the era when government prevented branch banking, the Panic of 1907 occurred in the fall, when country banks were pulling cash out of city banks so that rural customers could make withdrawals and then pay people to bring in the harvest. On top of the normal government-created annual autumn stress, in 1907 there were also the particular problems of a plunge in copper prices, which bankrupted some leveraged commodity speculators, and a general economic downturn. Railroads began to report losses, and United States Steel Company experienced a weakening of demand. Money grew tight.

One troubled institution, Mercantile National Bank of New York, which held deposits of about $11 million, applied to the New York Clearing House Association for assistance.[26] The clearinghouse provided illiquid member banks a loan certificate to settle accounts with other banks. This was borrowing backed by collateral that freed up precious cash for the bank.[27]

Mercantile received assistance, but in examining the bank's troubles the clearinghouse found links to another, much larger institution. Knickerbocker Trust Company had $35 million of deposits,[28] but, like other trust companies, held very little cash. Trust banks, chartered by states, accepted deposits from trust funds, wealthy individuals, and institutions and often made short-term loans to Wall Street brokerages wagering on stocks. The trust banks were allowed to operate with far less cash and riskier assets than the national banks, which had stringent capital and liquidity requirements.

But the leaders of even the strongest national banks figured that a panic among depositors at the trust banks could spread to other institutions. So they joined forces to see if they could save institutions that could be saved—in other words, firms that held quality assets but had a temporary need to borrow cash. Always prepared for a rainy day, Stillman's City Bank had the strength to play a leading role in the rescue effort led by J. Pierpont Morgan, who proposed to create a pool of funds to lend to struggling institutions. Also part of the rescue team were other leading bankers George Baker, president of the First National Bank of New York; George Perkins, a partner with J. P. Morgan; Henry P. Davison, vice president of the First National Bank; and Benjamin Strong, secretary of the Bankers Trust Company. The team determined which trust institutions were financially strong enough to support. Knickerbocker Trust was the initial institution experiencing liquidity difficulties. However, Knickerbocker closed its doors before even a cursory diagnostic review could be undertaken by Davison and Strong. Morgan was not overly disturbed by the failure or those who criticized his lack of will to intervene: "I can't go on being everybody's goat, I've got to stop somewhere."[29] Unable to receive assistance, Knickerbocker's president committed suicide.

Shortly after Knickerbocker's failure, a two a.m. phone call roused Strong at his home in Greenwich, Connecticut. He raced into New York City to help assess the next institution that was faltering—Trust Company of America. The team determined that the firm was solvent and had sufficient collateral to support a lending facility. The team members agreed to support it with $13 million, the first installment of which was $3 million extended entirely by Stillman's City Bank.[30]

Strong described how he personally delivered the collateral and the first installment of cash with the assistance of one of City's vice presidents. He first "dashed down to Morgan's," where he found Perkins and another banker "waiting anxiously for my report." After hearing his summary of the situation, they ordered the opening of the Morgan vault and gave Strong "bags of securities which had been left there the day before by the Trust Company

of America." Then a Morgan banker "called up Vice President
Whitson of the National City Bank and told him that we had to
have some cash at once." Strong was out the door again and racing
to prevent a panic:

> We ran down Wall Street to the National City Bank with some
> millions of securities, the street being thronged with sightseers
> and a long line of waiting depositors also extending down Wil-
> liam Street from the Trust Company of America and into Ex-
> change Place. A very hasty examination of the collateral was
> made at the National City Bank, and I remember giving Mr.
> Whitson a pencil receipt for a bundle of gold certificates—I
> cannot now recall whether it was $600,000 or $1,000,000—but
> I put them in my pocket, ran down Wall Street, and at almost
> exactly ten o'clock found Mr. Thorne [president of Trust Com-
> pany of America] walking up and down the gallery overlooking
> the banking room in the utmost anxiety lest he be disappointed
> in the loan. The minute he saw me he said that the trust com-
> panies had failed him, the money was not forthcoming, and that
> he expected to close the institution promptly at ten. The look
> of relief on his face when I handed him the first earnest money
> I shall never forget.[31]

Thorne wasn't the only one looking relieved as the crisis began to subside. But as fearful as many bankers and investors had
been as the trust banks began to falter, the Panic of 1907 ended
up causing little damage to other financial institutions. Very few
commercial banks failed during the panic, as the level did not
reach anywhere near the thousands per year that collapsed at the
height of the Depression (a peak of four thousand failures in 1933)
or the hundreds that went bust during the 1920s. Failures also
did not reach the level witnessed during the Panic of 1893 when
about five hundred banks failed in a single year. In contrast, only

six national banks, eighteen state-chartered banks and seventeen
state-chartered trusts failed during the Panic of 1907.[32] So at least
based on the benchmark of bank failures, commonly used to judge
the severity of a financial crisis, the Panic of 1907 was a relatively
mild event. (See Figure 1 on page 49.)

But a precedent was set that would prove to be very costly
indeed. The Panic of 1907 is commonly remembered as a crisis
managed and resolved by a private citizen, J. Pierpont Morgan. In
the years that followed, some urged a larger role for government
on the theory that the resolution of such financial crises should
not rest on the leadership of one wealthy banker—that it was too
much power for one man to hold. This view may strike some
modern readers as odd. Today, taxpayers can only dream that private individuals, rather than government, would be responsible for
coming to Wall Street's rescue in a crisis.

In any case, the truth is that while Morgan certainly led
the management of the crisis and put Morgan money into the
solution—and even helped rescue not only the New York Stock
Exchange but New York City itself—this was not a strictly private
undertaking. In one of the earliest historical examples of a federal
effort to support individual financial institutions, Treasury Secretary Cortelyou pledged $25 million on behalf of the US govern-
ment, with the funds deposited in City ($8 million), First National
Bank ($4 million), and National Bank of Commerce ($2.5 million)
among other New York banks. The idea was that these strong
commercial banks would then have more to lend to the firms that
were struggling.

The funding made available by the Treasury was extended in
large part to support borrowers like Trust Company of America.
But this new and larger role for Washington would ultimately
affect all Americans. In the wake of the crisis, public policy discussion focused on the possibility of the government creating a
central bank to serve as a lender of last resort in times of market

stress. Readers can probably guess who among New York bankers was an enthusiastic backer of the idea. Frank Vanderlip believed that Washington needed to organize and centralize financial power—and he would work very hard to make sure that the interests of City were well represented in the new world of American banking.

8

A City Banker Helps Create the Fed

Frank Vanderlip's role in the creation of the Federal Reserve would not become public for decades, but it would benefit City Bank almost immediately. The story begins with a secret message from James Stillman, who was spending much of his time in Europe as he began to pass control of the bank over to Vanderlip.

The cautious Stillman often wrote important business communications in code, to safeguard the bank's secrets against a curious cable operator or a disloyal secretary. While traveling, he kept his codebook in a valise that not even his most trusted servant was permitted to carry. Vanderlip kept the only other copy of the codebook back at City. The great men of finance and industry were assigned new names under the City code, so for example, William Rockefeller was Tumacar and J. P. Morgan was Zuckerat.[1] In 1908, Stillman sent a letter from Paris that concerned a man with the code name of Zivil.[2]

This was Senator Nelson Aldrich of Rhode Island. After the Panic of 1907, he had co-authored legislation to create a National Monetary Commission, and then assumed its chairmanship after his bill became law in May of 1908. That summer, Aldrich and his fellow commissioners visited England, France, and Germany, "the three countries of Europe in which conditions most closely resemble our own," to learn about banking in these countries through interviews with officers of the leading institutions.[3] The idea was to study how other countries dealt with financial panics and to consider, for example, the creation of a central bank to lend money to commercial banks in a crisis. Central banks were common in Europe. Along with its research value, the trip allowed Aldrich to leave behind American journalists, who might have reported skeptically on his meetings with wealthy bankers.

Even if reporters had been allowed to attend Aldrich's meeting in France with Stillman, they might not have learned much. Stillman, as usual, kept his cards close to the vest, telling Aldrich that he should not be influenced too much by "our Wall Street point of view."[4] But Stillman had more to say in his letter to Vanderlip. The aging City boss thought that a centralization of US bank reserves contemplated by Aldrich could be bad for banking and urged Vanderlip to stay in very close contact with the powerful senator. Stillman also said that during their meeting Aldrich had expressed regret that Vanderlip and Henry Davison, a partner at J. P. Morgan, were not able to join the commissioners on their European tour.

Vanderlip wasn't new to the issue. He had been publicly advocating for a banker-controlled central bank, but few members of Congress acted as advocates for the plan, possibly because it was seen as a Wall Street scheme.[5] Now here was a great chance to exert influence privately. Stillman discussed with Aldrich the idea of the lawmaker getting together at a remote spot, perhaps at a Rhode Island estate, with Vanderlip and Davison for some "uninterrupted" discussion. This was perhaps a euphemism to describe a meeting with no reporters around to ask uncomfortable questions.

Aldrich and his fellow commissioners continued their research on foreign financial systems while Vanderlip now had a bank to run. In January of 1909 he became City's president and Stillman became the bank's chairman. That year and the next, Vanderlip had his hands full thwarting mergers that might have threatened City's position as the country's largest commercial bank. Vanderlip appears to have kept City on top not by pulling political levers in Washington but by persuading J. Pierpont Morgan that City's leadership role was good for business.

Yet Vanderlip wasn't neglecting Washington, nor ignoring Stillman's advice to keep in close touch with Senator Aldrich. As a result, Vanderlip was among a select few bankers and government officials included in a secret meeting that to this day continues to inspire numerous conspiracy theories—and for good reason. "Despite my views about the value to society of greater publicity for the affairs of corporations, there was an occasion near the close of 1910, when I was secretive, indeed, as furtive as any conspirator," admitted Vanderlip in his memoir.[6]

Aldrich wanted the chieftains of New York finance to assist him in drafting legislation to reform the nation's banking system. But he knew that his plan would be doomed if the public knew that Wall Street helped write the bill. So he opted for a secret meeting of influential men pretending to be embarked on a duck-hunting trip. J. P. Morgan's Davison arranged for the clandestine group to gather at Georgia's exclusive Jekyll Island Club, a remote playground whose members included Joseph Pulitzer, William Rockefeller, and other barons of American industry.

Along with Aldrich, Davison, and Vanderlip, the group included Paul Warburg, a partner at the Kuhn, Loeb & Company investment firm who would later become vice governor (what we now call vice chairman) of the Federal Reserve, plus Assistant Secretary of the Treasury Piatt Andrew, and Aldrich's Senate aide Henry Shelton. None of these men would publicly admit their participation in the secret gathering for decades. They were told not to use their last names when communicating with one another and to avoid dining together on the night of their departure. "We were instructed to come one at a time and as unobtrusively as possible to the railroad terminal on the New Jersey littoral of the Hudson, where Senator Aldrich's private car would be in readiness, attached to the rear end of a train for the South," recalled Vanderlip.[8] Even after boarding, he and Davison went further than just avoiding the use of last names. They employed new first names as well. Wrote Vanderlip, "On the theory that we were always right, he became Wilbur and I became Orville, after those two aviation pioneers, the Wright brothers."[9]

Once in Georgia, "We were taken by boat from the mainland to Jekyll Island and for a week or ten days were completely secluded, without any contact by telephone or telegraph with the outside." After hashing out the details of a new American financial system, according to Vanderlip the group "returned to the North as secretly as we had gone South." But their work still wasn't done. Having dominated the construction of the Aldrich plan, the bankers were called on again to write an accompanying report due to Aldrich's ill health. Vanderlip reported that he and Bankers Trust boss and future Federal Reserve Bank of New York governor Benjamin Strong "went on to Washington and together we prepared that report. If what we had done then had been known publicly, the effort would have been denounced as a piece of Wall Street chicanery, which it certainly was not."[10]

Vanderlip, like the others, would attempt to rationalize the secrecy in which leaders from Washington and Wall Street wrote the initial draft of what would become the Federal Reserve System: "None of us who participated felt that we were conspirators; on the contrary, we felt we were engaged in a patriotic work. We were trying to plan a mechanism that would correct the weaknesses of our banking system as revealed under the strains and pressures of the Panic of 1907."[11]

It's possible they even believed this, but there's no doubt that the plan drafted by leaders from the nation's political capital and its financial capital ended up benefiting both. Their work would ultimately be submitted by Aldrich as his own product to the National Monetary Commission[12] and then on to Congress. With some modifications that enhanced the power of the federal government, the plan would eventually become law in 1913. Presented as a solution to the problems exposed in 1907, the reforms drafted by the handful of wealthy and powerful men left untouched policies that had contributed mightily to the crisis—and helped ensure the dominance of City and the other New York banks. At the same time, Washington greatly expanded its authority over the nation's financial system.

Unlike with the financial crises of the late nineteenth century, federal limits on issuance of banknotes could not easily be blamed for the Panic of 1907. The Monetary Reform Act of 1900 had eliminated a chronic threat to the availability of credit by making it much easier and more profitable for banks to issue notes, resulting in a big surge in issuance. Banknote circulation soared to $609.9 million in 1907—up from $242.9 million in 1899.[13] With the gold standard also restored in 1900, the credibility of the currency likewise could not be blamed for the events of 1907. Why did US finance suffer still another liquidity crisis?

The systemic problem that remained from the financial panics of the late 1800s—and that was ignored by the Jekyll Island gang—was a set of policies that encouraged banks nationwide to keep large deposits in New York. These policies were especially valuable to City in the Vanderlip era.

At the time of the Panic of 1907, the country's banks still largely consisted of single units with no branches. The federal government restricted interstate branch banking, and most states limited branching within state borders. This made it difficult for banks to diversify their risks and exposed them to local and regional shocks.[14] Branching restrictions made it more costly and difficult to move money around in a crisis, as banks had to act in concert with correspondent banks in other cities, instead of being able to simply transfer funds within their own firms. Country banks "kept interest-bearing accounts with Midwestern city correspondents, sending their surplus funds there during the off-season. Midwestern city correspondents, in turn, kept funds with New York correspondents, and especially with the handful of banks that dominated New York's money market. Those banks, finally, lent the money they received from interior banks to stockbrokers at call," writes financial historian George Selgin.[15] Call loans were ones in which banks could demand repayment from brokerages at any time, so the credit helping to support higher stock prices could vanish in an instant.

In short, there were powerful incentives to deposit in New York, where the money was often used to make short term-loans backed by risky investments in the securities markets. Beyond the branching restrictions, federal regulations on bank reserves also rewarded country banks for depositing their money in urban banks and rewarded banks in midsized cities for depositing their funds in the "central reserve cities" of Chicago, New York, and St. Louis. "Thanks to this arrangement, a single dollar of legal tender held by a New York bank might be reckoned as legal reserves, not just by that bank, but by several; and a spike in the rural demand for currency might find all banks scrambling at once, like players in a game of musical chairs, for legal tender that wasn't there to be had, playing havoc in the process with the New York stock market, as banks serving that market attempted to call in their loans," adds Selgin.[16]

National policy was pushing cash from the countryside into banks in big cities like New York, which also exerted a powerful demand for these funds with Wall Street's voracious appetite for credit. Depending on what else was going on in the world or the financial markets, this made every harvest season a potential source of instability for New York banks as the country folks started taking their money back. A decline in correspondent balances in turn put pressure on Wall Street's call loan market, causing such loan rates to rise sharply and stock prices to fall.[17]

Unstable though it was, this system was also highly lucrative for New York—and for Vanderlip's City Bank in particular. Thanks to his pioneering work in asking for accounts from out-of-town banks, City had become New York's market leader in correspondent banking, with nearly $100 million of its more than $200 million in deposits belonging to other banks. So the agenda for Vanderlip was to maintain regulations that encouraged the money to keep flowing to New York, but create a national lender of last resort to address the instability problem. And that's exactly what the Aldrich plan—and eventually the Federal Reserve Act—would do.

"Aldrich's preferences aligned with Wall Street's, for the Wall Street bankers, and Vanderlip in particular, had come to see a central bank as the best means for preserving their correspondent business whilst protecting them from the shocks to which that business exposed them," writes Selgin.[18] Of course, not *all* Wall Streeters shared this view. Stillman had been skeptical of what central banking would do to the industry, but Vanderlip's lobbying appears to have been just as effective inside the bank as it was in Washington.

The new rules would eventually require fewer reserves in the banking system, but still encourage smaller banks to send their deposits to New York. Also, branch banking restrictions would be maintained, but with one notable exception that helped City Bank most of all. US banks would now be able to open foreign branches.

Vanderlip had been pushing this idea for years. After a tour of Europe in 1901 during which he focused on US exports, Vanderlip began to speak in favor of foreign branch banking as far back as 1903 in a speech at the New England Club of Boston:[19]

> Let us suppose that we have an organization of great financial strength . . . energetically and intelligently representing broadly our exporting interests in the world's markets . . . Suppose such an organization should stand behind purchaser and producer, guaranteeing . . . the delivery of goods . . . [as well as] the credit of the purchaser. If such an organization were equipped with men of trained intelligence, keen observers of commercial conditions, who would be quick to see an opportunity and devise means of grasping it, and if that organization had behind it the cooperation of great manufacturing interests here, I believe wonders could be accomplished.[20]

To enable such wonders to occur, Vanderlip later initiated a lobbying campaign for foreign branching led by Milton Ailes, who had succeeded Vanderlip as assistant secretary of the Treasury. Ailes tried unsuccessfully to persuade the Department of the Treasury to allow foreign branching without changing the law and also floated the idea of exchanging City's national bank charter for a state charter since New York allowed foreign bank branches.[21] More fruitful was an effort to lobby executive branch officials up to and including President Taft to rewrite the law. The president even plugged the arcane policy idea in his 1910 State of the Union Speech.[22] Though it would not become law while he was in the White House, foreign branching was permitted in the Aldrich bill.[23]

How could one justify allowing a US bank to open a branch overseas but not in a nearby American city? At least as far as the freedom to open foreign branches, which was included in Section 25 of the 1913 Federal Reserve Act,[24] supporters could make a reasonable public case. Senator Claude Swanson of Virginia, who shepherded the bill through Congress for President Wilson, explained:

> By permitting the creation of branches in foreign countries we
> will enable the banks of this country largely to conduct our
> foreign business, with benefit and profit to the bankers and in-
> creased accommodation and the saving of many million dollars
> to the people of our country.[25]

How much tougher would it have been to sell this plan to the public if people knew that the benefiting and profiting bankers were also the plan's authors? This was probably just one of many reasons why legislative drafters decided that the genesis of this reform could under no circumstances be exposed to public scrutiny. Decades later, Vanderlip would cast the secrecy as necessary to solve a merely parochial issue for the financial industry: "Discovery, we knew, simply must not happen, or else all our time and effort would be wasted. If it were to be exposed publicly that our particular group had gotten together and written a banking bill, that bill would have no chance whatever of passage by Congress. Yet, who was there in Congress who might have drafted a sound piece of legislation dealing with the purely banking problem with which we were concerned?"[26]

It certainly was a banking problem, but one that affected all Americans, as did the alleged solution: a national safety net for banks. The Federal Reserve Act allowed the regional Reserve Banks to lend to Federal Reserve member banks, a power even the First and Second Banks of the United States did not explicitly wield. Section 13 allowed any Federal Reserve Bank to discount notes, drafts, and bills of exchange, in other words to provide cash loans to member banks that presented their noncash assets as collateral. This is often called lender-of-last-resort authority. In a different time and if the institution involved is weak, it might be called bailout authority. Vanderlip described this new power in his autobiography:

> It provided an organization to hold the reserves of all member banks and arranged that they would always be ready to relieve a member-bank under pressure by rediscounting loans that it held.[27]

The provision was patterned after similar lending authority that had been granted to central banks in Europe, in particular England, France, and Germany.[28] Although the exact language from the Aldrich bill was not used, the concept of a power to discount was a prominent feature of the Aldrich architecture.[29] The underlying details of the provision have been amended numerous times over the years, but the power to lend remains with the Federal Reserve. The authority was invoked during the most recent financial crisis, with the institution we now call Citigroup being one of the leading beneficiaries.[30]

In the days of Moses Taylor, customers large and small could rely on City Bank to stand rock-solid in the midst of a financial panic. In the bank's Stillman era, even the federal government could count on City for help in times of crisis. But thanks to the politically savvy Frank Vanderlip, these roles would be reversed. After 1913, it was City that could count on government for assistance when times got tough. And the times certainly would. In its second century in business, protected from disaster by a new national reserve system, America's largest bank would increasingly need it.

9

"Our Friendly Monster" Goes Global

War is hell. For some, it's also an opportunity. As Frank Vanderlip surveyed the world of 1914 and considered City's new freedom to expand overseas, he saw the potential to make America's biggest bank even bigger. Now backed by the Federal Reserve but increasingly without James Stillman around to offer words of caution, Vanderlip plunged into the world's most volatile markets.

Vanderlip could be forgiven for not seeing growth opportunities at home in the United States. Even in the best of times, state and federal restrictions on branching meant that growing a domestic banking business was a challenge. And these were not the best of times. The US suffered through a recession in 1913 and 1914. Along with creating the Federal Reserve, Washington had also created a federal income tax in 1913—not exactly a stimulus for the private economy. Then came the outbreak of war in July of 1914. Panicked European investors immediately wanted to convert their stocks and bonds into gold. Many of these investments were in the US, which caused a months-long closure of the New York Stock Exchange, lest foreign sellers drain the US of its gold supply.

But the economic destruction caused by the war was also creating demand for the services of New York banks, City in particular. The Allies, especially the British and French, borrowed huge
sums to buy food, weapons, vehicles, and all the other goods consumed by armies at war. Also, the Europeans were largely with-
drawing from the world as they focused their resources on killing
each other. "Something quite apart from the needs of the Al-
lied Armies was tempting us into a fantastic expansion," recalled
Vanderlip. "The bulk of European exports had stopped and there
was a correspondingly great world-demand for everything the
fighting nations formerly had been accustomed to make and sell."[1]

US businesses were rushing to fill the void. And if they wanted
a US bank to provide financial services overseas, one institution
was often the obvious choice. "We were the first major American bank to expand abroad,"[2] Citigroup correctly noted in 2012.
Vanderlip, who had successfully lobbied for foreign branching to
be included in the Federal Reserve Act, wasted no time in seeking to enjoy this new freedom to expand offshore. Even before
the law's passage, he had been sending executives on fact-finding
missions around the world, and he didn't like to hear that a foreign
market wasn't ready for a City branch.

One of the bank's vice presidents, John Kiernan, was dispatched
to South America and concluded that the timing wasn't right for
a southern expansion. So Vanderlip sent another vice president,
John Gardin, who returned with a conclusion only slightly more
optimistic. But that wasn't the end of it. Even though Vanderlip
had his own reservations about competition from German and
British banks—and wondered if he could find all the competent
managers he would need to oversee far-flung branches—he was
undeterred. Once the outbreak of World War I disrupted commerce between South America and both Germany and the UK,
Vanderlip was even more eager to seize what he saw as a competitive opening.[3]

In an earlier era, Stillman might have blocked the headlong rush into exotic markets, given the significant legal, political, and business risks. But heart disease was now taking its toll on City's sixty-four-year-old chairman. Vanderlip had made a pilgrimage to Europe in May of 1914 to get Stillman's blessing for an aggressive branching plan and seems to have met little if any resistance. By the following year, Vanderlip often could not even think of Stillman "as a banker at all, because sometimes for months on end he was completely an invalid, barred by the feebleness of his hold on life from receiving any news from the bank." At times in 1915, Stillman received so many injections of morphine that "it became difficult to find space on his legs where a needle could be inserted."[4]

As Stillman suffered, the bank he had built into a powerhouse seemed to be gaining even greater strength. An official corporate history published in 1985 says that Vanderlip's "new and more aggressive strategy" transformed City "from a specialized wholesale bank into an all-purpose intermediary providing a wide array of financial services to a variety of customers at home and abroad."[5] It was especially the business abroad that would now chart explosive growth.

By June 1914, Vanderlip had submitted an application to the Federal Reserve Board to set up shop in Argentina. The Fed's approval arrived in September, and two months later in Buenos Aires, City opened the first foreign branch of any nationally chartered US bank.[6]

During the next two years, the bank opened branches in Brazil, Chile, Uruguay, and Cuba, where City took over the Banco de Habana, which had counted Stillman among its investors. In the peak year of expansion in 1919, thirty-three branches were opened, and Vanderlip wasn't exactly a fanatic about diversifying his risks. Because the price of sugar had skyrocketed in the preceding decades—and especially during World War I—City wanted to go all in on Cuba's sugar trade. The island also offered opportunities in coffee and tobacco. Therefore, of those thirty-three branches opened in 1919, an almost unbelievable twenty-two of them were located in Cuba. By 1920, City had fifty-five foreign branches in the Western Hemisphere.[7] Although it was a pioneer among US banks, City wasn't the only American firm that was looking for international growth—and specifically off the coast of Florida. J. P. Morgan & Company had entered the Cuban market through the Trust Company of Cuba.[8]

Not satisfied with making a huge bet on the price of sugar, Vanderlip also saw opportunity where political risk was at its highest. With the enthusiastic support of the Wilson Administration in Washington, City opened a branch in the Russian city of St. Petersburg (then known as Petrograd) in January of 1917. The branch made money from the start and for a brief period appeared to be such a cash cow that the bank was planning to open another branch in Moscow. Unfortunately, the Russian Revolution intervened, and the Bolsheviks who seized power weren't particularly keen on American bankers.[9] The Russian debacle would lead to what appears to be the last conversation Vanderlip ever had with Stillman, and it could not have been a pleasant one.

But in the earliest years of City's foreign expansion, the effort appeared to be succeeding. "The bank was growing, growing, growing," recalled Vanderlip, who noted that his foreign branches "developed faster than we could find trained men to run them."[10] This had been a concern as Vanderlip prepared for his plunge into international markets and certainly should have been a red flag. To his credit, Vanderlip tried to address the problem and created programs in which college students would learn about banking while working at City during the summers. Sometimes they would get college credit for joining the bank in their final semesters. City's president simply couldn't find any other way to staff his overseas operations. "I am perfectly convinced that we have to grow our own stocks for foreign branches, if we are going to be in a satisfactory position to carry on this business. The men cannot be hired, they do not exist," said Vanderlip. But while his innovative recruiting and training programs would become widely employed across American industry in the decades that followed, they didn't arrive fast enough at City to prevent trouble offshore. The burgeoning effort to groom young talent simply couldn't keep up with the flood of branch openings.[11]

As if the challenge of staffing and managing a rapidly growing global bank weren't formidable enough, Vanderlip also sat as a director on the boards of some forty companies.[12] Then, while he remained City's president, he took an extended leave of absence to return to Washington to assist the government in selling bonds, even as he continued to participate in the management of the bank. This was after City had already exploded in size, such that Vanderlip wondered how to find the next generation of leadership: "There was a feeling on Mr. Stillman's part, and I shared it, that because I had seen the bank grow from $200,000,000 until it had increased five-fold that it would not be easy to get a man sufficiently young to make a change desirable, and yet capable enough to be master of our friendly monster."[13]

This billion-dollar monster wouldn't necessarily be friendly to taxpayers. But if all the ingredients for a banking disaster seemed to be combined in City's recipe—rapid growth, distracted management, hard-to-quantify risks concentrated in highly volatile markets—at least Vanderlip was eating his own cooking. He accumulated so much City stock that eventually his 12,500 shares would make him the bank's second-largest stockholder, though his stake was still significantly smaller than Stillman's 52,000 shares.[14]

The Russian venture was among the first of the international businesses to go south, and not in a small way. Once the new Soviet government nationalized all of City's assets in the country, the bank was then exposed to pay that branch's depositors with dollars held in New York. In February of 1918, Stillman summoned Vanderlip up to New York from his leave of absence in Washington. Perhaps the bank's largest shareholder summoned the strength to administer one last lesson about the careful banking that had allowed City to stand tall through every crisis. Had City itself now become the crisis? Vanderlip makes no mention of the meeting in his memoirs, but within a few weeks Stillman's health took another sharp turn for the worse, and he died in March.

If Vanderlip had failed to apply Stillman's lessons about building a sound bank that could thrive in any environment, he certainly seems to have understood them. Remembering Stillman, Vanderlip wrote, "All the years that I knew him he was concerned much more with the generation-to-come than with the one about to die."[15] After the passing of his mentor, Vanderlip faced an increasingly hostile board of directors. Given all the time he was spending to assist the government in Washington, William Rockefeller wondered aloud how Vanderlip could manage the giant bank working just one day a week. By June 1919 Vanderlip had resigned as president and was succeeded by James A. Stillman, son of the late chairman.[16]

That was around the time that federal regulators began to spot problems at City, even if they didn't appreciate their significance—or didn't want to. If the bank was struggling to manage its new international network of branches, government regulators had an even harder time trying to oversee and understand the sprawling financial giant. This was well before commercial air travel was commonplace. The Office of the Comptroller of the Currency, which to this day remains one of Citibank's regulators, was required by the Federal Reserve Act of 1913 to conduct on-site examinations of City and all other national banks two times each year. This meant that examiners had to spend time at a bank reviewing its assets and financial position and also visit key branches, as circumstances dictated.[17]

A major objective for regulators going on-site to a bank is to spot potential problems before they grow into major threats to the institution. Examiners generally review a large sampling of the loans at an institution and based on their review attempt to make generalizations about the management of the bank and to draw conclusions about the bank's direction: deteriorating, improving, or holding steady. The most seasoned and capable examiners can go into a bank and within a short period of time get a sense of the loan portfolio and the management.

The tendency for examiners at that time may have been to give City the benefit of the doubt. It was the nation's largest bank and, for over eighty years since the Panic of 1837, had been regarded as a squeaky-clean institution. Then, in June of 1919, a federal examination report disclosed problems with City's governance and its loan portfolio that were starting to appear as a result of foreign branching. Many of the loans were intertwined either directly or indirectly with the fates of shaky governments overseas.[18] Yet this ominous news seems to have been largely shrugged off by the feds. In a confidential section of the report titled "Loans and Discounts," the lead examiner, H. E. Henneman, gave a one-word response to the question of the general character of the loan portfolio: "Good."[19] Henneman later landed a job at City, where he stayed for many years, ultimately becoming the vice president of Latin American operations. Regardless of the strength of its loan portfolio at any given time, the bank has always seemed to have a knack for hiring key government officials.

A more aggressive regulator might have been concerned, for example, by the multiple overlapping bets City was making in Haiti. A loan for nearly $700,000 identified at the 1919 examination was extended to a firm called Caribbean Construction Company. It was classified as "doubtful" by examiners, who place loans in categories of descending order of condition: substandard, doubtful, and loss. A doubtful classification means that collection or liquidation of the loans is highly questionable and in fact improbable. The construction company was helping build a railroad, but its work was largely halted due to political strife. This can happen in places like Haiti, but City was also a major shareholder of the railroad.[20] And the loan was secured by railroad bonds that the examiners described as "of questionable worth."

Another example was a loan of over $200,000 to Mikhail Tereshchenko,[21] who was a lawyer, a publisher, and an industrialist who became the deputy to the State Duma of the Russian Empire, and was ultimately the minister of finance and foreign minister in the Russian Provisional Government after the February Revolution in 1917. However, he was arrested by the Bolsheviks in the Winter Palace, who stole his entire fortune and imprisoned him until 1918. Tereshchenko's loan had been past due since September of 1918, and was secured by rubles on deposit at City's Petrograd branch, which was nationalized during the Revolution.[22] Did anyone think the communists were going to send this money back to New York?

Examiners from the Office of the Comptroller of the Currency did go back to City's New York office for five weeks in February and March of 1920. The US regulators appear to have fallen behind on their mandate to examine banks like City twice each calendar year.[23] In any case, they noticed that the loan to Caribbean Construction had deteriorated further, with nearly $600,000 classified as loss and another $260,000 in the doubtful category. The loan to Mikhail Tereshchenko was nowhere in sight, possibly written off before the examination. Millions in defaulted bonds were detailed in the report, including a Russian issue and a Chicago Elevated Railway bond. And nearly $1 million was reported as owed to City's home office by the Petrograd, Russia, branch, along with a comment: "Value of this asset is extremely doubtful and should be charged off." Fair point.

Lucky for City, the bank now had a new partner ready to provide credit even during rainy days. The 1920 examination report shows that City's borrowings from the Federal Reserve Bank of New York had skyrocketed to $95 million, more than triple the $28 million reported during the 1919 examination. The bank that two decades earlier was strong enough to help bail out the US Treasury was now receiving more funding from the government than from its own shareholders. The bank's capital was just $88 million on the date of the examination.

This time the summary from the examination makes clear that at least one official was getting nervous about the Fed's increasingly cash-hungry customer:

> Taking the Russian experience as an indication of what can happen to foreign branches it might be well to consider what, if any, limit should be placed on the number of foreign branches which a bank be permitted to open and what, if any, limit should be placed upon the proportion of assets or of capital and surplus . . . when the world is apparently going through financial and political adjustment and whether or not it will prove advisable for banks of deposit to open up branches throughout the world to loan and discount and invest without limit when the parent bank is liable for debts of any or all branches . . . Bank has branched out all over the world and I believe they find it difficult to organize so that entire business is handled and controlled in comprehensive manner.[24]

City's increasing reliance on borrowings from the New York Fed clarified that this was no longer Moses Taylor or Chairman Stillman's bank. The examination team seems to have comprehended that, in the era of the Federal Reserve safety net, the days of "ready money" were long gone:

This Bank in the past has had an enviable record for keeping excess reserves and until lately has not been a large borrower, certainly not for any considerable period of time, but now its borrowings are unusually large and indications are this will be the case for some time to come.[25]

At the time of the 1920 exam, at least City's branches in Cuba appeared to be doing well. But the good times wouldn't last in Havana, either. Sugar and other cane products such as molasses and candy made up about 85 percent of Cuba's exports, so the island's economy was extremely sensitive to the price of sugar. Not unlike modern times, Americans were big consumers during this period, gobbling about a quarter of the world's sugar. Half of that consumption was produced domestically, while the other half was imported from Cuba.

Sweet-toothed Americans wouldn't be concerned about an alleged obesity epidemic for nearly a century, but that didn't mean there was no risk in the sugar market. In the years before City's big gamble, the price of this sweet commodity had been on a roller coaster of supply shocks and government price-setting. Trading for less than 4 cents per pound in 1894,[26] sugar rose above 10 cents and was surging higher during World War I as the invading German army turned Belgium's and France's beet fields into battlefields. With European sugar production plunging, and sugar's price on world markets therefore rising, the US and the Allies persuaded Cuba to accept price controls.

A brief golden age of Cuban sugar arrived after the war. Price controls were lifted and then, with Europe still largely absent as an exporter, an unrelated policy in the US created massive new demand. Numerous US states were prohibiting alcoholic beverages, and then a nationwide ban came into effect in January of 1920. Prohibition brought a surge in US consumption of soft drinks and candy. Sugar rose above 20 cents a pound, and Havana became a classic commodity boom town. Successful farmers headed into the city to shop for expensive baubles and enjoy the city's celebrated nightlife, which was also increasingly a magnet for thirsty American tourists denied the freedom to consume their chosen beverages at home. Real estate speculation was a favorite Cuban pastime, and heavy investment—including by institutions like City—powered a surge in the island's sugar production.

But the sugar bubble was short-lived. European production quickly returned to world markets and—combined with the expanded Caribbean supply—triggered a nearly complete collapse in the price of sugar. By the end of 1920, the sweet stuff was once again selling near its 1890s price of 4 cents per pound. By early 1921, sugar was trading below 2 cents per pound, devastating to farmers and refiners who had planted, built, and borrowed on the premise of 20-cent sugar.

Suddenly, Cuba was in the midst of a major financial crisis. Sugar-industry borrowers couldn't repay their loans, and depositors understood what that would mean for the banks holding their savings. The government put the entire banking system under a moratorium in October 1920, extending due dates on loans and placing strict limits on withdrawals. Rather than lasting days or a week, this bank holiday must have seemed like a permanent vacation. The moratorium endured well into 1921.[27]

Meanwhile, the US economy on which Cuba relied was slipping into a deep recession, what financial writer James Grant has called "The Forgotten Depression."[28] According to the National Bureau of Economic Research, the downturn started in January 1920 and lasted until the middle of 1921.[29] Real gross national product fell 9 percent, while industrial production fell by a staggering 32 percent. The comparative figures for the Great Recession of 2007 to 2009 were a 4 percent drop in real gross domestic output and a 17 percent drop in industrial production.[30]

City wasn't the only US bank to bet wrong on Cuba, nor of

course the only institution challenged by the struggling US economy. But federal regulators were finally starting to recognize that the country's largest bank, formerly a symbol of American financial strength, might now be a source of weakness. Regulators from the Office of the Comptroller of the Currency returned to City in January of 1921 for another examination. When they returned a month later to discuss the results with City management, they were led by the Comptroller himself, John Skelton Williams. The meeting started at ten a.m. on February 22, 1921, and lasted for the entire day. Inexplicably, City president James A. Stillman did not attend the meeting.[31] What was no doubt equally difficult to explain to regulators was how City had managed to take on $79 million of exposure to the sugar industry—a figure that rivaled the bank's entire capital—including a full $63 million of nonperforming loans. Borrowings from the New York Fed reached $144 million.

Thanks in large part to his predecessor Frank Vanderlip's big bet on Cuba, James A. Stillman would soon be absent from *all* of City's meetings. He resigned as president in May of 1921 with the bank "tottering" on the edge of failure.[32]

10

"Sunshine Charlie" Doubles Down on Sugar

E ven if he hadn't been going through a divorce, James A. Stillman would have struggled to clean up the mess at America's
largest bank. The United States was suffering through an
economic depression. When combined with Vanderlip's souring
foreign investments, it was a time that could try the soul of even
the most capable financier—which Stillman was not, according to
the bank's official history:

> The younger Stillman was a good banker, but he had neither the
> talent nor the self-confidence to fill his father's shoes. So little did
> James A. Stillman esteem his ability to take his father's place that he
> would not occupy his father's private office, preferring to retain his
> own desk on the platform. The father's shoes would have been hard
> for anyone to fill. The elder Stillman had been an extraordinary
> banker with few equals before or since and, according to a biogra-
> pher, he had once warned his son never to aspire to run the bank.[1]

In March of 1921, the younger Stillman filed for divorce from
his wife, Anne, better known as "Fifi." This commenced a decade-

long legal saga featuring public accusations of infidelity and out-of-wedlock births. He claimed that their youngest son was actually the result of an affair Mrs. Stillman had conducted with a Canadian outdoorsman, often referred to as an "Indian guide" in the voluminous newspaper coverage of the divorce.[2] Mrs. Stillman for her part argued that her husband had secretly fathered a child with a former Broadway dancer. Mrs. Stillman ultimately prevailed and received alimony as well as legal costs.

Back at the bank, the question was how to contain the costs of City's promiscuous investments in Cuba and elsewhere. The board's answer in May of 1921 was to fire Stillman and hire forty-three-year-old Charles Mitchell. Mitchell was a big, swaggering salesman who had grown up in a middle-class family in Massachusetts before attending Amherst. He later went to business school at night before embarking on a career in finance. But City's new boss had no experience as a commercial banker and knew little about taking deposits or making loans.

Mitchell came from the world of Wall Street stocks and bonds, and had even worked briefly at the Trust Company of America around the time it was being rescued by the other great financial houses during the Panic of 1907. Years later, he would recall that just five weeks of that crisis gave him "five years' training in banking."[3] He went on to start his own investment bank, C. E. Mitchell and Company, which ultimately led to a job as president of City's investment banking affiliate, National City Company.[4]

For a bank that was suffering for having strayed too far from its roots—and now desperately needed help with its commercial banking branches in Cuba—Mitchell might have seemed like the worst possible choice. Certainly this is how most historians view him. But to his credit, Mitchell knew his limitations and appreciated how much he needed to learn. A 1923 edition of the *Wall Street Journal* quoted from a profile of Mitchell in a periodical called the *American Magazine*:

When he was elected president of the bank, and moved his office downstairs to the main floor, he said to one of his friends on the board, "I know what I am up against. I'm like a chap that's going to learn to play the piano. I've got to begin picking out the simple tunes with one finger; then, after a while, I'll be able to use one hand, and then both hands. And some day I'll know enough to take it all apart, pull out the bad strings and put in good ones. But it's a long course of study, and I know it."[5]

After a year as president, Mitchell was asked if he was ready to play "Home, Sweet Home" and "Rock of Ages." "Hardly," he replied, "but I'm practicing."[6] Mitchell spent long days poring over City's repertoire of financial services, but he was also deeply curious about events outside the bank. If he was meeting a client with a manufacturing business, he would spend hours trying to understand the industry and its challenges.

Roughly a decade later, Mitchell would become a symbol of Wall Street excess. Much of the press would render him as a cartoon villain who helped engineer a credit-inflated stock bubble, all the while enriching himself as he peddled dodgy securities to unsuspecting investors. Politicians in the 1930s would use Senate hearings to help cast Mitchell in this role, but the truth was perhaps a little more complicated.

For example, reckless financiers who thrive on easy credit are usually the enemies of sound money. Companies that finance themselves with large amounts of borrowed money generally welcome inflation, because it makes their debt smaller as it reduces the value of each dollar they need to pay back.

But Mitchell was for hard money. He backed a gold standard, which allows people to trade their currency for a fixed amount of gold. This prevents governments from creating inflation because if the politicians print too much money, holders of the currency will simply trade it in and drain all of the government's gold reserves.

In 1922, Mitchell criticized plans by Henry Ford and Thomas Edison to take the US off the gold standard. Mitchell said that "the
old fallacies and heresies that have vexed society throughout all
history are hatched again in every time of disturbance and distress.
One of them, and from my viewpoint, one of the most important
of them, is that paper money delusion—the idea that governments
can make times good, by printing plenty of money." He added,
"There is an air of 'hocus-pocus' about the free operation of government money printing presses that ought to put men on their
guard, because we all realize that governments are not creators of
wealth, but have to be supported by taxation."

Once he became City's president, Mitchell acted to protect
the wealth of the bank's shareholders. Specifically, he made rapid
progress in treating the firm's Havana heartburn. Step one was
recognizing losses in Cuba on loans that were never going to
be repaid. This caused City's profits to plunge from more than
$12 million in 1920 to less than $4 million in 1921 and then all
the way down to $1 million in 1922. He also seemed to be more
careful than his two immediate predecessors in extending credit.
Total loans shrank from $650 million in 1920 to $469 million in
1923.[7] Aided by a recovering US economy starting in the middle
of 1921 and a modest rebound in sugar prices, City was able to
pay back every nickel it had borrowed from the Federal Reserve
Bank of New York. Sherrill Smith, the federal regulator in charge
of City's June 1921 examination, approvingly noted: "[T]here has
been a radical change in the handling of loans since the election of
Mr. Mitchell as President."[8]

There certainly had been. In his first few years at the helm,
Mitchell appears to have been among the most conservative of
bankers. After the explosive growth of the Vanderlip era, the
bank was shrinking during the early 1920s (see Table 3). This cycle of high growth, crash, and retrenchment would repeat itself

throughout City's history. Also unlike Vanderlip, Mitchell understood that he needed to focus on running the bank, not serving on myriad corporate boards. "He sticks to his piano," noted the *American Magazine*.[9]

Table 3: Asset Growth Rates for National City Bank v. All Banks

Years	City	All Banks
1914	27.6%	4.8%
1915	25.2%	3.7%
1916	39.5%	15.3%
1917	46.6%	14.8%
1918	8.3%	9.5%
1919	6.4%	15.8%
1920	-0.7%	11.5%
1921	-15.9%	-6.5%
1922	-2.1%	1.5%
1923	0.2%	7.5%

Source: *Citibank 1812-1970*, 321. Bureau of the Census, "Historical Statistics of the United States: Colonial Time to 1970," Part 2, (Washington, DC: Government Printing Office, 1975), 1019.

But even after writing off a lot of bad loans and slimming down City's balance sheet, Mitchell still hadn't fully solved the Cuba problem. As time went on—and once regulators were convinced that the bank had become more cautious in its lending—Mitchell would embrace more risk in Cuba, in other foreign countries, and most of all on Wall Street.

The biggest question facing Mitchell in the early 1920s, with City still holding tens of millions of dollars of Cuban loans on its books, was whether to bet on a rebound in the price of sugar. Additional investment might allow the bank to turn some of its questionable loans into winners if the sweet commodity staged a rally. On the other hand, writing down or selling all of City's remaining Cuban assets would have allowed the bank to close the book on its disastrous island adventure. But closing the book would mean recording more Cuban losses, reducing the bank's capital and limiting its ability to chase new business.

So Mitchell decided to double down on sugar. One month after the bank examiners visited City in 1921, Mitchell hired a few examiners of his own and sent them to Cuba to develop a plan for the bank's investments on the island. Gordon Rentschler, who had worked with Mitchell in the past, was at the time running a manufacturer of sugar-mill machinery and was trying to collect on a pile of bad debts in Cuba. So he knew the terrain, geographic and economic. The other adviser Mitchell sent to Cuba was Colonel E. A. Deeds, an executive at what is now NCR Corporation.

In late 1921, the two men reported back that additional investment could salvage the Cuban properties and make them profitable enough to repay City's loans. Rentschler and Deeds were essentially proposing that the bank become not just a lender but also a manager of Cuban sugar operations, or as Rentschler rationalized it in later testimony: "We were forced into the sugar business." Their recommendation was based on an optimistic assumption that the price of sugar would rebound to a more "normal" level. This was a gamble, and what did City know about running sugar plantations anyway?

It would be several years before Irving Berlin wrote *Blue Skies*.[10] But "Sunshine Charlie" Mitchell, as he would become known, liked to focus on the upside of any potential investment. Still, he wanted to see that potential for himself. So in January of 1922 he traveled to Cuba accompanied by Rentschler, Deeds, and a number of City directors. Mitchell spent his time inspecting plantations, analyzing records, and studying sugar mills. He liked what he saw on the sunny island. City approved the plan and created the General Sugar Corporation to take control of foreclosed Cuban properties and get them to start producing sugar again. The new City-backed venture also bought additional properties that had not gone bust because, as Rentschler explained: "We purchased adjoining estates to round out the property." The new General Sugar now controlled 325,000 acres, and the bank was not just taking over a vast expanse of cane fields. City had become "the reluctant heir to hundreds of miles of railroad track, a dozen locomotives, scores of railroad cars, several hundred thousand acres of plantation land, sixty sugar mills, and oversight of a small army of starving, disaffected campesinos."[11]

Could a bunch of New York bankers lead this ragtag army to victory in the battle for sugar profits? This financial adventure seems fit for a movie, or at least an interesting case study for students in business school. But it must have given pause to bank regulators, who tend to like solvency more than a well-told story. It was one thing for Frank Vanderlip's bank to start accepting deposits and making loans in countries where it didn't fully understand the political and legal risks. At least City knew banking. Now, in a market where its loans had already gone south—suggesting it struggled to understand local credit risks, too—the bank was piling on still more risk. City was betting it could figure out how to grow and mill sugar, while also managing all those starving campesinos.

For whatever reason, regulators allowed the gamble to proceed. There would have been a strong argument for making City acknowledge the bad loans and write them off, given that borrowers had been missing payments for years. If there were any future collections, they could then be counted as recoveries. But the Office of the Comptroller of the Currency exercised forbearance and allowed the loans to remain on City's books for much of the ensuing decade, as if repayment was still expected. Regulators also allowed City to expand its bet in Cuba. The bank had to extend even more loans to operate the sugar facilities, some of which had never produced any sugar before running out of money. Rentschler believed some of the accounts "were not good at all" and would "eventually" be written off, while others "were thoroughly good if they were given an opportunity to work their way out." He felt they had to be "rehabilitated," often with new equipment.[12]

For a while, the bet seemed to be paying off. The price of sugar recovered to 5 cents a pound in 1923 from its lows below 2 cents, and General Sugar turned a profit. Rentschler was rewarded with a seat on City's board in October 1923, while Deeds continued to work with General Sugar.[13] But the rally didn't last. European and US sugar production continued to rise and prices declined again in the mid-1920s, putting extreme stress on the Cuban operations. As the years rolled by, City's federal examiners were losing patience. They continued to criticize the troubled Cuban assets through the October 1926 examination.[14]

City developed a solution in February of 1927: a complex transaction to restructure the ownership of the sugar properties. The regulators might have lost faith that the loans would be repaid, but "Sunshine Charlie" still believed that the Cuban rebound was just around the corner: "[T]he cycle in the sugar industry will come around like it does in every agricultural commodity."[15] To exploit this potential opportunity, City would convert more of its risky debt into equity ownership.

To execute the strategy, City sold $50 million of newly issued stock to its existing shareholders. Half of this money was devoted to increasing the bank's capital, a prudent measure. But the other half was sent to the bank's securities affiliate to buy out the bank's Cuban sugar positions. The point was to get bad loans that were bothering regulators off the bank's books. But the potential Cuban losses didn't disappear—they just moved from City's commercial bank over to its Wall Street brokerage, where the assets would later be recognized as worthless and written down from $25 million all the way to just $1. But the bank received $20.9 million in cash from the transaction and $11 million of new General Sugar notes—essentially a five-year loan to the sugar company that would pay 6 percent annually and was secured by the Cuban properties.[16] The bank's balance sheet was now much stronger—assuming losses on the other side of the house wouldn't someday threaten the bank.

Federal examiners seem to have been happy to make that assumption. As part of the 1927 on-site examination of Citi, examiners from the Office of the Comptroller of the Currency shared Mitchell's optimism as they discussed the progress in reorganizing the Cuban debts, noting the "plan has been substantially carried out." Looking at the $11 million General Sugar balance on City's books, the examiners confidently stated that given their "prediction of [the] probable trend of [the] Cuban sugar industry" and that the corporation was now profitable to the tune of $1.7 million, the debt would be paid off by roughly $1 million per year. The regulators added that the loan would be "passed without criticism," meaning General Sugar's note would no longer be classified as a problem asset.

A section of the report titled "Loans and Discounts, General" had regularly referenced the dangerous concentration of Cuban sugar loans. In early 1927, these references disappeared, but not for long. The roller coaster that was the Cuban sugar market had more surprises in store for City and its federal overseers. By March of 1929, the remaining balance on the General Sugar note was again classified as a problem due to "slow" repayment.[17] Pretty soon, City was going to need prompt repayment from all its borrowers.

Cuba wasn't the only place Mitchell had been increasing his bets. "We are on our way to bigger things," he told City employees in a 1922 speech. "The Chief," as he was known inside the bank, said that after a "period of readjustment" for the firm, "We are getting ready now to go full speed ahead."[18]

That included expansion into new foreign markets, despite the ongoing Cuban debacle. City wasn't the only bank that had suffered from misadventures offshore, but Mitchell was among the few bank presidents who didn't want to change course. After losing money in the overseas expansion sparked by the Federal Reserve Act, some New York banks closed their foreign operations completely, blaming disruptions in world trade, the uncertainty of foreign markets, and the cost of operating a global financial network. With the US economy recovering, and banks gaining modest relief from domestic branching restrictions thanks to a 1918 law, some also argued that there were better opportunities at home in the US. The Federal Reserve estimated fourteen closures of foreign branches in the immediate aftermath of the 1920–1921 recession.[19]

Given that the fiascos in Russia and Cuba had put City on the brink of failure, one might have expected the bank to lead the retreat from exotic locales. And City directors thought about shutting down the entire system of foreign branches. But instead they decided to keep expanding it. Total foreign branches grew steadily from eighty-one in 1920 to ninety-seven in 1930 (see Table 4).[20]

Table 4: City Around the World

Year	Western Hemisphere	Europe	Asia and the Far East	Total
1920	55	8	18	81
1925	62	9	19	90
1930	67	11	19	97

Source: *Citibank 1812-1970*, 324. A foreign office is considered a branch if it accepts deposits, cashes checks, or approves loans.

Beginning in 1924, growth at home accelerated even faster. Whatever his faults—and politicians and the press would cite many of them in the years ahead—Mitchell was an innovator in serving markets that other bankers had long ignored. City began to bring many of the financial products that Americans now take for granted to small savers and borrowers. Until the 1920s, consumers had a hard time getting unsecured financing. Small personal loans from banks were rare, and gas stations and hotels were just starting to offer credit cards. Loan sharking was a scourge, inspiring government officials and newspaper editors to encourage banks to serve middle-class customers, who also had few options when it came to saving. Charles Mitchell's City embraced this mass market and business boomed. As of June 1922, City had 6,300 savings account customers with $2 million in deposits. By mid-1929, the bank had attracted more than 230,000 such customers with a full $62 million in deposits.[21]

Mitchell didn't just want to be America's banker, but its broker, too. His vision was to bring Wall Street to Main Street, selling financial services that had previously been available only to wealthy individuals and institutions to America's burgeoning middle class. Charles Mitchell was about to persuade millions of Americans to become shareholders.

And he would get paid very well to do it. Mitchell was not only an innovator in entering new markets and offering new services, he was also a pioneer in helping to make bonus season the most wonderful time of the year for bankers. He created such rich compensation packages for himself and his top lieutenants that "Sunshine Charlie" appears to have decided it was best to keep other employees in the dark about just how much compensation senior management was taking home.

The investing public would also have a hard time getting the whole story. Mitchell's annual salary through much of the 1920s was $75,000, about $1 million in today's dollars and not a particularly large sum for the head of the country's largest bank. A full decade before Mitchell took the top job at City, his predecessor, Frank Vanderlip, had received a salary of $100,000. This was in the range of what other leaders of the largest US corporations were making in that era.[22]

But Mitchell's compensation was not limited to his relatively modest salary. In May of 1923, City's executive committee quietly created a "management fund" that would eventually allow Mitchell's annual compensation to exceed $1 million. The creation of this new compensation scheme was not immediately apparent to the bank's regulators.

When federal examiners inspect a bank, a member of the team normally reviews all the minutes from meetings of the board of directors and the executive committee since the last examination. It's not the most exciting job and often falls to a junior bureaucrat because a bank's official summaries of such meetings often don't reveal too much. But in the case of the Office of the Comptroller of the Currency's inspection of City that began in November of 1925, an examiner discovered something relevant to Mitchell's compensation that was deemed so sensitive it was reported only in the confidential section of the exam report, which is not shared with the institution under review:

> The examiner wishes to call attention to the practice by the bank of setting up a reserve termed "Manager's Fund," a portion of the earnings for distribution to certain officers as extra compensation to salaries received. Aside from the following abstract taken from the Executive Committee minute book no data appears in the records.[23]

The examination report then showed disbursements that were rising rapidly, from around $660,000 in 1924 to nearly $1 million in 1925. The regulators don't appear to have taken any action to address the lack of transparency surrounding the management fund or question whether its structure could distort incentives in a way that threatened the safety and soundness of the bank.[24] City's official history, drawing on minutes from the 1923 executive committee meeting that created the fund, reports that it was a "contract between the owners and management of the firm.

Under its terms, the bank's annual net operating earnings were to be divided among additions to retained earnings, dividends to shareholders, and payments to executives participating in the plan."[25]

Assuming incentive compensation plans are clearly disclosed, at most businesses there's nothing wrong and a lot right with aligning the interests of shareholders and managers in the pursuit of higher profits. But banking was no longer just another industry, with its new government backstop via the Federal Reserve. Banks then and now have an obligation beyond just seeking to maximize profits. To varying degrees over the years, they have been playing with taxpayer money. Therefore, they have a special responsibility to try to avoid risks that could force them to call on the Fed as their lender of last resort.

If the regulators didn't do anything about City's new compensation system, that doesn't mean they liked it. A 1929 examination report referenced the manager's fund again and noted the oddity that the bonus recipients did not receive the money directly. Rather the payments were routed through two other financial institutions in New York City: Farmers Loan and Trust and Central Union Trust Company of New York. These institutions then paid out the compensation to City's managers: "According to verbal information at hand it is understood the amounts transferred to the two banks above mentioned were subsequently paid to executive officers of National City Bank as additional compensation." This complicated arrangement seems to have been constructed to ensure that City staff processing the payments would not become aware of the amounts paid to individual managers. By 1928, the amount paid into the fund was in excess of $1.4 million, which was "7.7 percent of the net profits for this period after losses and recoveries."[26] Company employees don't have an inherent right to know what their bosses make. But if a firm's leadership goes to such lengths to avoid disclosure, perhaps it's a sign that there's something wrong with the compensation plan.

Thanks in large part to Charlie Mitchell, a flood of new investors were coming into US capital markets. Meanwhile City executives had a poorly disclosed incentive to generate bigger profits, just as the government safety net was expanding around US financial firms, and the new Federal Reserve was learning to conduct the nation's monetary policy. What could possibly go wrong?

11

Mitchell and the Mania

Few people seemed to mind Charles Mitchell's mammoth bonuses and his fast cars and his yacht trips when the stock market was soaring. Of course, this was in part because few people were in a position to know that his annual compensation sometimes exceeded $1 million, a small fortune in the 1920s. But even those with access to the details of City's performance and paychecks were convinced that the bank's president was doing an outstanding job. For anyone who believes that the job of financial regulators is to take away the punch bowl just as the party is getting going, this period of history may be rather discouraging. The bank examiners overseeing City seem to have admired the fact that Mitchell was throwing one hell of a shindig.

While they continued to express concerns about the bonus fund for City managers and the Cuban sugar adventure, the feds generally opined on Mitchell's expanding financial empire in terms that ranged from complimentary to glowing. The following is a quotation not from City's public relations department but from a government official participating in the examination of the bank in November of 1924: "A wonderful bank, the largest in the United

States, apparently in very liquid condition and operated with great care along proper banking lines."[1]

Nearly six decades later, economist George Stigler would win a Nobel Prize in part by demonstrating the phenomenon of regulatory capture, in which government regulation is designed and operated for the benefit of incumbent firms in the regulated industry. For City in the 1920s, regulators may not have simply been captured—they seem to have been in a rush to surrender. In their defense, it's also possible that Mitchell was not quite the villain that politicians and the press would later portray him to be.

Regardless, Washington didn't object as the rising king of Wall Street helped propel an historic bull market. In a report from the October 1926 government review of City's books, an examiner commented: "As is well known, this institution is the largest and possibly, the best known bank in the U.S. . . . the investments as a whole enjoy splendid selection and evidence a good degree of liquidity . . . The Board comprises some of the keenest minds and a number of the outstanding financial resources in the country."[2]

The March 1928 examination inspired more gushing: "Under the aggressive leadership of President Mitchell this bank continues to maintain its place as the largest bank in the United States of America, and under its present policies and management, it is a reasonable presumption that it will continue to lead. Expansion of domestic branches is proceeding at a rapid rate, and all departments of the bank appear to be having proportionate growth . . . The affairs of this bank are well handled. Adequate reserves appear to be held to provide for contingency and no criticism is directed against the bank or its management."[3]

Certainly "Sunshine Charlie" did nothing to discourage the notion that City and the country as a whole were headed for even better days. "Mitchell Sees No Cause for Alarm," read a *Wall Street Journal* headline on October 11, 1928. The *Journal* quoted the City chief: "We are enjoying enormous prosperity in America and I am convinced that nothing can impede the progress we are making."

Mitchell believed that optimism was essential to personal success. An earlier profile in the *Journal*, published in 1923, noted that along with fifteen minutes of exercise before breakfast and a hot bath before dinner, Mitchell also made a daily habit of maintaining good cheer: "'No amount of brilliance or personal charm,' says Mr. Mitchell, 'will carry a man to the top and keep him there unless he can come up smiling day after day.'"[4]

Throughout the 1920s, Washington continued to smile upon his bank. And just months before the greatest financial crash in US history, the bureaucrats were still singing Mitchell's praises. "Bank's general condition is very satisfactory and its business continues to prosper under the able and aggressive leadership of President Mitchell,"[5] wrote an official who participated in the March 1929 exam. Mitchell and his bank were also enjoying rave reviews in the press. The *New York Times* described him as a "dynamic," "potent," "brilliant," "straight-from-the-shoulder" executive, and reporters regularly solicited his views on everything from "the state of the market to the state of the world."[6]

So what exactly were Mitchell and his colleagues doing to merit all the effusive commentary? They were bringing Wall Street to Main Street, and fueling a bull market in stocks that would roughly quintuple in value between Mitchell's ascension to the top job at City in May of 1921 and September of 1929.[7]

But first the City bankers had needed to go hunting for a loophole in federal law. They also had to overcome the fears of at least some government officials who, long before "too big to fail" became a household phrase, resisted putting too much financial activity under one roof.

For almost a century after its founding, City Bank had largely been in the business of accepting deposits and making loans. But

Vanderlip began to transform the firm into a financial conglomerate with both a traditional deposit-taking commercial bank and
an investment bank that would underwrite the issuance of stocks
and bonds and also trade in such securities.

Washington wasn't enamored of the concept. A 1902 opinion
by the Office of the Comptroller of the Currency determined that
national banks could not directly invest in stocks or underwrite
distributions of stocks or bonds. To get around these restrictions,
national banks started acquiring or creating state-chartered affiliates that were permitted to play in the securities markets. In 1908,
the First National Bank of New York, one of City's primary competitors, organized the first such securities affiliate for a national
bank.

Frank Vanderlip's City Bank wasn't too far behind. Building
on his knowledge of the market developed during his time at the
Department of the Treasury, Vanderlip had quickly made City's
bond department an important profit center for the bank. In July
of 1911, City established National City Company as its securities affiliate, and Vanderlip explained its importance in a letter
to shareholders: "The officers and directors of the National City
Bank of New York are of the opinion that it will be of material
advantage of the shareholders of the bank to unite in establishing a
corporation so organized that it may make investments and transact other business, which though often very profitable may not be
within the express corporate powers of a National Bank."[8]

No matter the spirit of the law, Vanderlip and his competitors
believed they had found a way to play on Wall Street while still
arguably following the letter of the relevant statutes and regulations. In fact, Vanderlip saw such huge potential in the capital
markets that he wanted to leave the commercial bank entirely. In
1914, he told his mentor James Stillman that he wanted to give up
his job running City Bank and lead the securities business as an
independent company separated from the mother ship. Stillman

did not approve.[9] National City Company would continue to be effectively controlled by the bank's shareholders even though the two institutions were presented as legally separate for the purpose of avoiding bank regulation.

In a move that would be echoed almost ninety years later with the creation of Citigroup, Vanderlip actually pushed City into the capital markets before it was formally permitted. After the bank created National City Company, President Taft asked his attorney general George Wickersham for a legal analysis. Wickersham in turn requested an opinion on the matter from his solicitor general, Frederick Lehmann. In a preliminary opinion in August 1911, Lehmann concluded that the creation of the Wall Street affiliate was prohibited "by the national bank act." In November of that year, he submitted a more detailed analysis that will likely resonate with many current critics of giant financial holding companies:

> I have reconsidered the question with the care demanded to its importance, and have reached the conclusion that both the bank and the company, whether considered as affiliated or un-related, are in violation of the law . . . because it embarks the bank in business and ventures beyond its corporate powers . . . The temptation to the speculative use of the funds of the banks at opportune times will prove to be irresistible . . . If many enterprises and many banks are bought and bound together in the nexus of a great holding corporation, the failure of one may involve all in a common disaster . . . I conclude the National City Co. in its holding of national bank stocks is in usurpation of Federal authority and in violation of Federal law.[10]

But just as in the era of financial crisis a century later, the Department of the Treasury sometimes seemed more concerned with the survival of Wall Street's giant incumbents than with fol-lowing established precedents. Secretary of the Treasury Franklin

MacVeagh had long been concerned that national banks, supervised by his department's Office of the Comptroller of the Currency, were at a competitive disadvantage against state-chartered banks and trust companies, which were allowed to engage in stock and bond underwriting and trading. MacVeagh argued that City complied with the letter of the law and pointed out that other national banks had had similar affiliates approved. At the same time, he seems to have contradicted this argument with what may have been an implicit acknowledgment that the law presented a barrier. MacVeagh said that a national bank "is, in some respects, unnecessarily tied hand and foot . . . [W]hy a national bank should not do all kinds of legitimate banking, it is hard to say."[11]

At least on the policy argument, he had a point. Even Moses Taylor, a model of financial caution and prudence, would make equity investments as well as loans. And even if a firm sticks to traditional bank loans, every extension of credit carries risk. One modern and persistent myth of the 2008 financial crisis is that Wall Street alone was responsible and that complicated derivatives were a root cause of the crisis. But plenty of small banks that never dabbled in complicated financial instruments failed because they had made too many loans to people who lacked the ability to repay them. The common denominator for failing financial firms was too much exposure to the US residential housing market. Bankers could find trouble with the most simple or the most complex investments tied to home mortgages. Too many bad real estate loans were an affliction for banks in the 1930s as well. City would also find trouble in territory far from its New York headquarters.

But back in 1911, as MacVeagh made his case for liberating the biggest banks to compete in the capital markets, City enjoyed fortunate political timing. Taft, who would make the government's final decision, was in the midst of a tough three-way reelection battle that he would ultimately lose to Woodrow Wilson. According to the *New York Times*, if President Taft decided against the banking giants, he might be creating what a later generation of government officials would call systemic risk: "If he decides holding companies are unlawful and proceeds to put them out of business he will strike a heavy blow at a great number of important business concerns closely connected with the financial stability of the country. If he decides they are lawful he will at once be accused of giving consent to the establishment of a money trust." Taft decided not to challenge the legal structure of City's new securities affiliate. It would not be the last time that Washington reluctantly ruled in City's favor out of fear of the systemic consequences of crossing the New York banking giant.

Vanderlip in turn threw Taft a bouquet and directed National City Company to sell its holdings in domestic bank stocks. But City's Wall Street affiliate continued underwriting and trading in securities issued by governments and nonbank corporations.[12] Therefore most of the potential markets in stocks and bonds were wide open for a firm that was already America's largest bank.

Initially, the bond market consisted mainly of the debt of foreign governments. Between 1914 and 1917, US securities firms and commercial banks formed nationwide syndicates to sell $2.5 billion worth of bonds issued by the Allied powers (primarily Great Britain and France), a pioneering effort by private firms to market securities to the public. After the US entered World War I in 1917, American banks and securities firms quickly shifted from selling Allied bonds to supporting their own government's efforts to finance the war.[13]

Table 5: Asset Growth Rates for National City Bank v. All Banks

Years	City	All Banks
1924	20.7%	6.1%
1925	12.4%	8.4%
1926	11.0%	4.6%
1927	20.0%	4.3%

1928	5.6%	4.8%
1929	27.0%	1.7%
1930	0.8%	2.7%
1931	-5.1%	-5.7%
1932	-20.5%	-18.2%
1933	-5.9%	-10.4%
1934	-0.6%	8.9%

Before long City would be selling much more than just government debt. By 1916, City's securities affiliate, National City Corporation, was already generating significant profits. It was bound to generate even higher profits after that year's acquisition of N. W. Halsey, a rising national brokerage. Vanderlip installed Mitchell at the top of the securities affiliate and further expanded his domain by transferring the bank's bond department over to the affiliate. Vanderlip would recall that Mitchell had "an astonishing capacity to generate energy,"[14] and in 1916, Vanderlip gave his new colleague significant capacity to chase both risk and reward on Wall Street.

Mitchell had been watching American households buy war bonds and decided that once the war was over, there was no reason the same customers couldn't be persuaded to buy other types of bonds. He was certain that there was "a large, new army of investors in this country who have never heretofore known what it means to own a coupon bond and who may in the future be developed into savers and bond buyers."[15]

No one could accuse Mitchell of lacking a vision for the future of personal finance. Having surveyed the consumer landscape, he described in a lecture to bank employees how he had come to see the potential for a mass market of investors:

> We felt that if we could tear from the investment banking profession the veil of mystery and false dignity that surrounded it;

if we could get the people to look upon securities as something they were themselves vitally interested in and could readily understand; if we could bring the investment banking house to the people in such a way that they would look upon it as a part and parcel of their everyday life; if, by advertising, we could spread the gospel of thrift and saving and investment; if we could, by developing a very large volume of business, reduce the unit cost—we then, by spreading the expense over this large volume, could afford to render a service to the individual investor and the bank investor such as had theretofore never been rendered. We felt that if we could take from the books of successful merchandisers and distributors, the country over, those pages that had spelled success for them, those that had to do with successful advertising, and those with successful education, within and without their organization, we could then, by adaptation of those pages, lift this investment banking business to a level it had never reached before.[16]

Under Mitchell, City aimed to become a sort of financial Walmart for America's growing middle class. National City Company opened brokerage offices across the country. By 1919, they were in fifty-one cities. Mitchell compared them to chain stores: "Our branch offices throughout the United States are already working to make connections with the great new bond-buying public. Our newer offices are on the ground floor . . . [W]e are getting close to the public . . . and are preparing to serve the public on a straightforward basis, just as it is served by the United States Cigar Stores or Child's Restaurant."[17] The latter has sometimes been described as the McDonald's of its day.

City was also getting closer to Wall Street, and not just with the booming securities affiliate that was trying to sell stocks and bonds to Main Street consumers. The bank itself was loaning increasing amounts of money to participants in the capital markets.

Specifically, City was lending heavily in the call loan market in which investors would buy securities from brokers with a small amount down, borrow the balance, and put up the purchased stock as collateral. For banks in the late 1920s, this looked like easy money. They could borrow at between 2.0 and 2.5 percent via corporate and interbank deposits or at a slightly higher rate from the Federal Reserve's discount window and then turn around and lend the money at more than 7 percent and at times more than 10 percent in the call loan market. During this period, call loans were seen as very liquid and nearly risk-free. Lenders could demand repayment, or "call" the loans at any time. Banks often preferred lending to private investors in this way instead of the federal government, given the long-term maturities and interest-rate risk of holding Treasuries.[18]

Such loans would grow as a share of City's asset portfolio throughout the 1920s and at times made up more than half the bank's loan book (see Table 6). This included loans from the bank

Table 6: Broker Loans, Total Loans, and Percentage of Broker Loans ($s in Millions)

Examination date	Broker loans	Total loans	Percentage of broker loans
February 1920	66.5	622.8	10.68
June 1923	138.6	356.4	38.89
November 1923	100.9	468.9	21.52
June 1925	179.5	424.0	42.33
November 1925	246.5	422.0	58.41
October 1927	406.8	849.7	47.88
March 1928	394.7	849.7	46.45
October 1928	299.4	921.8	32.48
March 1929	432.6	662.0	65.35
October 1929	618.9	1249.1	49.55

Source: *Citibank 1812-1970*, 131, 321. OCC examination reports, and authors' calculations. In some cases, there are timing differences between reporting dates for broker and total loan data.

to its National City Corporation (NCC) affiliate. The balance outstanding that NCC owed City fluctuated throughout the decade.
Initially at $4.8 million during the examination in June 1923, it rose
to a high of $18 million in April 1926. This was just under the legal
lending limit to NCC, which was around $20 million at the time.[19]

Credit was also extended to a maturing neighbor at 60 Wall
Street, just a few doors down from City. At that time, Goldman
Sachs was not the household name it is today, as evidenced by the
fact that regulators writing up their report on City's 1921 examination spelled the name of the nearby client as "Goldman Sacks
and Co." Broker loans to Goldman totaled $800,000 in November
1920, $2 million at the examinations in June 1921 and April 1924,
and $3.35 million in November 1924. After 1924, the balance of
loans to Goldman Sachs was no longer reported and it is unclear if
this meant the balances were no longer carried or if the federal examiners simply stopped reporting this data as a regular part of the
examination. Reporting over time was not entirely standardized.[20]

City's neighbor had been founded in 1869 by Marcus Goldman,
and in 1882 he transformed his sole proprietorship into a partnership with his son-in-law Samuel Sachs. They later began using
the name Goldman, Sachs and Co., and by the 1890s the firm was
the country's largest dealer of commercial paper—short-term debt
issued by corporations. Two decades later, then-partner Henry
Goldman's sympathetic views toward Germany during the First
World War caused a rift in the firm. He ultimately resigned after a thirty-five-year career when the financial house sold Liberty
Bonds for the US government to support the war effort. As he
departed, he withdrew his capital, which created "an enormous
financial problem for the firm."[21] It was around that time that
Goldman Sachs began to rely on City for some of its financing.
City would later provide funding as Goldman struggled to survive
during the 1930s.[22]

Just like Vanderlip's adventures in overseas banking, City's

expansion into the securities markets started off swimmingly. By
the late 1920s, National City Corporation's annual profits rivaled
those of the bank, with both in the neighborhood of $25 million.
Meanwhile, the bank continued to build its capital, which more
than doubled to $235 million from $94 million between 1925 and
1929.[23]

Things were also going swimmingly for Mitchell, who min-
gled with the elite families of New York (the Vanderbilts, Hearsts,
Astors) as well as the power brokers of 1920s Washington (the
Coolidges, Mellons). They could be seen at parties in his various
homes, which were located at some of the country's most coveted
addresses:

> With his celebrity and his wealth came all the trappings of Wall
> Street success—the limestone mansion on Fifth Avenue and the
> summer homes in Southampton and Tuxedo Park, all with their
> own live-in staffs. Mitchell lived flamboyantly and spent lav-
> ishly. He took annual European trips, shot grouse on the Scot-
> tish moors, and made six-week yacht cruises to the Caribbean.
> When Mitchell traveled for business, it was always by private
> railcar, complete with kitchen and chef.[24]

Decades later, Mitchell's children recalled the lifestyle as they
revisited the Manhattan home where they were raised:

RITA MITCHELL CUSHMAN: I can hardly believe that a family
   lived in this kind of house. I mean, today, it would be
   almost unbelievable. Six stories and these great big rooms.
CRAIG MITCHELL: Enormous. We counted it up the other day.
   We had 16 live-in help in this house.
RITA MITCHELL CUSHMAN: Not counting the chauffeurs and
   others.

CRAIG MITCHELL: —not counting the chauffeurs, yes, aside
   from all the help we had in the Tuxedo Park house and
   the Southampton house as well. But those days are gone
   forever.
RITA MITCHELL CUSHMAN: I should say.
CRAIG MITCHELL: But we never thought of it as being grandiose
   because practically everybody we knew seemed to live in
   the same way.[25]

One of the reasons Mitchell's kids could enjoy such opulence
was because Mitchell's financial empire was thriving. By 1929,
City was the largest bank on the planet, and its securities affiliate,
National City Company, "was reputed to be 'the largest agency in
the world for the distribution of securities.'"[26]
   The task of expanding City was certainly made easier by the
fact that the bank's regulators had great admiration for City's management. The feeling wasn't mutual. Not content with merely
capturing regulators, Mitchell also liked to point out their short-
comings. He was troubled by a general lack of competence in
government, a sentiment shared by his fellow Amherst College
alumnus Calvin Coolidge.[27] In a speech given to the American
Bankers Association just after Coolidge assumed the presidency,
Mitchell proclaimed: "We want the government out of every
other business, because every experiment in government management demonstrates its disqualification in that field."[28]
   In our own time—just as in Mitchell's—many commercial
bankers have been hesitant to publicly criticize their government
overseers. But in his regular dealings with City's primary federal
regulator, the Office of the Comptroller of the Currency, Mitchell
wasn't shy. Two days after receiving one of the bureaucracy's on-
site examination reports, he sent a letter that included the following observation:

The day before yesterday we received the report of the examination of our bank as of the close of business October 21,
1927. Now of course we get a good deal of value from the
verbal comments and criticisms of your examiners while they
are with us, but with the rapid turn of the wheels and the constantly changing conditions, a written report that comes in
three months after the examination is, as you know, of very
little value to us.[29]

Just because he thought government didn't work very well, that
didn't mean Mitchell wasn't willing to participate in its institutions. In fact, even while he continued to run his financial supermarket and rail against government intervention, he became
one of the most powerful figures in the Federal Reserve System.
And he used his influence to encourage the Fed to keep lending
to New York banks like his that were helping to finance the stock
market boom. This doesn't necessarily mean he wasn't advocating
a sound position. Some economists have since argued that despite
the booming stock market the Fed was actually running fairly
tight monetary policy and should have been lending more.

In any case, Mitchell would soon be in a stronger position to
influence such policy. Today, the Fed is dominated by the staff
and leadership in Washington, with heavy influence exerted by
the Federal Reserve Bank of New York, and much less influence
exercised by the eleven other regional Fed banks. But in Mitchell's
time, New York was even more powerful and at times dominated
Washington—no surprise given that the architecture of the system had been designed in Manhattan. Until the mid-1930s, there
was no Federal Open Market Committee driving policy and controlled largely by members of the Board of Governors in DC.

Fed historian Peter Conti-Brown refers to the period from the
opening of the Federal Reserve System in 1914 until a rewrite of
the Federal Reserve Act in 1935 as one of "institutional chaos."

Allan Meltzer explains that tension between the board and the reserve banks began even "before the System opened for business." He adds that various factions also developed within the board in Washington. This opened the door for a determined New Yorker to take practical command.

Benjamin Strong of Bankers Trust had worked with City to rescue other institutions during the Panic of 1907—and then worked with Frank Vanderlip to create the Fed. Strong was an obvious choice to lead the Federal Reserve Bank of New York. Since he had been deeply involved in designing the Fed, he understood it as well as anyone in or out of government. Meltzer observes that Strong was the "dominant personality in the early days of the System."[30] In 1914, Strong became the New York Fed's first governor (this position at the bank is now called "president").

The Fed's odd mixture of private ownership and public support guaranteed a complicated governance structure. The Federal Reserve Act provided that each regional Fed bank would be overseen by a nine-member board of directors, with the membership broken down into three classes of three board members each. Class A directors were nominated and chosen by the stockholder banks, acted as their representatives, and were generally chosen from the population of bankers within the given Federal Reserve district. Class B and C directors were barred from being officers, directors, or employees of any bank, with Class B directors chosen by the stockholder banks and Class C directors chosen by the Federal Reserve Board. The directors were appointed to three-year terms on a rolling basis with one member in each class rolling off or being reappointed every three years.[31]

Strong led the New York Fed for fourteen years. Toward the end of his tenure—and the end of his life—an open director seat occasioned a contest between Mitchell and Albert H. Wiggin of Chase National Bank. In an August 1928 letter to a New York Fed colleague, Strong said that he opposed Wiggin for reasons that were "ample and convincing and conclusive." Strong expressed his "high regard" for Mitchell. He wrote that:

> For a long time he was a very bitter critic of what we were do-
> ing. The influence of some of my friends outside of the bank
> has been quietly exerted to educate him a bit as to our policy
> and philosophy . . . For the last year Mitchell has been much
> more reasonable . . . The real point of this letter is to express my
> conviction that if Mitchell should be elected it would be best at
> the outset to have a very frank understanding with him on two
> points . . . One is that so long as he is a member of the board
> of directors he should be willing to accept the decision of the
> directors in all matter and not indulge in outside criticism but
> be loyal to the majority of his associates . . . The other point is
> as to the inevitable influence which his knowledge of what we
> are doing may exert upon his policy in running the City Bank.
> This is one of the oldest problems in central banking. How can
> a director who is interested in the other side of all banking prob-
> lems be disinterested and impartial in his attitude in the Reserve
> Bank as well as in his own bank, not take an unfair advantage
> of his confidential knowledge, and steer a clear course in a very
> delicate situation. Charlie Mitchell is one of these fellows who
> faces the facts honestly, and I think it can be discussed with him
> frankly and no possibility of misunderstanding rises."[32]

Based largely on Strong's recommendation, Charles Mitchell became a Class A director of the New York Fed in January of 1929.[33] But because Strong had died in October of 1928, he may never have had the chance to fully and frankly discuss with Mitch-ell the importance of avoiding conflicts. So there remained the possibility of a misunderstanding.

A misunderstanding by Mitchell could have significant con-sequences because he was not just another director at the New

York Fed. The young institution had already developed the custom of placing one head of a giant bank on its board. Mitchell's
seat had previously belonged to Jackson E. Reynolds, president of
the First National Bank of the City of New York. When Mitchell
completed his three-year term at the end of 1931, Chase's Wiggin
would finally get his chance. And whoever represented a giant
bank on the board immediately exercised outsized influence because upon joining the organization he became the resident expert
in high finance.

The other bankers who were Class A directors represented
places like Hoosick Falls, New York, and Montclair, New Jersey—
very small towns compared to Mitchell's Manhattan. Add to this
the force of Mitchell's personality and his international network of
high-level connections, and he was bound to be first among equals.
Were any bankers from Tompkins County in central New York
also serving as informal advisers to the president of the United
States? As for the Class B and C directors, they were industrial
heavyweights, but on matters of finance they might have been
inclined to defer to Mitchell as well. One of the Class B directors
who served with Mitchell was railroad car magnate William H.
Woodin, who a few years later would be named President Franklin Roosevelt's first Treasury secretary. But at the time he became
a director at the New York Fed in 1927, Woodin's experience had
largely been in manufacturing, not money markets.[34]

Almost immediately upon joining the board, Mitchell would
lead his New York Fed colleagues into a fight with Washington on an issue that represented a clear conflict of interest for the
City chief. The dispute involved how much credit the Federal
Reserve System should provide to member banks like City that
were providing financing to Wall Street. The experienced and respected Benjamin Strong might have forged a consensus between
Washington and the regional banks like the New York Fed. But
after he died, his successor, George L. Harrison, struggled to find

common ground. The Fed's Board of Governors, based in Washington, was increasingly convinced that bankers were taking cheap financing from the Fed and in turn loaning the money to stock speculators, possibly creating a financial bubble. Some of the Washington crowd also worried that all the financing for stock purchases was a misallocation of capital that otherwise could have gone to Main Street companies to build new factories and create new products. The board was inclined to stop lending money to member banks that were turning around and lending the cash to buyers of stocks.

As Milton Friedman and Anna Schwartz summarized it in *A Monetary History of the United States*: "The main battle was joined on security speculation [as there was a] division between the Board and the rest of the system. The Board believed the way to curb security speculation was to deny rediscounting privileges to member banks making loans on securities." The reserve banks argued for a narrower approach with "direct pressure" applied only in cases where member banks were borrowing for long periods or in outsized amount, combined with an increase in the rediscount rate.[35] Mitchell clearly had a vested interest in the outcome of this battle, given City Bank's pervasive role in this market.

In January 1929, the Federal Reserve Board deliberated over the issue. Board Member Adolph Miller argued that the "Federal Reserve System was drifting and that [a] rate increase was necessary to effect a curbing of speculation." He recommended a "public announcement that credit in the future would be available at reasonable rates for agriculture and business, but that the Board would watch the rise in discounts and prevent seepage into Wall Street." After Miller circulated a draft letter to the reserve banks, the chairman of the New York Fed, Gates McGarrah, pushed back, arguing "that it would be construed as a blow at the stock market."[36] Undeterred, the board in Washington sent what became known as the "warning letter" on February 2:

The Federal reserve act does not, in the opinion of the Federal Reserve Board, contemplate the use of the resources of the Federal reserve banks for the creation of speculative credit. A member bank is not within its reasonable claims for rediscount facilities at the Federal reserve bank when it borrows either for the purpose of making speculative loans or for the purpose of maintaining speculative loans.[37]

The message was straightforward: the Fed should be in the business of countering banking panics, not lifting stock prices and potentially creating dangerous financial bubbles. The letter requested details from reserve banks like the New York Fed regarding how they tracked the use of borrowings by member banks like City. Washington wanted to see that Fed credit facilities were not being abused and endangering member institutions and perhaps the Federal Reserve System itself.[38]

Chairman Harrison of the New York Fed met with the Federal Reserve Board on February 5. He and the other New Yorkers weren't interested in changing the terms on Fed lending. He essentially argued that the Fed should just focus on the rates it was charging, rather than what New York banks were doing with the money it loaned them. Harrison agreed that there had been excessive credit expansion but felt it could be solved with "sharp, incisive action" involving a temporary rise in discount rates that would "quickly control the long-continued expansion in the total volume of credit so that we might then adopt a System policy of easing rates." A day later, the Federal Reserve Board released the warning letter to the press along with the following release, which likely blindsided Harrison since he hadn't been told about it at the meeting:

During the last year or more . . . the functioning of the Federal reserve system has encountered interference by reason of the excessive amount of the country's credit absorbed in speculative security loans. . . . The matter is one that concerns every section of the country and every business interest, as an aggravation of these conditions may be expected to have detrimental effects on business and may impair its future.[39]

On February 14, Mitchell and the other New Yorkers still didn't want to put limits on what banks like City did with the money they borrowed from the Fed. The New York Fed tried to implement its approach of simply increasing the rate it charged. The reserve bank unanimously approved an increase in the discount rate from 5 percent, where the rate had stood since July 1928, to 6 percent. But under the Federal Reserve Act, such changes needed the approval of the board in Washington, and the board wouldn't budge. Until the New York Fed answered the questions in the February 2 letter, there would be no approval from Washington. In response, Mitchell directly criticized Fed governor Roy Young and said that Young would find himself in an "impossible position" if he had to run a bank like City amid such uncertainty.[40]

Young responded that the New York Fed directors "were trying to force upon the Federal Reserve Board the responsibility of taking action one way or another when they wanted time to think it over, that it was an important question which they needed time to consider."[41] After a flurry of phone calls between DC and Gotham, the Federal Reserve Board rejected New York's discount rate increase. This cycle of the New York Fed approving and then the Federal Reserve Board in Washington rejecting a rate increase was repeated no fewer than nine times in the ensuing meetings through late May.[42]

Mitchell certainly didn't want to put limits on what banks like City could do with the money borrowed from the Fed, and he didn't even want to raise interest rates. In 1929, he tried to persuade colleagues to keep rates steady to allow stocks to keep rising.

As John Kenneth Galbraith described Mitchell's stance: "He was for the boom. Moreover, his prestige as head of one of the two largest banks and most influential commercial banks, his reputation as an aggressive and highly successful investment banker, and his position as a director of the New York Federal Reserve Bank, meant that he spoke with at least as much authority as anyone in Washington."[43] Records of New York Fed meetings document his efforts:

> On June 5, 1929, Mr. Mitchell came before the Board and urged a more liberal discount policy and an easing of conditions by purchase of bills and Government securities, leaving the discount rate at 5%, to be increased only if speculation should revive.
>
> July 16, [1929]: Director Mitchell told Dr. Miller that an easing policy was absolutely necessary, although he said that Governor Harrison still favored an increase in the discount rate."[44]

Mitchell charted his own course in another case when the stock market began a descent in late March 1929. The Federal Reserve board was gathering daily, including an unprecedented Saturday meeting, but the board did not issue any statements, and the members were not talking to the press. The following Monday, March 25, brought a dramatic sell-off. Call loan volume was dropping, and interest rates to renew the loans were steadily increasing: 9 percent on March 25, 12 percent on March 26, and an eye-watering 15 percent later that week. There was heavy selling on the Chicago Stock Exchange beginning on March 21, which led to large withdrawals in New York. By one thirty p.m. on March 26, the volume of trading on the New York Stock Exchange exceeded 5.5 million shares, and the ticker tape, struggling to report an avalanche of market transactions, was fifty-eight minutes behind the market. Volume would eventually reach a record-breaking level of more than eight million shares.[45]

Charles Mitchell decided to stand athwart the market, yelling *Stop*. On March 26, City Bank advanced $6 million in the call loan market and Mitchell offered to make available $5 million if the call loan rate reached 16 percent and an incremental $5 million for each 1 percent increase in the rate up to 20 percent (for a total of $25 million). His comments in the press seemed to be taunting the Federal Reserve Board in Washington:[46]

> So far as [National City Bank] is concerned, we feel that we have an obligation which is paramount to any Federal Reserve warning or anything else, to avert, so far as lies within our power, any dangerous crisis in the money market. While we are averse to resorting to rediscounting for the purpose of making a profit in the call market, we certainly would not stand by and see a situation arise where money became impossible to secure at any price.[47]

In the words of Fed historian Allan Meltzer, Mitchell's "defiance made the System appear weak." At the same time, City was borrowing from the New York Fed.[48]

Meanwhile, Senator Carter Glass, who was a primary sponsor of the Federal Reserve Act when he was a member of the House of Representatives, demanded Mitchell's resignation based on the conflict he saw between his vision for the reserve banks and Mitchell's actions:

> The Federal Reserve Board has adopted the administrative policy of having Federal reserve banks remonstrate with member banks against permitting the facilities of the Federal Reserve System to be used for stock speculative purposes.
>
> This should have been done long ago, before the situation got out of hand. Now that it has been done, a Class A director of a Federal Reserve Bank, himself President of a great banking

institution, vigorously slaps the Board squarely in the face and treats its policy with contempt and contumely. He avows his superior obligation to a frantic stock market over against the obligation of his oath as a director of the New York Federal Reserve Bank, under the supervisory authority of the Federal Reserve Board . . .

The Board should ask for the immediate resignation of Mr. Mitchell as a Class A Director of the New York Federal Reserve Bank.

If the National City Bank in New York, or any other member bank of the System anywhere, imagines it is greater than the Federal Reserve System and may defy and reject the considered policy of the Federal Reserve Board, it should at least be given to understand that the President of such a bank will not be permitted to have an official part in the management of the Federal Reserve System.[49]

Opinion in the business and financial markets, as well as the *New York Times*, was that Mitchell had been correct, though his words were poorly chosen.[50] The week of Mitchell's intervention loan rates eased, and the market rallied. In early October 1929, while in Germany, Mitchell's optimism remained undiminished as he announced that the "industrial condition of the United States is absolutely sound . . . nothing can arrest the upward movement." Returning to the US, he made an additional announcement: "The markets generally are now in a healthy condition . . . values have a sound basis in the general prosperity of our country."[51]

Over the next thirty-two months, the stocks in the Dow Jones Industrial Average would lose more than 80 percent of their value.

12

Did City Bank Cause the Crash?

A t this point in the story it would be easy to place the black hat firmly on Mitchell's head and blame him for self-interested actions that inflated a financial bubble and ultimately created the worst economic calamity in US history. That was the conclusion promoted by leading politicians during the Great Depression, and it's been expressed by many historians in the years since. But the facts don't always cooperate.

Mitchell was no hero. Yet prosecutors and politicians struggled to make the case against him in the aftermath of the crash of 1929, and in the ensuing decades economists have found even more reason to question the Washington-made consensus. There's no dispute that an era of misery followed the crash. From 1929 to 1931, national income plummeted more than 30 percent and savings declined by 50 percent.[1] Unemployment surged from the low single digits in the late 1920s to nearly 26 percent in 1933.[2]

Three-quarters of a century later, when America faced a much less severe financial crisis, Dorothy Womble shared with the *Wall Street Journal* her childhood memories of the years following the crash. According to the paper, she "grew up in a small house on a dirt road in Winston-Salem, N.C. People around her were so poor, she says, 'They couldn't even get money to get seeds' to plant vegetables. She can still picture the strangers who wandered through with nothing but a bundle on their backs." The *Journal* also reported on another memory of that era:

> When the Great Depression hit, people came to the front porch of William Hague's home near Pittsburgh pleading for food. One well-dressed young woman asked Mr. Hague's mother if she would hire her for $2 a week. Why would she work for so little? his mother asked. "We have nothing to eat at home," she replied.[3]

In 1929, even sophisticated financial players had no idea of the agony to come. As the stock market tumbled in the autumn of that year, it was all they could do to record the chaos of each new day. Witnessing the spectacle at City was a team of federal bank regulators. On October 4, 1929, seventy-eight examiners from the Office of the Comptroller of the Currency and fourteen from the Federal Reserve Bank of New York showed up for the bank's semi-annual checkup. The regulators would remain at City for almost two months.[4] Their report had a very different tone from earlier dispatches:

> As a result of the recent break in the stock market, which began prior to and lasted during almost the entire period of this examination, the various departments of this bank with which the examining team came in contact, due to the excessive volume of business to be handled daily, were almost continuously in such a state of confusion and demoralization that very little co-operation could be had during practically all of the time under consideration . . . In fact, as a result of continuous margin calls, the volume of business of the [loan] department was increased

to the extent that the posting of records was at times several days in arrears, and employees of this department were on duty day and night for weeks.[5]

Despite the confusion and the anguish—and lots of all-nighters—examiners gave the bank high marks: "The general condition of this Bank is regarded as being sound and its investments on the whole are well selected with attendant high degree of liquidity."[6]

Back in Washington, senior regulators weren't so sure, and they began to get nervous about the relationship between City Bank and its Wall Street affiliate, National City Company. Could a collapsing stock market pull America's largest bank down with it? On November 18, while examiners were still camped out at City, Comptroller of the Currency J. W. Pole sent a letter to Owen Reeves, the chief examiner responsible for overseeing the New York district. Pole asked Reeves for the balance sheet on City's affiliate as well as details on its liabilities. Reeves replied, on December 4, that the lead federal examiner at City had tried unsuccessfully to meet with City Bank president Gordon Rentschler on November 19. Reeves added that Rentschler "was even reluctant to furnish me with a current balance sheet of the National City Company." At the time, City "was carrying an unsecured loan to NCC of approximately $5.7 million."[7]

In our own time, it would be unthinkable for a bank to refuse to provide basic financial information to its regulator. But the Comptroller's office continued to struggle throughout 1930 as it tried to pry information out of City about the Wall Street exposure created by its securities affiliate. Frustration was building among the bank's federal overseers. The open section of the September 1930 examination report said that National City Company "was not examined, and neither an operating statement nor a list of assets is available . . . Schedules supporting its statement of condition were denied to the Examiner." The confidential section of the report, which was only viewed within the Comptroller's office, carried a more harsh assessment: "The bank has gone rather far in financing the National City Company, its securities affiliate . . . The denial to furnish us with schedules supporting the company's statement of condition would appear almost reprehensible."[8]

Amazingly, a year later the bank was still keeping its regulators in the dark. According to the report from the 1931 examination, "A statement of [National City Company] as of the close of business 9-30-1931 was submitted to your examiner without any supporting information. The statement without supporting data is of practically no value."[9]

A year after that, City was still playing this game. According to the September 1932 exam report, "There is included in this report a condensed statement of the National City Company. Supporting information is not available to your examiner and accordingly no comment on this company is possible."[10]

This appears to be a case of regulatory capture so severe that not even Stigler could have imagined it. How did City get away with it, especially in the aftermath of a market meltdown and in the midst of an historic economic decline? The US economy entered a deep downturn in August 1929 and would remain in recession until March 1933, nearly four years.[11]

Perhaps the answer is that despite Mitchell's unwillingness to share important information with shareholders and regulators, despite his questionable management of potential conflicts of interest and his wildly inaccurate market predictions in 1929, his bank appears to have done a decent job of insulating itself from the US financial and economic catastrophe. Overseas catastrophes would be another matter. But what's striking about Mitchell is that, while he did many things deserving of criticism, they generally received less attention from his critics than other alleged offenses for which the evidence is dubious.

Whatever the particulars of his management, Mitchell became

an irresistible target for politicians determined to regulate and separate Wall Street from commercial banking. Given his market boosterism prior to the crash, he became a highly useful symbol of alleged 1920s excess. Senator Carter Glass, who had urged the New York Fed to get rid of Mitchell and claimed the City boss had slapped the board "squarely in the face" in an effort to promote "a frantic stock market," sought in late 1929 to pin the country's troubles on City's chairman:

> The recent trouble is due largely to Charles E. Mitchell's activities. That man more than 40 others is more responsible for the present situation. Had the Federal reserve acted and dismissed him, the trouble might be less. The crash has shown that stock gambling has reached its limit.[12]

Glass added that Mitchell was "more responsible than all others together for excesses that have resulted in this disaster."[13]

But what exactly caused the disaster—and why did it last for so long? As to the cause, the popular political explanation at the time was that inflation, a speculative fever, and reckless lending had fueled a financial bubble, which upon its bursting wrecked the economy. And even Mitchell largely accepted this view of events, based on Senate testimony he offered in 1931, though he believed the root cause was located far from the United States:

> Essentially, one factor—the war. The situation as it exists today is a backwash of the war and all that it brought about in the way of inflation—inflation both in the volume of production and in the price level. It caused a great flow of gold to this country which became the basis of a great overexpansion in real estate and the stock market . . . All the activities of production and distribution, banking, investment banking, consumer buying, went on without perhaps as heavy curbs as might have been

put on them . . . [the banks' credit policy] was undoubtedly too liberal. They were too ready to loan . . . It came about in part by reason of the public's interest in and fever and fervor for investments and speculation, if you will.[14]

Certainly, the flow of gold into the US could have enabled a binge of money printing once commercial banks deposited the gold at regional Fed banks. That certainly could have fueled inflation and a financial bubble. But that's not what happened. In an effort to prevent such inflation, Fed banks acted to offset the incoming gold by selling their holdings of other assets—draining cash out of the financial system. In their landmark *A Monetary History of the United States*, Milton Friedman and Anna Schwartz explain:

The widespread belief that what goes up must come down . . . plus the dramatic stock market boom, have led many to suppose that the United States experienced severe inflation before 1929 and [that] the [Federal] Reserve System served as an engine of it. Nothing could be further from the truth. By 1923, wholesale prices had recovered only a sixth of their 1920–21 decline. From then until 1929, they fell on the average of 1 percent per year . . . Far from being an inflationary decade, the twenties were the reverse.[15]

It's also clear that 1920s prosperity was not simply built on a speculative frenzy for the instruments of Wall Street, but on remarkable vitality in the Main Street economy. Innovations from entrepreneurs like Edison and Ford were driving a productivity revolution. In just the six years from 1923 to 1929, US automobile production doubled. Financial historian Amity Shlaes notes that unemployment, which was running at 5 percent when Coolidge was elected president in 1920, declined to 3.2 percent in 1925 "and then into the twos and ones."[16]

In a 1999 paper, Federal Reserve Bank of San Francisco senior economist Timothy Cogley showed that while stock prices were surging in the 1920s, it was largely because companies were generating higher dividends for investors and therefore deserved higher valuations.[17] He notes that only late in the decade did stocks become historically expensive relative to the payouts they were generating for investors, but not wildly so. The price-dividend ratio of New York Stock Exchange issues peaked in early 1929 at "roughly 20% above the long-term average. Dividends had grown rapidly through 1928, and investors projecting similar growth rates forward may have been willing to settle for dividend yields somewhat below the long-run average." If stocks had only declined 20 percent from that point, the crash would have been forgotten long ago.

The Fed, concerned about speculation, was aggressively tightening monetary policy by 1928, raising interest rates and selling assets to reduce the supply of money. The Fed would continue to do so into the Great Depression, with a brief pause in the first half of 1929 while it was fighting with Mitchell and the other New Yorkers.

While Mitchell may have been completely self-interested in opposing the Fed's effort to restrict the availability of credit on the eve of the crash, he appears to have been advocating the correct policy. Unfortunately, he did not maintain a consistent position. Once the stock market crashed, the country could have used a forceful champion to persuade the Fed to make credit more freely available. Instead, the central bank would reduce the country's supply of money by a quarter to a third over the next four years. According to Cogley, the "depth of the contraction in economic activity probably had less to do with the magnitude of the crash and more to do with the fact that the Fed continued a tight money policy after the crash." The nation's relatively new central bank was starving the economy of the cash needed to fund an economic rebound.

We normally think of a gold standard as a natural brake on the desire of a government to print too much money to pay its bills. If consumers decide the currency isn't worth much, they will trade it for gold and drain the country's reserves of the precious metal. This will discourage money printing. But a gold standard also serves to prevent the creation of too little money. If the government's gold reserves keep rising, it's a sign that the currency is too scarce, as people are eager to trade in their gold for it. The Fed was stubbornly ignoring this sign.

Richard Timberlake, author of *Monetary Policy in the United States: An Intellectual and Institutional History*, calls this period "a deflationary disaster." He adds, "By February 1933, owing to the Fed's tight money policy, the economy was in shambles and constricted to the point of monetary suffocation." More than a third of the nation's banks failed.[18] Smaller banks that were not Fed members were especially vulnerable during this period. Thousands closed their doors. (See Figure 1 on page 49.)

City endured, but whereas the bank of Moses Taylor and James Stillman had thrived in times of crisis and had even seen its reputation enhanced, the Fed-backed giant of Mitchell's era achieved a different kind of renown. An official history of Citibank published in the 1980s describes the destructive impact of the Great Depression on the country in general and the bank in particular:

At the trough, the US real gross national product was little more than two-thirds of the peak reached in 1929. By 1933 prices had fallen 25 percent and unemployment had risen to one-fourth of the labor force . . . Worst of all fared National City's reputation, and that of commercial banks in general. As the *New Yorker* quipped in 1933, "We regret to announce the loss of a handsome set of iridescent halos. Finder will kindly return to the officers of the National City Bank." As the depression deepened the press increasingly pictured banks as villains rather than victims.

Bankers, Charles E. Mitchell foremost among them, were re-
viled as "banksters."[19]

Of course, many bankers of that era lost much more than their
reputations. And even being one of the lucky members of the Federal Reserve System with access to emergency loans wasn't always
enough to prevent disaster. The New York financial market was
badly shaken in late 1930 when Bank of United States, a lender
heavily invested in real estate, bank stock, and insider loans, experienced a run on its deposits and failed. Especially popular among
immigrants, the bank's name may have misled some unfortunate
depositors into thinking that it was actually an institution of the
government. And it did receive some government assistance. The
Federal Reserve Bank of New York—just as it had during the deep
1920–1921 recession—opened its discount window to a large, weak
institution and loaned $19 million to the struggling Bank of United
States. But it wasn't enough to prevent a collapse.[20]

The slow-motion collapse of National City Company had also
begun (see Table 7). The value of City Bank's Wall Street affiliate
followed the path of the stock market on which it had relied for
profits. Over three years beginning in September of 1929, its stockholders' equity would decline by more than 80 percent. National
City Company's customers and shareholders suffered mightily, but
to his credit Mitchell had largely insulated his bank from the troubles at its stock-trading affiliate. National City Company was not
directly owned by City Bank, but was separately owned by the
bank's shareholders, so when its value imploded, the bank didn't
have to record a loss. And National City hadn't borrowed all that
much from the bank. Its loans from City had peaked at $18 million
in 1926 and were usually at least partially collateralized, for example with Liberty Bonds. So despite the fears of bank examiners and
Mitchell's ominous unwillingness to share information, the Wall
Street operation wasn't going to take down the bank.[21]

Table 7: National City Company, Assets and Equity Balance 1929 to 1932

Examination report	Bonds and Stocks	Stockholders' Equity
October 1929	$133 million	$130 million
March 1930	$130 million	$114 million
October 1931	$75 million	$71 million
September 1932	$19 million	$23 million

Source: October 4, 1929, examination report, 11-A-2; March 14, 1930, examination report, 11-A-2 to 11-A-3; October 9, 1931, examination report, 11-A-4; September 30, 1932, examination report, 11-A-2.

Adding more difficulty to the task of characterizing Mitchell as a reckless architect of financial ruin, he had consistently increased the funds City would have on hand for a rainy day. The bank's capital grew steadily from $90 million in the wake of its near-failure in the early 1920s to $235 million in 1929. After a merger with a smaller competitor early that year, the bank's reported capital to assets ratio stood above 11 percent, where it remained through 1935.[22] In our own time, very few big banks have this large a cushion to absorb losses.

Given that the entire worldwide economy was imploding, it may seem amazing that City's capital levels held up throughout the early years of the Depression. But that's not the whole story. Problem loans were rising, as one would expect when many borrowers were in desperate straits. Eventually, the bank would record significant losses.

Federal bank regulators reviewed a large share of the dollar volume of loans at each examination. Then the exam team labeled each loan in one of the following categories: Slow, Doubtful, Loss, or Pass. The last category usually means that the borrower is on time and expected to pay the debt in full.

To regulators, every loan that isn't marked Pass is considered "classified." There's a problem and the loan may not be repaid. As a gauge of the quality of the portfolio, the amount of classified assets is generally either compared to total assets or to capital, which is the difference of assets minus liabilities. And of course the more that classified assets are in the Doubtful or Loss categories, the greater threat there is to the solvency of the bank. As City's troubled loans increased in the early 1930s (see Table 8), the percentage of classified assets climbed into the danger zone of 20–25 percent of total assets and peaked at more than 100 percent of capital. If all the classified loans went unpaid, the bank would be broke, with more liabilities than assets.

Table 8: Assets Classified as Slow, Doubtful, or Loss by OCC Examiners

Examination Date	Total Classified Assets
March 1931	$114 million
October 1931	$202 million
April 1932	$346 million
September 1932	$285 million
June 1933	$289 million
June 1934	$173 million

Source: October 9, 1931, examination report; April 22, 1932, examination report; September 30, 1932, examination report; June 1, 1934, report.

Today, the FDIC develops a "problem bank" list of institutions "with financial, operational, or managerial weaknesses that threaten their continued financial viability." As you can imagine, these problem children get a lot of increased supervision from regulators, but the names of these troubled institutions are not publicly released for fear of triggering a bank run. The quality of institutions is not graded on a curve. During times of calm, there may be fewer than a hundred problem banks, while during a crisis there might be one thousand or fifteen hundred. Every commercial bank is rated from one to five under a system known as CAMELS, and the weakest institutions, those with scores of four or five, are generally classified as problem banks.[23]

During the 1930s, there was no such system. The FDIC was not created until 1933, and the predecessor to the current CAMELS system didn't exist until 1979. But, based on the City examination reports from the 1930s, the level of classified assets, and the snarky commentary about management, City probably would have been graded a four and classified as a problem bank. Given the wretched state of the economy and financial system at that time, a lot of other banks would have earned the same grade or worse, and of course many failed.

But despite media and political parables about the greed and excess of the Roaring Twenties in the US stock market, the exam reports suggest that many of City's troubles originated offshore. An April 1932 examination report warned darkly, "The well-known economic chaos existing abroad presents potentialities for very substantial losses in the liquidation of these investments."[24] City Bank had $20 million in direct exposure to Chilean government debt. A September 1932 exam report noted that the "eventual outcome cannot be determined at this time" and the classification was evenly split with $10 million considered doubtful and $10 million projected as a loss. There was an additional exposure of $11 million to the Anglo-Chilean Consolidated Nitrate Corporation with about $4 million classified as Doubtful.

By 1934, some of the Chilean credits had turned around, but a larger problem would take much longer to fix.[25] Along with thirteen other Latin American countries, Chile experienced a sovereign debt crisis that began in 1931 and would not be resolved for seventeen years. Smaller amounts of sovereign debt classified by examiners emanated from Cuba ($5 million), Hungary ($1 million), and Greece ($1 million).[26]

These were small potatoes compared to another overseas risk. In hindsight, it's clear that being long on Germany in the early 1930s was a dangerous place to be. But by 1932, City had amassed $65 million of lending exposure in a country that was undergoing a crisis of both government and private credit—and would soon inflict a much greater crisis on the entire world.

City's examiners from the Office of the Comptroller of the Currency classified the German debt as Slow and reported:

> An acute situation developed during July [1931]. As it was virtually impossible for the German debtors to meet the demand of the foreign creditors, an agreement known as the "Stillhaltung Agreement" was consummated during September . . . a moratorium of the German banks and industrial firms with the foreign bank creditors.[27]

The "*Stillhaltung*" or "Standstill" moratorium, essentially a time-out on enforcement of the underlying loans, was a deal struck in Basel, Switzerland, by negotiators including Chase National Bank's Albert Wiggin. The negotiations were limited to short-term foreign credits on banks' books as of July 31, 1931. The moratorium was structured to last for six months but was later extended until March 1933.[28]

Meanwhile, City was still playing the game of extending and pretending in Cuba. Specifically, the bank continued to resist recognizing losses on its sugar investments. Mitchell and his team continued to pretend that low sugar prices that had persisted for a decade should be seen as merely temporary. In July 1931, federal examiner O. W. Beaton explained the problem that he considered too sensitive to include in the recently submitted report of examination:

> The General Sugar Corporation is for all practical purposes a wholly owned subsidiary of National City Bank . . . The bank has been financing the corporation since [1920] by advancing yearly funds necessary to grow and harvest each crop. Unquestionably, the bank anticipated that they would be able to divest themselves of their business within a relatively short time after 1920. Instead, eleven years of operation has resulted only in further losses . . .

From 1927 to 1930 the operating losses of this corporation totaled $9,829,000. On the basis of current prices, a further very substantial loss is apparent from 1931 operations. The total debts of this corporation to the bank at present are $20 million.[29]

And if it weren't bad enough that the bank was still losing money and still only begrudgingly recognizing losses, Beaton also saw potential self-dealing as members of City's board got the bank to finance their own separate sugar ventures:

In addition to the above, the bank finances other sugar producers which are interested with various directors of the bank. These companies because of the same adverse conditions in the sugar market have lost very substantial sums from operations, and appear to be in a position where receivership and reorganization are unavoidable.[30]

In October of that year, an exam report shows that the bank still didn't want to accept that sugar was a loser for City:

The policy of carrying "sugar loans" at values which make no allowance for the long continued depression in the sugar industry seems contrary to conservative banking practice. The past five years' experience indicates that in forced liquidation, the value of capital assets is extremely problematical, no market whatever existing for properties or securities . . . It would seem to be time to inaugurate a vigorous charge-off policy on these loans.

Further, it is questionable whether or not the management is according the stockholders and depositors the proper protection in continuing to operate these properties at a loss of several millions each year, further depleting what equity may exist in the real property.[31]

The September 1932 exam report described the sugar loans as "the subject of repeated criticism . . . the unliquidated portion of accumulated advances to mills which management has previously conceded have little or no realization value. Other than writing off $2.9 million on the Cuban Dominion Sugar Company, which was recently reorganized, the management of the bank will not concede any loss on these loans."[32]

It makes sense that City's regulators in the US were highly concerned about the bank's Cuban sugar plantations and a freeze on German debt repayment. The economic calamity in the 1930s was global. In *A Monetary History of the United States*, Friedman and Schwartz argue that to find a comparable downturn it's necessary to go all the way back to the depression of 1839 to 1843, a similar period of "worldwide crisis."[33]

But US politicians remained focused on other issues. Senator Glass, probably unaware of how the Fed had been starving the economy of cash, was taking aim at Mitchell's business model. Even though City's securities affiliate wasn't threatening the bank, Glass demanded a total separation of commercial and investment banking:

> These affiliates were the most unscrupulous contributors, next after the debauch of the New York Stock Exchange, to the financial catastrophe which visited this country, and were mainly responsible for the depression, under which we have been suffering since, and they ought to be speedily separated from the parent banks, and in this bill we have done that.[34]

Ferdinand Pecora, chief counsel to the Senate Committee on Banking and Currency, would clash with Mitchell in celebrated hearings in 1933. A former assistant district attorney in New York City, Pecora had experience prosecuting bucket shops peddling fraudulent securities. He now had the opportunity to hunt for much bigger game. Pecora explained in his memoir of the Banking Committee investigation:

> National City was one of the very largest banks in the world and had but recently been surpassed in this country by the Chase National. The prestige and reputation of these institutions were enormous. They stood, in the mind of the financially unsophisticated public for safety, strength, prudence and high-mindedness, and they were supposed to be captained by men of unimpeachable integrity, possessing almost mythical business genius and foresight.[35]

To many observers, Pecora versus Mitchell must have looked like a perfect David and Goliath confrontation. Pecora was making $255 a month, directing a staff of similarly compensated government attorneys. In the years before the crisis, Mitchell had been making more than 350 times as much, and was represented by a blue-chip legal team including Garrard Winston, a former undersecretary of the Treasury, and James Harry Covington, a former member of Congress and later chief justice of the Supreme Court of the District of Columbia. The outfit that still bears his name, Covington & Burling, is a major international law firm.[36]

In the days prior to Mitchell's appearance before the Banking Committee, Pecora spent long hours poring over documents subpoenaed from City, while Mitchell took his wife to Bermuda. An experienced and confident veteran in speaking before congressional committees, Mitchell didn't seem particularly concerned about this one.[37]

Pecora was inspired by hundreds of letters he had received from former customers and investors that blamed Mitchell and City for staggering market losses.[38] And by the time of the hearing, the country had been suffering through a rolling series of financial disasters with no end in sight. After the stock market crash of 1929 and the failure of Bank of United States in late 1930, another crisis of bank depositor confidence came in 1931. Still another panic occurred during the last quarter of 1932 and the first quarter of 1933. A wave of bank failures started in the Midwest and the West. By the first week of March, bank holidays had been declared in about half of the states.[39]

As for stocks, investors had suffered through a series of additional crashes in the years after 1929. The Dow Jones Industrial Index finally bottomed in the summer of 1932, having lost nearly 90 percent of its value since September of 1929. The Dow stocks would not recover their lost ground until 1954.[40]

It can be hard for people in our own time to appreciate the physical and psychological devastation wrought by those years of financial catastrophe. But it's perhaps easier to see why the highly compensated boss of a giant New York bank would make an especially appealing target for a congressional inquiry. David's aim was true, and Goliath's reputation would never recover. Under questioning from Pecora and the assembled lawmakers, Mitchell was portrayed in the press as a selfish and dishonest financial operator.

But in hindsight, the hearings did not nearly prove that Mitchell was the person most responsible for the Great Depression and the early days of the hearings were largely focused on trying to establish that Mitchell was self-interested and overcompensated rather than proving customers had been abused. Also, many of the allegations against Mitchell that received significant attention from politicians and the press didn't fare as well when tested later in the legal system.

Pecora focused heavily on Mitchell's huge compensation and highlighted several issues intended to demonstrate Mitchell's greed. Among the most politically explosive was a late 1929 transaction in which Mitchell sold some of his stock in City Bank to his wife, and then subsequently bought it back. "I sold this stock, frankly for tax purposes," he admitted in response to a question from Senator Smith Brookhart of Iowa. Mitchell had been spending his own money buying City shares as the market was collapsing. The reason, he said, was to support the stock price and try to help prevent a calamity for the bank and its shareholders. He described his stock purchases as "throwing my fortune into the breach" for "the benefit of this institution."

Since the value of the shares kept dropping, he realized that by booking a sale of some of the shares he could record a loss and reduce his tax bill for that year. But he wanted to continue increasing his stake in City. He decided that he could both support the stock price and book a loss for tax purposes by executing the sale-and-repurchase deal with his spouse. He ended up paying no income tax for 1929, and he continued accumulating City shares. By the time of the hearing in 1933, he could say, "Today I hold the largest amount of stock of the National City Bank that I have ever held."[41]

Pecora and the legislators succeeded in publicly defining Mitchell as an overpaid tax cheat. After his first day of testimony, a headline in the *Washington Post* announced, "Huge Pay Told." The *New York Times* proclaimed, "Mitchell Avoided Income Tax in 1929 by $2,800,000 loss." The *Wall Street Journal* also focused on Mitchell's purchases of City Bank stock and the sale in which shares never left the Mitchell family.[42]

By the end of the first week of hearings, the US attorney general and the US attorney in Manhattan announced investigations into whether the transaction involved a violation of law, perhaps even criminal tax evasion. The Bureau of Internal Revenue also initiated an investigation and claimed that Mitchell had made statements during the hearing that contradicted previous declarations to the bureau. Within a month Mitchell was arrested for tax evasion.

Yet after a six-week trial he was acquitted. In separate proceedings, he ultimately settled the government's civil case for $1.1 million.[43] Whatever one thinks of Mitchell's conduct in this matter, it's hard to argue it had anything to do with causing the stock market crash or the economic depression that followed. The same can be said about the Cuban sugar debacle. Pecora labored at length in the hearings in an effort to show that National City Company had bailed out the bank. The point was to persuade the public that shareholders of the securities affiliate hadn't been given the full story when their company bought struggling sugar assets from its corporate cousin City Bank. Since City shareholders typically owned shares in both the bank and the securities affiliate, it's not clear how they were harmed by this, or whether such disclosure was even required under the laws of the time.[44]

Pecora also spent time highlighting Mitchell's differences with his colleagues in the Federal Reserve System. Mitchell countered that the differences were not as great as they were portrayed in press accounts. At the time it looked bad for a banker to be at odds with regulators who were concerned that too much bank lending had fueled a speculative bubble. But with the benefit of hindsight modern students of the period may conclude that Mitchell didn't argue with his Fed colleagues nearly *enough* as they choked off the supply of credit. In a discussion with Pecora and Banking and Currency Committee chairman Peter Norbeck, Mitchell appropriately raised the question of whether it's worth wrecking the economy to eliminate what the Fed believes is undue speculation.[45]

This message was right on target. Starving the whole economy of capital was too high a price to pay to satisfy the Fed that stock prices were reasonable. But the messenger was not credible to much of the public. And Mitchell didn't help his credibility by making the dubious argument that City's call loan business wasn't supported by the money City borrowed from the New York Fed. Money is fungible, and more funding for City, even if technically used for home mortgages or industrial loans, freed up City's other cash to be lent to buyers of stocks. Yet Mitchell tried to argue the point anyway, suggesting that Fed loans were only used to support other types of loans.

One line of questioning that arguably approached the heart of the market crisis was the question of whether management fund bonuses, tied to the level of profits at the bank and at National City Company, gave executives too big an incentive to peddle risky shares to consumers and pursue lucrative but unsound banking business. There's a legitimate debate, joined in our own time since the financial crisis of 2008, about how to structure compensation so that it encourages employees to pursue not just short-term profits but also the long-term success of their institutions. At the hearings in 1933, lawmakers and their counsel explored similar questions. Mitchell said that while he understood that the potential for a big bonus could inspire reckless sales of securities to the public, he didn't recall seeing it operate that way in practice. He argued that the bonus system "establishes an esprit de corps and an interest in one officer in another officer's work that is to me most noticeable."[46]

Pecora then went into the details of Mitchell's compensation and showed that in the years leading up to the crisis he had been making more than $1 million annually. In current dollars, his annual management fund payments would have been about $15 million in 1927, $18 million in 1928, and $16 million in 1929.[47] The enormous sums shocked a struggling public. But the underlying question of whether City's bonus incentives had driven Mitchell and his colleagues to recklessness is not easily answered.

It's even harder to prove that Mitchell and his men led the way in creating a bubble leading to a market crash and then economic depression in light of historical evidence of Fed culpability—some of it presented by researchers at the Fed's own regional banks. Moreover, Fed policies in the era after the financial crisis of 2008 were largely driven by Chairman Ben Bernanke's determination— largely shared by his successor, Janet Yellen—not to repeat the

Fed's errors during the Great Depression. Our recent era of ex-
pansive monetary policy was forged in part by the lesson that the
Fed had been too restrictive after the stock market crash of 1929.
Put another way, the policies of the contemporary Fed are an implicit rebuttal of the case that the excesses of bankers like Mitchell
caused the agony of the 1930s. Whether recent Fed officials have
lately gone too far in the other direction will be a question for
historians in the future.

As for the cause of the stock market crash itself, the precrash
market looks less like a bubble the more one looks at the underlying economic and monetary conditions. Still, after the huge gains
of 1927, 1928, and the first eight months of 1929, perhaps a correc-
tion should have been expected to bring valuations back toward
historical norms relative to company earnings and dividends. But
if 1929 had seen the beginning of a bear market in stocks and
a typical economic recession lasting a year or perhaps eighteen
months, Mitchell would not have been getting grilled by senators
in 1933 about his 1920s paychecks. It was the depth and duration of
the market and economic decline that fueled the search for scape-
goats. And, as we've seen, there is compelling evidence to show
that the depth and duration of the catastrophe were Fed creations.

But the Pecora hearings instantly made Mitchell public financial
enemy number one. Eugene Meyer, head of the Federal Reserve
Board in Washington, urged Mitchell's removal.[48] On February
26, 1933, the weekend following the initial four days of hearings,
Mitchell submitted his resignation letter to City Bank, which read
in part:

> As the chief executive officer of the National City Company
> as well as National City Bank, I personally have been brought
> under a cloud of criticism from which I conceive that the insti-
> tution should not be permitted to suffer by my continuance in

office. [City's] financial strength is such that it needs no restate-
ment by me, but it will always be my deepest source of pride.[49]

So Mitchell had tendered his resignation, but City Bank's
board was reluctant to accept it due to fear that the chairman's
departure might further erode customer confidence. City directors contacted the outgoing Hoover and incoming Roosevelt Administrations for advice. Hoover thought that accepting Mitchell's
resignation would likely *increase* customer confidence. Roosevelt
told William Woodin, his Treasury secretary designate, who sat
along with Mitchell on the board of the New York Fed, that he
thought Mitchell should resign immediately. As a City customer,
Roosevelt appeared to be personally aggrieved by the large bonuses: "My gosh I feel Charlie took my money . . . These New
York bankers haven't any more notion of public psychology than
a chicken."[50]

In his inaugural speech just a few weeks later, Roosevelt de-
monized bankers like Mitchell:

> Practices of the unscrupulous money changers stand indicted in
> the court of public opinion, rejected by the hearts and minds
> of men . . . They know only the rules of a generation of self-
> seekers. They have no vision, and when there is no vision the
> people perish. The money changers have fled from their high
> seats in the temple of our civilization. We may now restore that
> temple to the ancient truths. The measure of the restoration lies
> in the extent to which we apply social values more noble than
> mere monetary profit.[51]

Roosevelt would later claim that businessmen had no "moral
indignation" about the sins of their peers: "Did they denounce
Charles E. Mitchell or Harry Sinclair? They did not!" The president

of the United States was lumping Mitchell in with the founder of Sinclair Oil, who had been convicted of jury tampering and served prison time after the Teapot Dome Scandal.[52]

It wasn't just the president targeting Mitchell. A day after he resigned, Mitchell and various members of City's management team were named as defendants in a lawsuit brought by Celia Gallin and other plaintiffs. This was just one week after Mitchell's first day of testimony before Pecora.[53] The plaintiffs claimed the defendants had breached their duty as directors and officers of City Bank and National City Company in several transactions that had been discussed at the hearings. A judge of the Supreme Court of New York County later denied almost all the claims, but ruled that there had been a computation error in awarding some bonuses and ordered managers to return the overages.[54] The lawyers on the case took home nearly half a million dollars from the pioneering shareholder derivative suit,[55] a legal creation that would enrich trial lawyers for generations.

All of this is not to say that Mitchell was wonderful or blameless, only that the charges against him were frequently off target or overblown. Not that there weren't plenty of grounds to criticize him. His bank enjoyed an advantage over many smaller competitors. City could and did borrow directly from the Fed, although it was not as significant a funding factor as in the early 1920s. Also, Mitchell made a habit of refusing to recognize problems in the overseas loan portfolio. His bank and its Wall Street affiliate disclosed very little to regulators or even to their own investors. And when all was said and done, after Mitchell had railed against Washington, his bank accepted one of the biggest bank bailouts of the Great Depression.

There is something of a debate about the bailout, however, as it occurred after Mitchell had resigned and James H. Perkins had been named City's chairman. An experienced banker who had worked at City and elsewhere, Perkins was perhaps more importantly a friend of President Roosevelt. The two had met two days after Roosevelt's inauguration to discuss legislation to separate commercial from investment banking, and to consider how City Bank would sever its ties with National City Company.[56]

The debate is over whether City really needed Washington's money, or was persuaded to participate in a broader program intended to show that the government was shoring up the nation's banking system. Just as in 2008, federal officials in the 1930s wanted even healthy banks to accept government investment so that the weak banks that really needed it would not be stigmatized by accepting federal assistance. So which category did City fall in?

Jesse Jones was chairman of a government agency called the Reconstruction Finance Corporation, which had been created by President Hoover to lend money to banks and other businesses. After Roosevelt became president, the agency's remit was expanded in March of 1933 to allow it to inject capital into banks through the purchase of preferred stock.[57] In the fall of that year, Jones invited City's Perkins, William Potter of Guaranty Trust, and Percy Johnston of Chemical Bank to meet with the president.

Just before the meeting with the three bankers, Jones suggested to the president that he not ask them to do anything. This would leave the banks free to suggest the structure and amounts of the federal capital injections. As described by Jones, Perkins "broke the ice" with a specific request: "Mr. President, to be perfectly frank, I would like very much to have $50,000,000 new capital for our bank."[58]

On Monday, December 4, 1933, at four forty-five p.m., the executive committee of the Reconstruction Finance Corporation met at its offices at 1825 H Street NW in Washington, just a few blocks from the White House. As Perkins had requested, the committee agreed to subscribe to up to $50,000,000 of City preferred

stock paying 5 percent annually. After the approval, Jones wrote
to President Roosevelt that "this new capital should multiply itself
many times in credit for agriculture, business and industry." Perhaps liberated to acknowledge how much City had needed the
help, the bank charged off a massive $129 million of problem assets
over the course of a year ending in mid-1934.[59]

Then again, new managements sometimes like to recognize
big losses if they can blame them on predecessors, because it makes
future results look better by comparison. Adding to the mystery
of how much City needed help is a Perkins letter to shareholders,
which presented the acceptance of government investment as a
sort of patriotic gesture:

> Our Directors feel that the Bank should support the President
> of the United States in his program of strengthening the cap-
> ital structure of the banks of the country and in his campaign
> to bring about business and industrial recovery. They also feel
> we should accept the offer which the Government has made to
> purchase preferred stock in national banks . . . The Comptroller
> of the Currency and the Federal Reserve Board, which have ju-
> risdiction in the matter, have given their approval on condition
> that the capital . . . be applied to writing down assets, and that
> no distribution on account thereof be made to shareholders.[60]

In the letter, Perkins also quoted the president, who was trying
to calm fears that the government wanted to undertake a wholesale nationalization of the banking industry:

> The government only wants to help provide banking capital
> adequate to meet the credit needs of the country, and through
> buying and lending upon preferred stock and capital deben-
> tures, it accomplishes this without undue demands upon present
> shareholders.[61]

The government's purchase of preferred stock in City was one of its largest bank investments. Only Chase and Continental Illinois received as much. All three were among the large banks that had imposed on investors the biggest dividend cuts, write-offs, and stock market declines during the period.[62]

Each of the three banks openly offered $50 million in preferred stock and in some cases private parties bought some of the available shares. But Continental, clearly the weakest of the three banks, sold all $50 million to the government. City sold $49 million to Uncle Sam and Chase sold $46 million. As a result of the transaction with Continental, the Reconstruction Finance Corporation gained control of the bank and required the installation of a new chairman, but Perkins was allowed to keep running City. In a historical preview of a controversy that would rage after the 2008 crisis, Jones had to certify the appropriateness of salaries paid at institutions that received government funding.[63]

City wasn't as bad off as Continental, but it was getting a giant taxpayer investment. A number of large banks, including Irving Trust, Central Hanover, and Bankers Trust each sold just $5 million of stock to the feds. These three institutions, along with others, such as First National Bank of Chicago and Guaranty Trust Company, were considered the most liquid large banks.

So it seems likely that City really did need the money. But there's also the question of whether it would have remained healthy if not for the Fed's monetary policy mistakes of that era. James Grant, publisher of *Grant's Interest Rate Observer*, argues that, compared to the condition of institutions like Citigroup after a much less severe crisis in 2008, Mitchell's City Bank held up remarkably well given the circumstances of the 1930s, and was in fact solvent at the time it accepted Washington's investment. Grant sees other virtues in the onetime City chairman: "Mitchell, who resigned in disgrace from National City and lost his houses to foreclosure, refused to file for personal bankruptcy. Rather, he honorably worked to pay every last dollar of debt. Later he built Blyth & Co into a thriving investment bank."[64]

The historical debate seems likely to continue. But one national argument *was* settled in 1933—at least until the successor to Charlie Mitchell's City Bank would reignite the debate more than six decades later. Pecora's hearings had succeeded in persuading the public that stock trading and commercial banking did not mix. The Banking Act of 1933, commonly known as the Glass-Steagall Act, was signed by President Roosevelt on June 16, 1933, and barred firms like City Bank from playing on Wall Street.[65]

Banks were given a year to cut ties, and City explored different options for jettisoning National City Company.[66] With time running out before the deadline, Perkins communicated a plan to liquidate the securities business in a letter to the Comptroller of the Currency:

> Present book worth of the City Company of New York is about $15,000,000 . . . pending the settlement of claims, disposition of litigation and realization of slow assets, we propose to take its stock on our books at a purely nominal figure of $1 for record purposes.[67]

Mitchell had dreamed of turning America into a nation of shareholders, and of serving millions of them with a new type of financial supermarket. He went a long way toward achieving both goals, but thanks to his mistakes overseas and the Fed's at home, his bank was hobbled and his brokerage was hardly worth a dollar. Yet City had endured another crisis, with help from a big slug of taxpayer capital.

13

Bank for the United States

Bankers who still had jobs by the late 1930s were generally so scarred by the experience of the Great Depression that they had little interest in risk-taking. And for any who were still inclined to lend to questionable borrowers, federal regulation was there to discourage them. The flurry of legislating and rule-making that followed the election of President Franklin Roosevelt in 1932 not only separated banks from Wall Street but essentially turned them into public utilities. The result was a banking system largely protected and controlled by the federal government. Then, in the 1940s, Washington would repeat what it had done in the 1860s—regulate US banks with the primary goal of funding a war.

After Mitchell was forced out of City Bank and Roosevelt's chum Perkins took over in 1933, the bank got along very well with the feds. Bank regulators became as complimentary of Perkins as they had once been of his predecessor. Just as examiners had been impressed by Mitchell's housecleaning of troubled assets when he first arrived in 1921, City's federal overseers now proclaimed another promising new chapter in the history of the tarnished bank.

In 1934, staff for the Office of the Comptroller of the Currency
wrote:

> The report of examination discloses this bank to be in a more
> sound condition than at any time since the beginning of the
> world wide depression . . . Since J.H. Perkins was elected Chair-
> man of the Board in February 1933, a complete change in the
> policies prevalent during the Mitchell regime has been brought
> about. Mr. Perkins is entirely familiar with the problems of the
> bank. It is evident that Mr. Perkins is endeavoring to carry out
> the conservative policies which he inaugurated.[1]

After recognizing significant losses and accepting a big government investment, City's books were showing solid improvement.
Nonaccrual assets—primarily loans in which the borrower was
not making payments—declined from $120.9 million at the end of
1933 (52 percent of common stockholder equity) all the way down
to $16.6 million (11 percent of common stockholder equity) by the
end of 1939.[2]

Along with an improving balance sheet, it seems that City's
reputation was also on the mend. "Under the guidance of present
management the bank has steadily progressed since February 1933
and has regained its prestige," according to a 1935 examination
report.[3] The following year brought a similar message: "It appears
that the present policies of this bank in regard to loans and investments are definitely much better than in the past."[4] In 1937,
federal examiners were particularly keen on City's management of
its overseas business, which had frequently been a source of trouble
in the preceding decades:

> Up to a few years ago this department was operated more with
> ambition than discretion. The old "expansion" policy left this
> bank with material losses and with an accumulation of frozen

loans and work outs. Present policies appear to be wholly concerned with strictly commercial loans in the foreign branches
and with the movement of merchandise along the various principal trade routes of the world, at the same time salvaging as
much as possible of the frozen credits.[5]

While the regulators were happy with City's new managerial
regime and even with the bank's foreign exposures, there was
one overseas jurisdiction that was making them nervous. German
debtors owed City $44 million and bank examiners figured a sig-
nificant portion of that total should be written off as losses. Bank
executives for their part were not exactly optimistic that they were
going to be repaid in full. After a visit in 1934, Perkins wanted
City out of its German exposures as quickly as possible. But City
managers pleaded with examiners not to make this pessimism official. The bankers worried that acknowledging that the German
borrowers might default could encourage them to do just that.
The confidential section of the 1934 exam report explained the
dilemma:

> The executive officers seemed to feel that if the German debtors
> ever became aware that the New York banks had been required
> to write off their loans in whole or in part, serious difficulties
> would eventually occur in any program for liquidation in that
> the Germans would try to bargain for a settlement on the basis
> of the book value of the assets rather than the claim value.[6]

The regulators insisted on a 40 percent write-down of the German credits. But elsewhere overseas the bank's prospects were
improving, and so rather than a wholesale retreat from foreign
markets, Perkins opted to prune those offices that weren't profitable and reduce the bank's exposure to geopolitical risks. The
number of foreign branches fell from a 1930s peak around one

hundred down to forty-five branches at its lowest point during the early 1940s.[7] Yet even after its retrenchment, City remained the US bank with the greatest global branch network.[8]

Shareholders were fortunate that Perkins didn't entirely abandon risky markets abroad. According to financial historian Phillip Zweig, during the Depression the bank "was able to maintain its dividend only because of some $7 million in profits—about 40 percent of the gross earnings of the overseas network—generated by its Chinese branches, mostly from silver trading and speculation."[9]

Also, since state and federal limits on domestic branching limited City's US business to the confines of New York City, foreign markets offered City the only potential to grow its territory. Moreover, the friendly confines of its home field weren't what they used to be. While the bank dominated its market in New York City, the branching restrictions prevented the firm from following its customers as they increasingly moved to the suburbs or to faster-growing cities in the South and West.

The year he took over as City chairman in 1933, Perkins had made the case to shareholders that they should continue to benefit from the overseas investments made years earlier:

> Under anything like normal conditions the foreign branches make handsome earnings and contribute largely through their services to the building up of domestic deposits. In building up this foreign organization a great deal of money has been spent, for which values over and above those appearing in the Statement have been created. These values consist of our experience in the foreign field and our facilities for foreign commercial business, which would take any other bank many years and great expense to duplicate.[10]

Regulators were satisfied, and the bank was taking other actions to please their federal overseers. Limiting executive compensation is always a crowd-pleaser in Washington, and City learned from the Pecora hearings just how much the general public enjoyed reading about windfalls for Wall Streeters during a time of hardship. After that debacle, City bosses were paid more like the utility executives they had become than the financiers they used to be. An examination report from 1935 makes no mention of the kind of bonus fund for managers that had raised eyebrows in Mitchell's day. Examiners seem to have been pleased to learn that Chairman Perkins and President Rentschler were each making $100,000 in annual salary, with the next-highest-paid executive making $75,000. The exam report said City Bank's management compensation "is not considered excessive."[11]

Deciding what was excessive and what was not fell to regulators for many aspects of a bank's operation. The new Federal Deposit Insurance Corporation now had taxpayers standing behind each insured depository. Banks were prohibited from paying interest on checking accounts. The Federal Reserve decided how much interest banks could pay on other types of accounts. Federal law also limited how much of a bank's capital could be loaned to any one customer. At City and elsewhere, advertising and marketing were kept to a minimum. In tune with the times, City had traded in a star salesman at the top for a quiet and well-connected plodder.

City and most of its competitors suffered during the economic downturn of 1937 and 1938. Perhaps explaining why he and Roosevelt got along so well, Perkins appears to have been the rare businessman of his day who didn't think the federal government was intervening *enough* in the US economy. He blamed the slump on a lack of fiscal stimulus from Washington. In the language of the day, he called for more of FDR's "pump-priming"—government spending intended to boost the economy.[12]

Despite the downturn, the banking system was generally stabilizing during this period. After nearly fifteen thousand bank failures during the 1920s and early 1930s, the fittest had generally survived. By the time Perkins died in 1940 while still chairman, City had largely recovered from the depths of the Depression.[13] Gordon Rentschler, who had been president since 1929, succeeded Perkins as chairman and was no more eager than his predecessor to chart an adventurous course. Across the industry, the years of financial crisis had made risk aversion almost a religion, whether self-imposed or dictated from DC.

Zweig notes that at least into the late 1940s, lending policy at the bank reflected the searing experience of the financial crash and economic depression: "No loan could be made without the signatures of three officers. If a loan request exceeded a certain level, it might require the approval of a more senior officer and a review by the credit policy committee."[14]

But as cautious as bankers had become, they were still just as likely to respond to incentives as any other group of humans. When Washington needed to focus this boring world of banking on the single task of providing the money to defeat Germany and Japan, a combination of patriotism and regulatory persuasion helped transform the capital markets. From 1941 to 1945, US government debt more than quintupled, as financiers across the country agreed to sell Treasury bonds without taking profits.[15] And the buyers were mostly banks, in part because the Fed relaxed reserve requirements for any institution holding Treasury bonds.[16] As cautious as they had become, bank executives still appreciated the opportunity to convert more of their cash to profit-generating assets, for example by buying even more Treasury bonds. This would not be the last time that regulation encouraged private banks to loan money to government—nor the last time that bankers seized the opportunity to get regulatory relief for doing so. The combination would become a recurring theme in the era of government-backed banking.

But unlike in some later years, in the 1940s this policy mix worked out well for City, for the United States, and for Western civilization. Funding the world's arsenal of democracy led to the liberation of Asia and Europe and to stability for the formerly troubled bank:

> The National City Bank of the 1940s was less a bank than a bond portfolio. Of its total $5.59 billion in assets, National City held $2.93 billion in U.S. government obligations and just $1.24 billion in loans. Although it might have been patriotic to finance the nation's war debt, it certainly required little or no banking skill. Bank profits in the forties were not large, but they were virtually guaranteed.[17]

Just in case City and other banks wanted to invest in things other than US Treasury bonds, Washington didn't make it easy. The wartime Regulation W largely prevented consumer finance, and in any case, the War Production Board generally didn't allow the manufacture for civilian use of things for which a consumer might seek financing in the first place, such as automobiles and durable goods.[18]

While the assets on the balance sheet during the war became almost uniformly dull, the people who watched over these assets were becoming more diverse. As in other industries, the war created new opportunities for women in banking. By the end of 1942, a full 43 percent of City employees were female, up from 23 percent just two years earlier.[19] Still, the bank's senior leadership would remain entirely or almost entirely male for decades.

Meanwhile in the overseas offices, employees could scarcely have imagined how far from dull their workplaces could become. In 1940, German bombs destroyed a church next door to City's London branch. Bank employees came into work to find missing walls and pieces of the church embedded in their desks. "But the bulk of the building remains OK and they are carrying on in the most splendidly urbane and unperturbed manner," wrote a visitor from City's trust company affiliate. "I saw one of the accountants sitting at his desk . . . almost entirely in plain air—clad in mackintosh and bowler hat—dictating a letter to a stenographer in coat and hat—while an umbrella lay handily on top of the desk . . . Really, the people of London are quite amazing."[20]

City's contribution to the war effort went well beyond maintaining a stiff upper lip while providing the financing. Back in the US, numerous City employees enlisted or were drafted into the armed forces after the Japanese bombing of Pearl Harbor in December of 1941. At the end of that month the bank had 10,000 employees, but the total would fall to 8,650 by the end of 1943. The bank's official history suggests that many did not return home, because after the end of the war those returning to the payroll were notably fewer than the number who had left. At the end of 1945, about 790 of the bank's onetime employees had been released from military service, and 673 of these decided to return to the bank.[21] City seems to have made every effort not just to rehire men who had spent years serving their country, but also to offer new opportunities befitting those who had in many cases exercised enormous responsibilities on the battlefield.

After victory in the war, the men who ran City Bank could easily have gotten into trouble given the financial turbulence of the period. In 1946 and 1947 inflation was spiking even as the economy was shrinking. The rapid financial transition from war to peace had begun in 1945. Germany surrendered that May, followed by Japan in August. Consumers and businesses that had been taking direction from Washington for years could suddenly pursue private opportunities.

During the three years beginning in June of 1945, City's commercial and industrial loans surged to $661 million, up from $279 million. The bank's loans to consumers more than tripled, to $167 million from just $47 million.[22] Still, by the end of the period, US government securities added up to most of the bank's domestic earning assets,[23] underlining how much the bank had become above all a vehicle to fund the federal budget.

Now City was starting to move back toward servicing the private economy, with all the opportunities and risks that came with it. During the war, the Fed had sought to keep interest rates low and stable, ensuring that banks like City could collect deposits, provide cheap financing for Uncle Sam, and predictably make a nice, if unspectacular, return. While a heavy regulatory burden remained, the bank would have more opportunities to succeed or fail in a business that was about to get more complex and volatile.

One thing that kept City out of trouble in the years immediately after World War II was the collection of memories held by executives of the tough times that had followed the previous war. Many veteran bankers expected another deep economic downturn in the late 1940s once the boys had returned home from Europe and the Pacific. The bank's vice chairman wondered out loud whether "we can avoid a boom and bust. We are set for it, just as after World War I."[24] Even though commercial and consumer loans were surging and inflation and interest rates became less predictable, the bank remained strong in part because of an institutional caution, a healthy fear of the potential for financial crisis among City executives. Eventually, they'd get over it. And the man who would lead them through a radical cultural change was already in the building.

14

Walter Wriston and the Culture of Risk

Walter Wriston didn't arrive at City Bank with painful childhood memories of 1930s deprivation. He didn't share the fears of his new colleagues about the potential for financial ruin. And he was, truth be told, not particularly interested in banking. All of which may help explain the business revolution he began to foment almost from the moment he walked in the door.

Wriston had participated in his high school math club in Appleton, Wisconsin, but when he went to college at Connecticut's Wesleyan University he focused on foreign affairs, history, and political science. Not an outstanding student but by all accounts a diligent worker, he won a prize for public speaking and worked as a stringer for the nearby *Hartford Courant* newspaper.[1]

The lanky kid who enrolled at Wesleyan in the fall of 1937 was not a child of the Great Depression, because it had largely passed him by. The Appleton of Wriston's youth had managed to muddle along despite the national catastrophe because the local paper mills had for the most part continued to operate. And the Wristons were not just another local family. Appleton was also home to Lawrence College (now Lawrence University), where Wriston's father served as president. Instead of wondering where the next meal would come from, young Walter was wondering which important personage from the worlds of academia, business, or politics would be the next visitor at the family dinner table. When Wriston was a senior in high school, his father became president of the Ivy League's Brown University.[2]

Wriston's parents didn't spoil their children. They set high standards and taught the importance of thrift and self-reliance. At the age of fifteen, their son Walter had become the youngest Eagle Scout in the country.[3] But given his upbringing, Wriston was not governed by the extreme caution that would mark so many Americans of his generation who had grown up in an age of scarcity and fear.

Yet especially after he became a college student, certain moments would be engraved on Wriston's memory forever. They would remind him of the danger of allowing anyone to have too much power to govern others. Wriston's parents, especially his father, had for years been staunchly opposed to Roosevelt's New Deal, viewing it as an attack on individual liberty in favor of bureaucratic central planning. Wriston shared this view. But it was a family vacation before his junior year at Wesleyan that would confirm for him the danger of surrendering too much authority to the state.

The Wristons traveled to Europe in 1939, just weeks before Hitler's Germany invaded Poland. Wriston biographer Phillip Zweig explains that the family "found themselves standing outside the Frankfurt railway station watching in horror as waves of Nazi Youth units goose-stepped by, waving swastika banners and singing 'Deutschland uber Alles,' the Third Reich's national anthem."[4]

For the young Wriston, the lesson was clear: "I saw what happens with total regulation of people's lives, which starts with economic regulation and leaps over into politics and abolition of free speech." While he conceded that some regulation was necessary to protect health and safety, he generally opposed government intervention in the economy.[5]

Back from the disturbing visit to Europe, Wriston was elected president of Wesleyan's Willkie for President Club. The candidate lost the election of 1940 in a landslide, but Wriston's own candidacy for graduate school was successful. The future banker studied at Tufts University's Fletcher School of Law and Diplomacy and then in 1942 started a career as a junior foreign service officer in the State Department. The next year, he was drafted into the army. Wriston waited an extended period in the US and ended up as a signal officer on a remote Pacific island. After several years in uniform, he became a civilian again.

Thanks to his father's friendship with City Bank vice chairman W. Randolph Burgess, Wriston landed a position as a junior inspector in the Comptroller's division of the bank at $3,000 a year. One can assume that he had not been fielding too many other job offers. He later admitted: "If I were to sit up at night making a list of everything dull, banking would come out on top." Wriston began work in 1946 and, not surprisingly, did not exactly fall in love with the highly regulated, staid world of post–New Deal banking. He later recalled, "Banking was kind of a nice club. You had your inventories under control because the government told you how much you could pay on deposits."[6] Many other returning veterans weren't falling in love with City, either:

> Having risked their lives on the battlefields of Europe and Asia, the returning GIs had little patience with the silly bureaucratic conventions perpetuated by those who had stayed behind. Wriston himself was once slapped with a written reprimand for reading the *Wall Street Journal* at his desk.[7]

Some office rules are simply beyond the pale. The 1940s dress code for men at City Bank demanded black shoes, no exceptions.

Button-down shirts were forbidden; starched collars were required. The bank president at the time, William Gage "Iron Duke" Brady Jr., once called out a young war veteran in City's training program for his choice of neckwear, saying, "You know I don't like bow ties." The aspiring young banker replied, "I guess that's why I'm wearing one and you're not." Wriston would recall that the veteran, who was independently wealthy, was the hero of the bank's young staff.[8] In time, Wriston would attack many other City conventions, some of which weren't so silly.

By 1948, Wriston was working in City's credit department and learning about the three Cs: character, capacity, and collateral.[9] When considering whether to extend credit, a banker must know whether the potential borrower has both the integrity and the financial wherewithal to repay a loan, but also understand which assets of the borrower can be seized and sold by the bank if the loan is not repaid. Wriston perhaps could have spent more time in this course of study.

The next year he received a call from George Moore, a vice president who would eventually run the entire bank. Moore was looking for rising stars to groom for executive leadership and he was intrigued by Wriston's background. Moore got right to the point, telling him: "You look like a pretty smart guy, so you're coming to work for me tomorrow morning."

Wriston became immersed in the business of providing credit to the transportation industry, especially railroad companies, and he also began a long and fruitful business relationship with Greek tycoon Aristotle Onassis. Much of the shipping and steel industries of the time thought Onassis was crazy when he sought financing for the construction of giant ocean tankers to carry oil. But Texaco agreed to pay him to move the cargo, and Wriston arranged the financing to build the massive vessels, along with long-term loans from the insurer MetLife. The rest is energy-market history.[10] City became the world's leading bank in financing shipping. Wriston was generally not in the habit of drinking, but his achievements in this area certainly gave everyone involved a reason to cheer. Zweig explains:

> The launching of a new Onassis tanker was always a cause for celebration. Early on, a number of the tankers were built by Bethlehem Steel, which obviously became comfortable with supertankers, at its Sparrow Point yard in Quincy, Massachusetts. Wriston recalls that Bethlehem's president customarily chartered a train to bring people up for the launching of a ship. "Fueled almost entirely with Scotch," Wriston recalled later, "they were blowouts like you couldn't believe."[11]

Before long Wriston was overseeing the entire City unit serving transportation firms. This domain grew larger in 1955, when City Bank bought its similarly named rival First National Bank of the City of New York. First National's blue-chip clients included the railroads Burlington Northern, Great Northern, and Northern Pacific. Like the banks of the time, it seems the railroads were not particularly creative when it came to naming themselves. After City completed the acquisition, the combined firm was called the First National City Bank of New York.

Bank names, of course, are usually intended to be boring and to project an image of stability. But inside, the place was changing. Wriston was helping to transform City from an owner of government bonds to a real bank, extending credit to finance the growth of global business. By the early 1950s, for the first time in twenty years, loans were a bigger part of the balance sheet than investments.[12] The 1955 acquisition and Wriston's charge into new types of transportation financing accelerated this trend.

Now City was ready to once again charge into overseas markets. US banking was still heavily regulated by both state and federal governments, and an ambitious banker would naturally set his gaze on places that offered the chance for growth. In 1956, Walter Wriston joined the international division.

City's overseas operation had been erratic to say the least, from the initial success during the Vanderlip years to the Russian and Cuban debacles, to the partial revival under Charles Mitchell before the disasters of the Depression era. When Wriston signed on, the international division was not in crisis but barely profitable. His new colleagues were not entirely thrilled to see him. Division head Leo Shaw told Wriston at their first meeting: "You've got to be born into this business, and I'm sorry you're here." He added: "You're too old to learn anything. I didn't want you, so here we are. Good-bye." Another senior banker described Wriston as "about as popular as a skunk at a tea party" among the long-time international staff who had long worked under Shaw. The division head, who had been on board during both the Russian and Cuban disasters, epitomized a culture fearful of new ventures and resistant to change.[13]

Shaw didn't exactly warm up to the new employee foisted on him by headquarters. He didn't invite Wriston to key meetings, assign him any work, provide leads, or share information about overseas markets. But by traveling around the far-flung branch network, Wriston figured out on his own that City was virtually unknown in the local markets where it operated. Shaw had been making sure the bank earned a modest profit on currency trades and seems to have done almost nothing to build the bank's brand overseas.

Just over a year after Wriston's arrival, Shaw was demoted and Moore took over as head of the overseas division. Wriston became his chief lieutenant and went to war against the old guard and its risk-averse, bureaucratic culture. He and Moore started a system of rotating staff between domestic and overseas assignments so that employees couldn't spend an entire career in just one country. New managers arrived in many of the foreign branches.[14] Wriston blended his transportation and overseas work. Aristotle Onassis continued as a client during this period, with Wriston helping to finance his purchase of Olympic Airways from the Greek government.[15]

By 1959, Wriston became head of the overseas division.[16] He had a mandate from City's new president, Moore:

> Around 1960, we in Citibank took a new position. We would not be merely a bank. We would become a financial service company. We would seek to perform every useful financial service, anywhere in the world, which we were permitted by law to perform and which we believed we could perform at a profit.[17]

This was in many ways a return to the strategies of Frank Vanderlip and Charles Mitchell, and (spoiler alert!) there would be some similarity in the results. Particularly strong markets for growth included Latin America. Although it was not a "paragon of managerial excellence and efficiency," Wriston's overseas division was setting the standard for global banks. As always, the potential rewards of banking in developing countries came along with significant risks, for example the possibility of bloody Marxist revolutions and the resulting state-enforced theft. City lost $45 million when Fidel Castro overthrew the Batista government in Cuba and nationalized the bank's assets.[18]

Such setbacks didn't deter Wriston. In 1963, he made it clear that City was playing offense all over the planet:

> The plan in the Overseas Division was first to put a Citibank branch in every commercially important country in the world. The second phase was to begin to tap the local deposit market by putting satellite branches or mini-branches in a country. The third phase was to export retail services and know-how from New York.[19]

The global focus of the bank only sharpened when Wriston became president in 1967, taking over after Moore's ascension to chairman. Unlike past presidents Mitchell and Perkins, Wriston did not have an overhang of bad assets to clean up starting on day one. But he would have to face an economy and a financial system that were lurching into one of the most difficult periods in US history. And he was sailing into the storm with less caution than some of his predecessors.

Banking isn't like other industries, because, as we see in the history of Citigroup, the taxpayer is often forced to stand ready to offer assistance when a banking giant stumbles. Wriston was a highly innovative leader who would go on to drive the adoption of ATMs and credit cards, among other consumer services. But the entrepreneurial spirit that is so valuable in other industries is not so beneficial when public money is at stake. Being innovative by conducting more and more financial activities above the taxpayer safety net is often innovation the US economy can do without.

As we've seen, Citi was often at its least stable during periods when it was most politicized. Therefore those who knew the bank's history may not have been happy to see Wriston developing significant political ties. This is in some ways unavoidable when running a giant bank, but City's boss took an active role in national debates about financial policy. He was twice offered the job of Treasury secretary under President Nixon and twice turned it down. The first offer came in 1968, just a year after Wriston had taken over as City's president. The second arrived in 1974 after George Shultz resigned.[20] Six years later, shortly after President Reagan's election, Wriston would attend a meeting of the Co-ordinating Committee on Economic Policy, tasked with laying the groundwork for the incoming administration. The thirteen-member committee was chaired by Shultz and included the likes of Milton Friedman, Alan Greenspan, Jack Kemp, former Treasury secretary William Simon, and former Fed chairman Arthur

Burns.[21] Wriston was once again on the short list for Treasury
secretary, but eventually lost out to Merrill Lynch chairman Donald Regan. Wriston would later also come under consideration to
take Paul Volcker's spot as chairman of the Federal Reserve when
his term was up in 1983. Regan, who had inched out Wriston for
the Treasury secretary job, described the potential for his fellow
financier to be a "brilliant" Fed chairman. In the end, President
Reagan decided to reappoint Volcker.[22]

Back in Nixon days, the highly connected Wriston ran into
the first of a series of crises involving his megabank. It must have
come as quite a shock because in Wriston's first few years at the
helm City saw steady growth, with profits regularly breaking
the $100 million mark. Then came problems at the Penn Cen-
tral railroad.[23] The resulting intervention by the Federal Reserve
revealed the lengths the central bank would go to in attempting
to maintain financial stability. City had a long history of financing transportation—railroads in particular—dating back to the
restructuring of the Union Pacific Railroad during the 1890s and
even further back to the days of Moses Taylor's investments in the
country's early rail lines. More recently, Wriston had made City
the king of transportation financing among the major banks. But
this was one deal the bank should have left alone.

Penn Central resulted from the 1968 merger of the Pennsylvania and New York Central Railroads, a response to competitive
pressures from interstate highways and the Saint Lawrence Sea-
way. Penn Central had to live under the heavy regulatory hand of
the Interstate Commerce Commission (ICC), so it was a company
with little operational flexibility. City had led a syndicate of banks
supporting the merger with a $100 million revolving credit line.[24]
The merger carried the hope that two troubled entities could
jointly find enough cost savings to transform themselves into one
healthy enterprise.

Unfortunately for Penn Central and its bankers, the cost savings and some hoped-for operational improvements never materialized, even as the new firm took on a heavy debt load. About a year after the deal closed, Penn Central chief financial officer David Bevan met with City officers to talk about increasing the revolving credit line from $100 million to $300 million. Bevan claimed that the increase was needed, among other reasons, because the integration of the two railroads was taking longer than expected. Penn Central's debt to City would ultimately grow to $63 million (see Table 9), the most of any bank, but lots of other big institutions had followed City into the deal, so they were now exposed, too. The syndicate of fifty-three banks led by City ultimately approved the increase.

But it wasn't enough. Another meeting with City later in 1969 was focused on increasing the amount of commercial paper funding for Penn Central up to $250 million. The company's overhang of debt and commercial paper financing translated into interest

Table 9: Penn Central Ten Largest Lending Banks

Bank	Loan Balance ($s in millions)
First National City Bank	63.2
Manufacturers Hanover	40.0
Chase Manhattan Bank	34.2
Chemical Bank	31.2
Irving Trust Co.	30.0
First National Bank of Chicago	28.0
Morgan Guaranty Trust Company	25.8
Mellon Bank	22.0
Continental Illinois National Bank	19.0
Bankers Trust	15.0
SUBTOTAL	**308.0**
All participating banks	494.0

Source: SEC Staff Report on the Collapse of the Penn Central Company, balance as of June 1970, 226.

Note: Balance excludes certain loans such as direct equipment loans.

costs of nearly $50 million a year. The debt burden became such a concern that City began to seek additional collateral to support the syndicate's loans and Penn Central announced a large quarterly loss in early 1970.[25]

As Penn Central's financial situation worsened, management needed to draw down the final $50 million on their revolving credit facility with the banks in May 1970. City was blamed by the syndicate for not staying on top of the railroad's financial standing. CFO Bevan then started talking to City and Chemical Bank, one of the other major lenders in the syndicate, about approaching the government for a guarantee of its debt, which was a red flag for the banks. Taxpayer bailouts are often the last refuge of a mismanaged failure. Within a week Penn Central's management was headed to Washington for meetings with Treasury Secretary David Kennedy, Nixon aide Peter Flanigan, and newly installed Federal Reserve Board chairman Arthur Burns.[26] The discussion focused on the possibility of up to $750 million in federal loan guarantees. To justify propping up a private company, bailout supporters planned to argue that allowing potential disruptions in domestic railroad operations would put national security at risk.[27]

Two days after the high-level meetings in Washington, a *Wall Street Journal* story revealed the mounting problems at Penn Central. The following day, Bevan and City met with the banking syndicate to discuss the potential government guarantee.[28] Wriston told the Penn Central board that heads should roll, particularly Bevan and the railroad's chairman Stuart Saunders. On June 3, Wriston met with Bevan, who wanted more money from the syndicate. Wriston's reply was immediate: "There's no way. You don't have any assets. You're down the slippery slope."

The banks would not move forward with any additional funding until the government stepped in with a guarantee. Wriston, who was a frequent and articulate advocate of open markets free of government intervention, supported the idea of a government rescue at a meeting of bankers organized by the Federal Reserve Bank of New York. Wriston even backed the preposterous argument that a railroad bankruptcy was a threat to national security. With City on the hook for financial losses—and a potential loss of prestige as leader of the banking syndicate—Wriston seems to have decided that his beliefs about the proper role of government were becoming a little too expensive.

Within a few days, Bevan, along with Penn Central chairman Saunders, who had appeared on the cover of *Time* magazine only a few years earlier under the heading "Railroads of the Future," were relieved of their duties. Vice Chairman Alfred E. Perlman was also dismissed.

Fortunately for taxpayers, influential officials in Congress as well as the Nixon administration weren't buying the argument that the country couldn't afford to let the Penn Central guys fail. After Treasury Secretary Kennedy advised the president that he thought the market could absorb a collapse of the railroad firm, Nixon refused to back the government guarantee. On June 21, Penn Central filed for bankruptcy.[29]

The bankruptcy filing hit the commercial paper market hard. Issuing commercial paper was a relatively new way for big corporations to borrow money for short periods of time instead of getting bank loans. The corporations were issuing securities similar to bonds, but because they were only borrowing for perhaps sixty or ninety days, some buyers thought that holding commercial paper was almost like having cash, rather than an investment that could fail. The market had doubled in size to $40 billion in just a two-year period from 1968 to 1970. Penn Central had an estimated $84 million of commercial paper outstanding at the time of its bankruptcy, with much of the balance coming due that summer. As commercial paper is unsecured, creditors holding it would fare much worse in a default than banks, which typically demanded that loans be partially or fully secured with collateral.

The problems at Penn Central sparked worries that perhaps other big companies also might not be as solid as they seemed. This led to a run on the commercial paper market. With the economy wallowing in a recession, there was concern that other firms would also be exposed to losses.[30] As their debts came due, corporations might not be able to issue new paper and could face an acute shortage of cash.

To counteract the run on the commercial paper market, the Federal Reserve made it easier for banks to borrow from the discount window so they could in turn provide loans to nonfinancial companies. Federal Reserve chairman Arthur Burns said that if necessary, the central bank would even lend directly to industrial companies.[31]

It never came to that, as increased liquidity to the banks calmed markets. Investors realized that industrial companies would be able to borrow to make payroll and take care of their other pressing needs for cash. Lending through the discount window expanded by $1 billion during this period and peaked at about $1.7 billion during July 1970.[32] Although this reveals a dramatic increase in lending in the period surrounding Penn Central's collapse, it is a far cry from the $2.7 billion in discount window lending during 1920 and 1921, a full fifty years earlier. City would later announce $28 million in losses related to Penn Central, a tiny fraction of its $1.4 billion in capital as of year-end 1969.[33]

But at least two results of the minicrisis should have been of deep concern to anyone worried about taxpayer risk and the stability of the financial system. The new leader of American banking, despite his big talk about the virtues of free markets, had been happy to welcome government intervention to prevent private losses—especially his own. And the chairman of the Federal Reserve was more than willing to rescue not just the banking system, but even companies entirely outside the world of finance.

15

Not That Big, but Too Big to Fail?

Too big to fail" didn't become a household phrase in the United States until the financial crisis of 2008, but it became very familiar to anyone following banking policy in the 1980s. And whether or not they knew what to call it, Americans in the 1970s had the misfortune of witnessing this category of government-favored enterprises expand into more of the financial economy.

Commercial paper is not banking, but rather a market of securities, where investors are supposed to understand that they can lose just as easily as gain. Just like stocks and bonds, short-term debt instruments issued by companies can rise or fall in value, and buyers should know that. Railroads are also not banking, and as the bankruptcy of Penn Central proved, the country can survive a railroad company taking on too much debt. Bankruptcy doesn't cause the tracks and the engines and the cars to explode; it just changes their ownership, or allows the same old owners to operate with a lighter debt burden.

Fortunately, the government didn't end up bailing out Penn Central or directly lending to issuers of commercial paper. And there's a case to be made that the Fed did what it should as a lender of last resort: providing liquidity in a financial crisis to healthy banks able to offer good collateral as they seek to borrow. But the reaction to the railroad's failure showed that financial leaders in both New York and Washington were getting more comfortable with the idea of federal rescues of giant corporations. And in the world of banking, the idea of a taxpayer rescue was catching on for a broader group of firms. The government would soon be bailing out an enterprise that nobody would call a giant of American finance.

The trouble started overseas, as it often does in financial crises. City's Walter Wriston wasn't the only American banker who figured out that foreign markets offered much more upside than his home turf. As for the downside, one of City's New York rivals would be among the first to learn all about it.

The difference was that while megabanks like City felt constricted by state and federal regulation in the US, Franklin National Bank of New York seems to have been upset that its home market wasn't regulated *even more*. Starting in 1960, the large New York City banks were allowed to start invading its Long Island territory. Franklin first tried defending its suburban stronghold the old-fashioned way—with lawyers. For example, it sued to try to block City's entry into New York's Nassau County.[1] The legal warfare didn't work. Franklin tried to retaliate against the Manhattan giants by moving into their wholesale banking market in New York City, taking on borrowers that had a difficult time getting credit. But the real growth opportunity for Franklin, as for so many other US banks, was overseas.

Franklin opened a branch in the other Nassau—the one in the Bahamas—and also opened one in London. The bank was diving into the Eurodollar market, which involves accounts and transactions denominated in US dollars but held overseas, sometimes to avoid US regulation. Franklin also embraced foreign exchange trading. Its foreign branch deposits leapt from 8 percent to more than 30 percent of total deposits, and foreign branch loans grew from 2 percent to 20 percent of total loans from 1969 to 1973. For a while, the aggressive push for international growth seemed to be working. Franklin had become the twentieth-largest bank in the US, an increasingly important financial institution though still nowhere near as big as a megabank like City.

Franklin's ownership also had a foreign orientation—Italian financier Michele Sindona was a significant shareholder. Unfortunately for both himself and the other owners, Sindona would end up being indicted and convicted on no fewer than sixty-five of sixty-nine federal criminal counts in the United States, including bribery and fraud. Many of the convictions related to his work at Franklin.[2]

The transactions at Franklin that were perfectly legal didn't work out so well, either. Fast growth in banking can be especially dangerous because it may be the result of weak underwriting—loaning money to build bank assets without carefully vetting the creditworthiness of the borrower. On the other side of the ledger, safety requires stable sources of funding—whether long-term loans or depositors who are unlikely to withdraw all their funds in an instant. But Franklin had problems on both sides of the balance sheet. It relied heavily on short-term borrowings to fund a troubled domestic loan and investment portfolio. When combined with heavy losses in foreign exchange trading, the result was an insolvent bank and a run by depositors in 1974.[3]

Almost as ugly as the bank run were the regulatory failures that preceded it. Sometimes after a financial disaster or a massive fraud, an obscure whistle-blower will emerge to explain how his or her warnings went unheeded by an institutional hierarchy. Often the whistle-blower is a midlevel employee or perhaps a quirky outsider who didn't buy the official story that was accepted by the rest of the industry. But in the case of Franklin, it seems that whistles were being blown all over the place, from top to bottom in the organization, and even in the press. Yet the feds had taken hardly any action.

Later congressional hearings would be especially embarrassing for regulators in highlighting that among those trying to get the attention of regulators was a man who had run the whole bank. Former Franklin chairman Arthur Roth testified before a sub-committee hearing of the House Committee on Government Operations. He discussed the warning letters he had sent to regulators with Congressman Elliott Levitas of Georgia:

> MR. LEVITAS: I'd like to try to clear up this chronology again, Mr. Roth. Mr. Brown suggested that the first communication you had with the regulatory agencies may have occurred in 1973. Did you send copies of your April and July 1972 letters to FDIC and the Comptroller of the Currency?
>
> MR. ROTH: I surely did.
>
> MR. LEVITAS: So they would have had this information brought to their attention early in 1972.
>
> MR. ROTH: And you should have seen the newspapers at that time. All of the newspapers carried big stories about this. They could not have missed it . . .
>
> MR. LEVITAS: Can you shed any light on why the regulators did not identify Franklin as a problem bank in time and take the necessary steps to avoid the ultimate failure?
>
> MR. ROTH: No, I can't. After all, when I wrote my letter on April 27, 1972, I indicated that it was a problem bank—if you read between the lines. It was a very strong letter. I don't know whether they had Franklin down as a problem bank at that time or not, but certainly I did.

The Office of the Comptroller of the Currency eventually figured out that something was amiss. The agency's examination of the bank in November 1973 resulted in an overall rating of "extremely poor." But the regulators didn't move to seize the bank before the run started in 1974. First the large depositors, including foreign customers, started to flee and finally the government acted.

Regulators often seek more authority over the firms they oversee, but this doesn't mean they always want to exercise this authority if it means being accountable for the results. If Franklin had been a tiny community bank, regulators likely would have cleaned up the mess by shutting it down, selling what could be sold to other banks, and if necessary, paying to make insured depositors whole. The FDIC had been doing this for decades. But the closure of a small local bank for idiosyncratic reasons is not going to reverberate throughout the larger financial system. As has often been the case, regulators were fearful that the system was too fragile to withstand the failure of even a large bank like Franklin, never mind a megabank like City.

After the May 1974 run, both the Federal Reserve and the Office of the Comptroller of the Currency were hesitant to shutter Franklin. The Fed explained later that they kept the bank open "first to prevent the severe deterioration of confidence, at home and abroad, that would have resulted from an early failure of the bank, and second, to provide time to permit Franklin National Bank itself, or if necessary the bank regulatory authorities, to achieve a more permanent solution to the bank's difficulties."[4] The FDIC put the bank up for bid.[5] But the regulators agreed that failure should not be an option. In May the Federal Reserve Bank of New York began propping up Franklin, ultimately putting out $1.7 billion in discount window lending while regulators deliberated on what to do next. This allowed many of the big depositors to flee the bank without any losses according to Anna Schwartz, who argued that the lending "shifted discount window use from short-term liquidity assistance to long-term support of an insolvent institution pending final resolution of its problems. The bank was insolvent when its borrowing began and insolvent when its borrowing ended. The loans merely replaced funds that depositors withdrew," with the "inflow from the Reserve Bank matching withdrawals."[6] The Fed was no longer simply providing liquidity in times of general market stress to otherwise healthy banks offering good collateral. It was lending to a failing bank that would spawn criminal convictions because regulators were afraid of what might happen if they didn't. America's central bank was now putting taxpayers on the hook for an indirect rescue of uninsured depositors.

This was not the way regulators were supposed to clean up such a mess, and of course regulators bore some responsibility for allowing the creation of the mess in the first place. Franklin represented among other things a massive supervisory breakdown, and Comptroller of the Currency James Smith was looking for the quickest, easiest way to make the problem go away. So he began to pressure Wriston and the other top New York bankers to help find a buyer for Franklin. Meanwhile, Fed chairman Burns wanted Smith to strong-arm the banks into funding a bailout, but Smith balked at that suggestion. There were also legal factors impeding the ability of regulators to market Franklin to the full range of US institutions—specifically 1970s limits on interstate banking. For example, the largest US bank, Bank of America, was not allowed to bid. This was fine with the New York banks, who didn't want more competition in their neighborhood.[7]

After five months of negotiations, the financial regulatory agencies ultimately decided to prevent any losses for uninsured depositors or creditors at Franklin and to sell what was left of the bank. City put in a bid only because of pressure from Fed chairman Burns and offered the least among the four bidders. The winner was expected to be Manufacturers Hanover, which had been interested in Franklin even before it began to falter. But Franklin was ultimately sold to European American Bank and Trust, a bank chartered in New York State and owned by a consortium of European financial institutions. The FDIC accepted the loans extended by the Federal Reserve Bank of New York with a three-year term for repayment. Because regulators weren't willing to allow private creditors to accept the consequences of their decisions, FDIC losses totaled $59 million. Franklin was the largest bank failure in history to that point. A study by the House of Representatives Committee on Government Operations concluded that the failure of Franklin "brought to a conclusion half a decade of financial mismanagement and regulatory neglect."[8]

Perhaps the staff of the committee was being too kind. Franklin was not an isolated incident in terms of lax oversight of the overseas activities of US banks. More fundamentally, it was a signal event in the growth of what economists call moral hazard. Human nature being what it is, creditors are less likely to worry about the soundness of a borrower if they think the government will be there to help in the event the borrower stumbles. Whether they intended it or not, regulators had just sent a message to both banks and their creditors that any institution as large as or larger than Franklin would get special help if it ran into trouble. This was one of several destructive messages sent by regulators just as all the largest New York banks were becoming increasingly aggressive in expanding overseas and increasingly reliant on foreign operations to support their bottom lines (see Table 10).

Walter Wriston's City Bank was leading the way. City and the other big US banks would naturally search for new markets and profit opportunities, but their highly regulated home markets were particularly unattractive for new investment. Industrial companies were increasingly issuing commercial paper instead of taking out bank loans. This reduced share of a market that banks used to dominate placed additional pressure on banks to seek new sources of revenue offshore.

The highest rewards—along with the highest risks—were

available in the Third World. Outstanding loans to less developed countries at the eight largest banks increased from $33 billion in 1977 to nearly $60 billion in 1984, with such loans representing more than 10 percent of total assets and more than 250 percent of capital and reserves for the eight money-center banks at their peak.[9]

Table 10: Percentage of Total Earnings, Foreign Operations, New York Banking Corporations

	1970	1971	1972	1973	1974	1975
First National City Corp.	40	43	54	60	62	70
Chase Manhattan Corp.	22	29	34	39	47	56
Manufacturers Hanover Corp.	13	24	29	36	47	50
J. P. Morgan & Company	25	29	35	46	45	60
Bankers Trust NY Corp.	15	19	31	40	52	62
Chemical NY Corp.	10	17	14	19	34	45

Source: Salomon Brothers, *United States Multinational Banking: Current and Prospective Strategies* (New York: Salomon Brothers, 1976), 13, as quoted in Joan E. Spero, *The Failure of the Franklin National Bank* (Washington, DC: Beard Books, 1999), 40.

For a while, lending to developing countries allowed the US banking giants to post the kind of wins that were increasingly difficult to find at home. City was the biggest winner of all. During and after World War II, City had downsized its foreign presence from the heights reached during the early 1930s, but it retained a formidable foreign branch system. It enjoyed an established customer base, knowledge of local conditions, and experienced staff. The bank rebuilt this business during the postwar boom years. Its combination of branch banking, foreign exchange trading, and dollar-based services for foreign customers in New York combined to make City the only bank with a true worldwide network. The branches also allowed City to act as a local bank, accepting local currency deposits and making loans to local firms and subsidiaries to US multinational corporations. By the mid-1960s, City had one hundred foreign branches, matching its 1930s height. By 1969, it had more than two hundred. Its megabank rivals, Chase Manhattan and Bank of America, had nothing like City's international empire.[10]

By 1973, foreign deposits exceeded domestic deposits at the bank, which had been operating in the United States since 1812. But just like City's founding directors, managers in the 1970s were accumulating significant risks. In the early 1970s, an issue of City's own *Monthly Economic Newsletter* raised red flags about developing-nation debt when Mexico's outstanding loans stood at a mere $4 billion. Mexico, Brazil, and Argentina were three of the markets where City fought for the top spot with other New York banking giants, like Morgan, Bank of America, and Manufacturers Hanover. Around this time, Wriston and Gesualdo Costanzo, who supervised City's international operations, were starting to worry about the growing risk in the international portfolio. Wriston had met Costanzo in Argentina in 1960 when he was working with the International Monetary Fund as deputy director of the Latin America department. Shortly after that meeting, City hired Costanzo, who had a PhD in economics, to be the bank's lead on Latin American policy.

The bank had long had a process on the domestic side for judging credit risk. Together Wriston and Costanzo determined that the bank lacked a system for assessing the unique risks for lending in each foreign country. In May 1974, right around the time that Franklin was suffering a bank run in large part due to overseas losses, City hired Irving Friedman, another IMF veteran, to ramp up a country risk unit. Friedman quickly determined that the bank did not even have a formal system for totaling up the exposure to a given country across all its business units.[11] The bank was just beginning to take its foreign risks seriously—years after the foreign operations had become the largest source of bank profits.

Regulators weren't any quicker to spot the potential problems. In 1977, Federal Reserve Board chairman Arthur Burns warned in a speech at Columbia University's business school about the "distinct possibility" of some countries having extremely high borrowing needs for years to come. The economic recession of the 1970s had him wondering out loud how the financial system could weather another one:

> Under such circumstances, many countries will be forced to borrow heavily, and lending institutions may well be tempted to extend credit more generously than is prudent. A major risk in all this is that it would render the international credit structure especially vulnerable in the event that the world economy were again to experience recession on the scale of that from which we are now emerging . . . commercial and investment bankers need to monitor their foreign lending with great care, and bank examiners need to be alert to excessive concentrations of loans in individual countries.[12]

It may have been a compelling speech for the guests who had assembled for an annual dinner at Columbia, but back in Washington almost nobody acted on the warning from the Fed chairman. The bank regulators, including Fed officials reporting to the speech maker, were implementing a disorganized and inconsistent system for assessing country risk. Each of the agencies was applying its own criteria to evaluate bank loans and other claims owed by foreigners. In the mid-1970s, the Office of the Comptroller of the Currency had determined that loans to several countries should be classified as "substandard," but the Fed gave that label to just one country. The three federal bank regulatory agencies finally took action to more closely monitor the buildup of exposure to developing-country debt by adopting uniform examination procedures in November 1978, due for implementation by the spring of 1979. The regulators created the Interagency Country Exposure Review Committee to coordinate assessments of country risk as part of their bank examination process and developed a uniform system, which divided seventy-five monitored countries into four groups. The weakest countries were classified if they had actual or imminent arrearages; the remaining categories ranged from Weak to Moderately Strong to Strong. The ready availability of this information allowed examiners to add "special comments" into their reports on exposures above a certain size in countries with debt-servicing problems and highlight weaknesses in other risky countries.[13]

So the regulators now had a system for flagging problems. But did they use it to prevent overseas risks from endangering bank capital and ultimately taxpayers back in the United States? One objective was to prevent too much exposure to just one country. A bank's loans to "one borrower" would normally be limited to 10 percent of a bank's capital and surplus. However, when a commercial bank extended credit to multiple government agencies and corporations in the same country, bankers argued that the 10 percent limitation should apply to each separate entity. This was especially relevant in the cases of lending to Mexico and Brazil. The Office of the Comptroller of the Currency weighed in on this issue in 1979, concluding that individual agencies and corporations could be treated separately, each with its own individual 10 percent limit. As if they hadn't already caved enough to the big bank lobby, the regulators also deferred to the banks' judgment on whether the individual entities had the means to service the debt.[14]

Examiners were inserting their "special comments" into reports that consisted of the country write-up and a paragraph on the composition of the bank's exposures. But a General Accounting Office analysis published in 1982 noted that special comments had little impact in restraining the growth of the relevant assets.[15] The comments turned out to be not very special, or perhaps special only for banks that wanted to keep building up risks in a particular country. Federal Reserve governor Henry Wallich summarized the process for enforcement:

> It's really regrettable that we didn't put any teeth in the country-exposure regulations. The banks reported to us regularly, but we didn't do anything about it. Examiners raised questions. In some cases, they got a response. Other banks said, "These stupid examiners—what do they know?"[16]

The exposure review committee came into existence when the Fed was going through one of the most turbulent periods in its history. Chairman Burns had departed in 1978 after presiding over an era of spiraling inflation. The Fed and the US dollar were suffering diminishing credibility in international markets and punishing American savers. America needed the next Fed chair to be a respected figure who could restore faith in the dollar and bring stability to prices of goods and services that had been skyrocketing. Speculation focused on three potential successors to Burns: Paul Volcker, president of the Federal Reserve Bank of New York; Robert Roosa, chairman of the Brookings Institution and a former undersecretary of the Treasury under President Kennedy; and Bruce MacLaury, a former president of the Federal Reserve Bank of Minneapolis.

President Jimmy Carter surprised and mystified the markets by selecting G. William Miller, who led an aerospace conglomerate. "Many bankers' first reaction to the appointment was: "G. William who?'" reported the *New York Times*. The dollar sold off on the news and investors' initial instincts turned out to be right. Miller's brief tenure was known for a dramatic plunge in the dollar and a spike in inflation to double-digit levels, which to be fair to Miller merely continued a trend initiated under Burns. Miller left the Fed in August 1979 to become Treasury secretary. While

President Carter was pondering a replacement, he called Walter Wriston for advice.

Wriston, who had renamed his institution in 1976 and given it the stylized brand Citibank, was at the time perhaps the most respected man in global finance. He told the president: "You have to get someone who foreign central bankers don't say, 'Who dat?' The guy whose name they know is Paul Volcker." Carter picked Volcker and, at least initially, Wriston and Citibank were supportive of the new Fed chairman's policies.[17]

Paul Volcker stands six foot seven, and his reputation was even bigger. He had been appointed to key financial oversight roles by presidents of both parties. John F. Kennedy named him deputy undersecretary of the Treasury for monetary affairs in 1963 and Richard Nixon entrusted him with the same job in 1969. Six years later, after being passed over for Treasury secretary when he was under consideration along with Walter Wriston, Volcker became president of the Federal Reserve Bank of New York, the preeminent regional organization within the Federal Reserve System. The president of the New York Fed serves as vice chairman of the Federal Open Market Committee, which conducts monetary policy. Also, given that its territory includes the financial capital of the world, the New York Fed oversees most of the largest bank holding companies in the system. Having earned high marks in New York, Volcker as Fed chairman would achieve almost legendary status as the slayer of inflation during his eight years running the central bank, from 1979 to 1987. Volcker biographer William Silber writes that after the demoralizing inflation of the 1970s, "Volcker did nothing less than restore the reputation of an American financial system on the verge of collapse."[18]

Volcker deserves great credit for reducing inflation during his tenure at the Fed from double digits to low single digits. It's hard to find any fault with his conduct of monetary policy. But as for the rest of the Fed's job description—regulating banks—there are grounds for criticism. Volcker's earlier jobs in Washington had focused on the money supply and the macro-economy. It wasn't until he became president of the New York Fed that he had line responsibility for banking supervision. William McChesney Martin, a predecessor as Federal Reserve chairman from 1951 to 1970, would later issue a report card on Volcker as the nation's top central banker: "[V]ery good on monetary policy, a complete flop on bank supervision."[19]

In his defense, at both the New York Fed and at the Fed's headquarters in Washington, Volcker inherited broken supervisory systems with regard to judging the risk in developing-country loans. He didn't fix them. Even when the Fed and other federal agencies agreed on approaches to monitoring risk, political considerations could override questions of financial safety and soundness. Former deputy comptroller William Martin recalled that when a country was classified under the uniform procedures, "the bankers would tell the countries. They'd tell their ambassadors. The ambassadors would tell [former secretary of state Henry] Kissinger and Kissinger would call the [Office of the Comptroller of the Currency]." Argentina was constantly on the borderline of being classified, which would sometimes trigger a visit to the Comptroller's office by the Argentine ambassador.

When asked about the new process for evaluating foreign exposures, Volcker replied that it was a "very intelligent system. Did it work? No. It tried to give cautionary signals where human beings were either looking for a green or red signal. It said we want to give you various degrees of amber. It was intended to moderate [foreign lending] without killing it. It fell short of moderating, and sure didn't kill it."[20]

Volcker would soon face the question of whether foreign lending, unmoderated by Washington, could end up killing New York's giant banks. One bank in particular had hardly been moderate in its overseas expansion and had more to lose than anyone if developing countries suddenly stopped paying their bills.

16

When Countries Fail

Walter Wriston's most remarkable achievement at Citibank was persuading Washington that lending money to governments in developing countries was nearly risk-free. He certainly had help from ambassadors and lobbyists. Plenty of inhabitants of the Beltway swamp were happy to explain why it made all kinds of sense, both financially and morally, for banks like Citi to loan money to Latin America. And if not much could go wrong loading up on the debt of foreign governments, then Wriston's corollary argument—that banks actually don't need much capital to absorb losses—also would seem to make sense.

In hindsight both premises may seem laughable, but Wriston and his team at Citibank maintained straight faces as they relentlessly pressed their case with regulators. When Fed chairman Paul Volcker began to express concerns about the rising pile of money that Citi had lent to relatively poor countries, Wriston replied: "They're the best loans I have. Sovereign nations don't go bankrupt." Volcker would later recall hearing Wriston at a conference proclaim that lending to less-developed countries "is like lending on U.S. Treasury bills." Before this argument was proven false,

Citi's boss seems to have promoted it even more aggressively in private than in public. Former deputy Comptroller of the Currency William Martin recalled: "[Wriston and his officers] were tough. I was a lowly little government clerk. They were just eating me up. There were bears to the left of me, bears to the right of me. There was blood all over the place, and it was all mine."[1]

Even among people who weren't paid or intimidated into accepting Citi's point of view, there had for years been a tendency among many government officials to look with favor on loans to less-developed countries (LDCs). The big American banks were taking "petrodollar" deposits from Middle Eastern despots and recycling them into loans for countries rising out of poverty. FDIC chairman Bill Seidman recalled: "Back in the mid-1970s we in the Ford Administration had a chance to deal with the creation of the LDC debt problem, as well as other problems in the financial system, but we just did not see the magnitude of the trouble ahead. We saw only the short-term benefits of the loans to our industry and finance. But then, long-range planning has never been an outstanding attribute of our governmental process."[2]

Meanwhile over at the Federal Reserve, it was only by solving its problems in the conduct of monetary policy that the Fed realized the size of its errors in bank regulation. By growing the money supply, the Fed had enabled the great inflation of the 1970s. While it had been brutal for consumers and savers in the US to see the value of their dollars continually declining, it was a godsend for borrowers including Latin American governments. They could pay back their loans with currency that was worth less than when they had borrowed it. Also, if their local economies depended on producing commodities—as many poor countries did—they benefited from surging prices for their principal exports.

Americans can probably never adequately thank Paul Volcker for ending the inflation of the 1970s, but his medicine did come with side effects. Limiting the money supply began to cure inflation, but restraining the growth of credit was also restraining the US economy. And this was not just a problem for people in the United States. Slow growth or even an outright decline in the US economy meant less demand for the commodities that poor countries were exporting. Lower inflation also meant no more price surges on these commodities. And lower inflation meant that borrowers now had to pay back their loans with real money. All of these related phenomena represented bad news for governments in developing countries. Their debts were becoming more expensive at the same time their economies were having a harder time generating the cash from exports to service these debts. Oil-producing countries like Mexico had been borrowing large sums from banks like Citi on the premise of a gusher of petroleum revenue. Oil prices peaked in 1980, and over the next five years would experience a sharp decline.

As he tackled the inflation problem it's not clear how much Volcker thought about the likely impact on the banks that the Fed had allowed to gorge on developing-country loans. Silber's Volcker biography references bank supervision in the context of the Latin American debt crisis. However, the reference is not to efforts to address building problems, but rather to congressional hearings after the fact, when Volcker suffered withering criticism from lawmakers of both parties.[3]

Before Latin American governments began buckling under the strain of their financial obligations, some journalists began to warn of the coming storm. In January of 1981, a story in the *Wall Street Journal* noted that "developing nations have run up a mountain of debt totaling nearly $500 billion." The report added that many countries were struggling to make payments, and that "there's mounting nervousness about the biggest international borrower, Brazil. The dangers are casting a cloud over large commercial banks and possibly over economies throughout the world."

Walter Wriston might have disagreed, but the story described the simple and disturbing math:

The nine largest American banks had $38.6 billion on loan to
developing countries (excluding the oil-exporting states) at the
end of 1979, according to the latest Federal Reserve figures.
Moreover, these banks' capital totaled only $21.9 billion. So, in
theory at least, they could all be forced into insolvency if only
about half of their Third World loans were thrown into default
and had to be written off.[4]

A crisis was about to move out of the realm of theory, and of
course Citi and the other banks also had loans out to oil export-
ers, who were suddenly feeling less flush. What would happen if
countries began to violate Wriston's maxim and go broke? Although the term was not yet in wide circulation, it seems that both
governments and big banks were now viewing themselves as too
big to fail. Executives at giant American financial institutions increasingly didn't believe the government would allow their firms
to become insolvent:

> Privately, senior U.S. bankers insist that the Fed never would
> let that theory be played out. "They go on the assumption that
> they aren't going to be let go down the drain, at least if they're
> big," observes Nathaniel Samuels, Advisory Director at Lehman
> Brothers Kuhn Loeb Inc. Third World governments tell them-
> selves much the same thing—that they will be sustained by the
> international system—Samuels notes, but he adds, "The system
> is getting a little stretched."[5]

The relationships between Citi and its regulators were also getting stretched, given the lengthening shadow that sovereign debt
was casting over the bank. Wriston and Volcker argued over capital
levels, the terms of the 1979 federal bailout of automaker Chrysler,
bank powers and of course that mountain of debt to developing
countries. One developing country in particular was causing in-

creasing concern among regulators. Mexico had "borrowed heavily from banks in the United States and Europe to develop capacity as an oil-exporting country. American bankers, led by Walter Wriston of Citibank, could not lend them enough, and reaped the rewards during the inflationary surge of the 1970s," notes Silber.[6]

But now oil prices were sliding at the start of the 1980s. In 1981 Volcker asked his staff at the Fed's Washington headquarters for data on Mexico exposures among major US banks. The reports, preserved in Volcker's personal papers, showed that defaults in Mexico alone could knock out a significant portion of capital at the major US banks (see Table 11). Citibank had the highest total exposure of $2.6 billion, although in percentage terms it was not as vulnerable to problems just south of the border as Manufacturers Hanover, where Mexico exposures equaled a full 80 percent of its capital. System-wide, US banks were on the hook for $21.4 billion, up from $15.9 billion the previous year.[7]

Table 11: Exposures to Mexico of the Largest US Banks (Year-End 1981)

	Exposure ($s in millions)	Capital ($s in millions)	Exposure as a percentage of capital
Citibank	2,609	5,390	48.4%
Bank of America	2,206	4,596	48.0%
Manufacturers Hanover	1,834	2,284	80.3%
Chase Manhattan	1,617	4,206	38.4%
Chemical Bank	1,079	2,158	50.0%
Morgan Guaranty	1,052	2,611	40.3%

Source: Board of Governors of the Federal Reserve, Table from Sandy Wolfe to Paul A. Volcker, "U.S. Bank Claims on Mexico (end-1981; adjusted for guarantees)," undated; Paul A. Volcker Papers, Princeton University; and handwritten list of bank direct and indirect exposures, undated, Paul A. Volcker Papers, Princeton University.

Note: Direct exposures include funds actually loaned and recorded as assets on the balance sheet; indirect exposures include off-balance sheet items such as commitments to lend, letters of credit not yet negotiated. For example, for Citibank the direct exposures added up to $2.264 billion and indirect exposures were $0.345 billion.

By now the Fed was trying to get its arms around the threat of countries going bankrupt. Its Division of International Finance developed still another warning system with yet another set of classification categories to highlight "financial trouble spots." The worst of these categories were Actual Trouble Spots, defined as countries where debt servicing had been interrupted, access to new credit had become problematic, or debt restructuring was highly likely in the near term. As of September 1981, Mexico and Argentina did not appear on the list of Actual Trouble Spots, but they would appear under that classification in an updated memo in May of 1982 due to their difficulties accessing credit.[8]

Some early warning. In 1982 the unraveling of Mexico's financial system marked the start of a "lost decade." The year started with a devaluation of the currency in February. The Mexican government allowed the peso to float, leading to a drop in value from 27 pesos per dollar to 45 by August. It would plummet to 150 by December. Mexican president Portillo sacked his finance minister and the head of the central bank. Given its exposures down south, Citi was meanwhile starting a rough decade of its own by losing some credibility in financial markets. Credit ratings agencies downgraded its debt.

In Washington, Chairman Volcker was urging the Mexican government to seek funding from the International Monetary Fund. He also led an effort to give the Mexican central bank some breathing room by executing $700 million of swap agreements at the end of April and June. The swaps made the Bank of Mexico's balance sheet look stronger than it was. Volcker would later regret this accounting trick: "This 'window dressing' disguised the full extent of the pressures on Mexico from the bank's lenders and from the Mexicans themselves."[9]

In the spring of 1982, the US Department of the Treasury was also concerned about Mexico when Treasury Secretary Don Regan met with his counterpart, Finance Minister Jesus Silva Herzog. Regan asked Herzog to give him "some warning" if there was going to be trouble. Herzog reportedly replied: "Don't worry, Don, we'll give you plenty of warning."

Herzog probably should have replied, "Don, consider this your warning." From August 1982 to December 1984, about $20 billion in loans to Mexico were coming due, and in just the three months beginning in August, Mexico was scheduled to pay close to $8 billion. For some reason Washington had figured the Fed's swap agreements would be enough to get Mexico through September. But on August 12, Regan received a phone call from Herzog, who asked the Treasury secretary if he remembered their discussion earlier in the year.

> REGAN: Yeah, I remember it.
> HERZOG: Well, the time is here. I need money.
> REGAN: How much do you need?
> HERZOG: About a billion.[10]

Right after his conversation with Herzog, Regan called Fed chairman Volcker and asked: "Do you know what's going on?" Volcker had already been called by his counterpart at the Bank of Mexico. Over the next several days, Regan, his deputy Treasury secretary McNamar, and the heads of the world's central banks put together a $4 billion rescue package that included a $1 billion advance payment from the US on Mexican oil, central bank credit lines of $1.5 billion, and a $1 billion US credit line for food imports. Chairman Volcker appointed Bank of America and Citibank as co-heads of a fourteen-member advisory committee, and the banks were expected to provide further funding. Representing Citibank was William Rhodes, a senior international banker who had worked previously with Mexico on negotiations with the government of Nicaragua. Rhodes had also extended his fair share of bad loans to Mexico that were now on Citi's books.

One of Rhodes's first tasks was to help determine how much Mexico owed and to whom. The answer was it had borrowed too much from most of the world's leading international banks. When a deal with the IMF was finalized a few months later, it was an $8.3 billion package. As for new loans from private banks in the US—needed to allow Mexico to pay interest on the old loans—Chairman Volcker promised they would not be classified. Citibank was expected to contribute the largest share.[11]

Wriston had proclaimed that countries don't go bankrupt. This turned out to be true only in the sense that Washington wouldn't let them fail, especially when they owed so much to banks like his.

Even with the terms of foreign assistance being negotiated, the Mexican economy and financial system continued to melt down. Inflation was raging. Mexico nationalized its banks in September. The following month back in Washington, Volcker told his Fed colleagues at a meeting of the Federal Open Market Committee that "we sorely need a victory, or a series of victories, in terms of stability in some key countries. We would like to have that in Mexico." The Fed chief believed the stakes could hardly be higher:

> If it's not going to be in Mexico, there had better be dikes built pretty promptly around some of these other countries so that there is not a feeling of absolute inevitability, which is developing rapidly in the market, that all of these countries are going to go down like a bunch of tenpins . . . Extraordinary things may have to be done. We haven't had a parallel to this situation historically except to the extent 1929 was a parallel.[12]

Many of the tenpins had borrowed heavily from Citi and the other US banking giants. Considering the debts run up by Mexico, Brazil, and Argentina, Silber writes: "Defaults by these three countries could wipe out the capital of the nine largest banks in the United States."[13]

Although the major US banks were not lent up as much to Brazil and Argentina as they were to Mexico, exposure was still massive at $16.3 billion for Brazil and $8.1 billion for Argentina by the end of 1981, compared to $21.4 billion to Mexico.[14] Such debt was also a high percentage of capital at the big banks (see Table 12), with Citibank's exposure for all three countries adding up to about 100 percent of its capital. Of course this threat to its solvency did not even include any other foreign risks or the potential downside in Citibank's domestic US business.

Brazil was next up in negotiating a new loan agreement and an IMF program in February 1983, followed by Argentina in August.[15]

Table 12: Exposures to Brazil of the Largest US Banks
(Year-End 1982 Plus Estimate)

	Exposure ($s in millions)	Capital ($s in millions)	Exposure as a percentage of capital
Bank of America	1,983	4,799	41.3%
Citibank	1,931	5,989	32.2%
Chase Manhattan	1,242	4,221	29.4%
Manufacturer's Hanover	1,156	2,592	44.0%
Morgan Guaranty	1,271	3,108	40.9%
Chemical Bank	779	2,500	31.2%

Source: Office of the Comptroller, memo and table from C. Stewart Goddin to Robert R. Bench, Deputy Comptroller, "Brazil Exposure," September 20, 1983, Paul A. Volcker Papers, Princeton University.

Note: Exposure is calculated as amount outstanding to the Brazilian public sector as of 12/31/82 plus an estimate of commitments based on terms of Brazil's debt rescheduling during 1983 and 1984. These exposures are not fully comparable to Mexico exposures in Table 11 on page 213 as to date or calculation of exposures. Other estimates of the Brazilian exposures vary.[16]

More than a few Americans were wondering why the US government was coming to the aid of spendthrift foreign governments—and the bankers who had lent them money. The people's representatives wanted to know how bank regulators who were supposed to be overseeing the financial giants had allowed them to put so much money at risk in the developing world. Senator John Heinz, Republican chairman of the Subcommittee on International Finance, and Democratic Ranking Member William Proxmire presided over a February 1983 hearing at which Volcker was the chief witness. In his opening statement, Heinz laid the blame on Volcker and his fellow supervisors:

The role of the nation's bank regulators in the current crisis is very direct and significant. Indeed, many critics have argued that the U.S. bank debt problems would not have gotten to their present dangerous stage had our bank regulators not been asleep at the switch. The primary mission of our bank regulators is the safety and soundness of our banking system. Yet, we have been told of bank after bank whose entire capital is exposed in one or two or three countries, shaking international borrowers.[17]

Proxmire joined the attack:

Mr. Chairman, as we go through these hearings, I think we must get the answer to a very simple question: Where were our regulators? How is it possible for our banks to have become so overexposed on foreign loans without the regulators blowing the whistle? As far as I can tell, the regulators were not unaware of the problem. They advised, they monitored, they cajoled, they encouraged—in fact, they did everything except what they are paid to do, and that is to regulate.[18]

Volcker didn't offer much of a defense of the Fed's supervision of Citibank and the other giants:

SENATOR PROXMIRE: You stated in response to a question of Senator Heinz that a legitimate question in international lending is: Were the regulators forceful enough? But what is the answer to your question? Were they?

MR. VOLCKER: I suppose, in retrospect, probably not.[19]

The megabanks were faced with an overhang of exposure from their commitments to the LDCs. Then as now, Washington regulators enjoyed broad discretion in applying capital rules to the banks they oversaw. The Fed, the Office of the Comptroller, and the FDIC had basically two alternatives. The first was to take a hard look at the capacity of Mexico, Brazil, Argentina, and the others to repay their loans and reduce reported capital levels for the megabanks accordingly. This meant requiring the banks and their shareholders and creditors to accept the consequences of their bad decisions, but also accepting any collateral damage that might occur in the financial system. The alternative option is to look the other way and decide not to enforce the capital standards, allowing the megabanks years to work through their problems. Federal officials went for option two and exercised "forbearance" in the parlance of bank regulators. They decided that to do otherwise was to allow a cascade of failures of giant financial institutions. According to then–FDIC chairman William Seidman:

The Latin American loans were so formidable that they had placed the world's largest banks in jeopardy. US bank regulators, given the choice between creating panic in the banking system or going easy on requiring our banks to set aside reserves for Latin American debt, had chosen the latter course . . . Regulators use forbearance when they exercise judgment in applying normal supervisory mandates. They do this when, in their judgment to do otherwise would unnecessarily cripple a bank financially. When the Third World Debt Crisis broke in 1982, regulators were slow to require banks to build up reserves against potential losses; if they had not exercised judgment, seven or eight of the ten largest banks in the United States probably would have been insolvent. It is not hard to imagine what kind of economic, and then political crisis that would have created. The regulators had looked over the abyss and decided to take a different path.[20]

As Seidman notes, a primary argument in favor of forbearance relates to the fear of systemic collapse. As in 2008, in the early 1980s virtually all the major banks were suffering to some degree from the same problem. In the first case they had overdone it lending to Latin American governments; years later they would shovel too many loans to US home buyers. In the 1980s, forbearance was not only the solution for too much sovereign debt. Regulators also argued that it was appropriate in cases where strict enforcement of the rules would close a large number of institutions serving a particular industry—the basis for decisions to avoid the closure of hundreds of agricultural banks in the Midwest.[21]

Exercising forbearance is a roll of the dice. If the banks can make their way back to solvency, a sort of no-harm, no-foul rule applies. But if an institution continues to deteriorate, as often happened in the savings-and-loan crisis later in the decade, then the losses can grow much larger than if a full, up-front enforcement of the capital rules had been employed. The history of forbearance also shows that, not surprisingly, it is often particularly appealing to government officials when it allows them to avoid having to manage the closure of a giant firm. Regulators didn't cut any slack to hundreds of smaller banks that failed during the 1980s and were summarily shuttered. Lawmakers in the 1990s enacted reform measures intended to reduce such regulatory discretion. But ensuring the survival of megabanks like Citi would continue to be a preoccupation of their federal overseers.

As for the Latin American debt crisis of the early 1980s, forbearance clearly allowed a number of the great money-center banks to live on, essentially by allowing them to fudge the value of their assets:

> Had these institutions been required to mark their sometimes substantial holdings of underwater debt to market or to increase loan-loss reserves to levels close to the expected losses on this debt (as measured by secondary market prices), then institutions such as Manufacturers Hanover, Bank of America, and perhaps Citicorp would have been insolvent.[22]

The New York megabanks were not the only ones permitted to join the forbearance club. But as shown in Table 13, the nine money center banks that had the largest concentrations of troubled international loans were allowed to make much slower progress in cleaning up their messes than smaller institutions that were also required to reduce their exposures to deadbeat countries.

Table 13: Exposure to Countries with Debt Servicing Problems

Reporting Date	9 Money Center Banks	13 Other Large Banks	All Other Banks
December 1982	$63 billion	$20 billion	$18 billion
September 1988	$55 billion	$12 billion	$9 billion
Raw Change	-$8 billion	-$8 billion	-$9 billion
Percentage Change	-13%	-40%	-50%

Source: Office of the Comptroller of the Currency, Board of Governors of the Federal Reserve, Federal Deposit Insurance Corporation, "Study on the Risks to the U.S. Banking System Posed by Troubled Foreign Loans," March 31, 1989, 10.

Note: The nine money center banks are Bank of America, Bankers Trust, Citibank, Chase Manhattan Bank, Chemical Bank, Continental Illinois, First National Bank of Chicago, Manufacturers Hanover, and Morgan Guaranty.

Walter Wriston retired in September 1984, his legacy tainted by the crisis that would continue to haunt Citi for years. Wriston would later blame the Fed chairman: "What nobody knew was that Volcker was going to lock the wheels of the world. And when he threw the U.S. into the deepest recession since 1933, it spread to the whole world. And that's what started the, quote, international debt crisis: Export ratios that looked very good the month before he took office looked like a disaster a year later."[23]

What bankers should know is that operating with thin capital levels while assuming that countries always pay their debts is a recipe for financial catastrophe. If the average taxpayer was looking for someone to blame for having to bear an increasing share of the risk of such catastrophes, there were plenty of candidates in both New York and Washington.

17

The Banker Who "Never Made a Loan"

J ust before his retirement from Citi, Walter Wriston played a supporting role in one more taxpayer bailout drama. And if there were any more observers of American banking who still wondered whether the federal government would rescue a stumbling giant, this episode should have removed all doubt.

Continental Illinois was the nation's seventh-largest bank in the early 1980s, less than half the size of Citi in terms of assets. Most Americans—if they had even heard of Continental—probably would not have said that it was indispensable to the US economy. Corporate executives had heard of it. The bank had been growing rapidly by taking on risky and volatile short-term liabilities and using this funding to loan money to businesses. By 1981, it was the largest commercial and industrial lender in the country. Like Citi and the other big banks at the time, Continental's equity amounted to only about 4 percent of its assets—not much room for error if some of those assets turned out to be loans that didn't get repaid. Now backed by the federal government, none of the big banks had large capital cushions like those maintained in an earlier era by the likes of Moses Taylor or James Stillman. As the federal safety net had broadened underneath the banks, the banks were devoting fewer of their own resources to ensure their safety and soundness. This is moral hazard in one easy lesson. With taxpayers backing the banks, bank investors were comfortable with banks operating at higher levels of risk. At Continental in particular, an increasingly large majority of the assets was composed of loans—so the bank's exposure to default risk was rising.[1]

An official FDIC history acknowledges that "intimations that Continental's lending style might be overly aggressive had not been altogether lacking. The bank's growth was attributed partly to its 'zeal for occasional transactions that carry more than the average amount of risk.' One bank officer stated, 'We hear that Continental is willing to do just about anything to make a deal.'"[2]

Banks that will do just about anything to make deals probably ought to fail. But for a number of reasons Continental was an outfit that the feds were willing to do almost anything to save. As we have seen in a number of modern crises, just because government officials have been handed significant authority doesn't mean they want the responsibility that comes with exercising it.

In theory, the FDIC should seize a failing bank over a weekend and sell it to another institution ready to open Monday morning. The FDIC is supposed to see to it that insured depositors are protected while uninsured creditors bear losses. But in 1984 regulators doubted their ability to pull it off, or perhaps didn't want all the headaches that would come along with making creditors live with the consequences of their decisions. Among the uninsured creditors were scores of other banks in the Midwest. Would some of them also need help if their Continental balances were suddenly worth much less than expected? Also, Continental was bigger and more complex than other banks that had been subjected to weekend closures.

Regulators at the Office of the Comptroller of the Currency essentially ignored the problem until a run on Continental in May of 1984. Then the FDIC and the Federal Reserve intervened, not with a closure, but with a bailout. Regulators assembled a $2 billion assistance package, the Fed said it would meet Continental's liquidity needs, and the FDIC said it would protect all depositors and general creditors—not just the ones covered by FDIC insurance.

After the details of the bailout of creditors became public, Wriston made it clear that he favored market discipline—at least for banks other than Citi. Said Wriston: "My instinct is that bondholders are not entitled to protection, neither are equity owners, and neither are depositors with more than $100,000. The perception has grown up that everybody's entitled."[3]

The regulators intended their assistance to be temporary, but they couldn't find a private merger partner for Continental that they considered suitable. At one point in the rescue drama, FDIC chairman Bill Isaac and Fed chairman Paul Volcker met with representatives of the top seven banks and urged them to join with Uncle Sam in making investments in Continental. Citi executive Thomas Theobald, sitting in for the soon-to-be-retired Wriston, blurted out: "Why would I want to help a competitor?" This comment inspired Volcker biographer William Silber to write that "Citibank advocated free enterprise, especially when it applied to others."

Volcker called Wriston in the middle of the night to plead for support for Continental. When the topic of Theobald's remarks came up, Wriston said: "Well he's probably trying to protect the shareholders of Citicorp, which is what we pay him for." Three years later, Theobald would become chairman of Continental, which by then was operating as a nationalized bank.[4]

Would other banks be rescued by the government if they ran into trouble? A junior member of the New York congressional delegation, Representative Charles Schumer, wrote in the *New York Times* in June of 1984 that the Continental debacle "could happen to any of our biggest banks. None of them has a capital cushion large enough to withstand a sustained round of rumors. Many have greatly overextended themselves in lending to Latin America and other third world countries."[5]

In the end, the FDIC was on its own investing in Continental. In July of 1984, it bought $4.5 billion of the bank's bad loans, then hired the bank to service them. Uncle Sugar also received $1 billion of preferred stock in the bank's holding company.

Two months later, a senior bank regulator made the implicit lesson of Continental explicit and official. The *Wall Street Journal* reported on September 20:

> WASHINGTON—Comptroller of the Currency Todd Conover told Congress that the federal government won't currently allow any of the nation's 11 largest banks to fail.
>
> Mr. Conover made the statement reluctantly during hearings before the House Banking Committee on the $4.5 billion government rescue of Continental Illinois National Bank & Trust Co. of Chicago. Mr. Conover expressed discomfort with the concept of blanket protection for only the largest banks. He declared, "we've got to find a way" to deal with potential failure of the large multinational banks that doesn't give those banks more favorable treatment than smaller institutions receive.
>
> Mr. Conover's statement was met by jibes from committee members, who said the government had created a new category of bank: the "TBTF" bank, for Too Big To Fail. Many banking observers had said the Continental rescue in July indicated that regulators already had adopted such a policy, but Mr. Conover's testimony yesterday was the first time a government official acknowledged that such a policy existed.

Mr. Conover didn't name the lucky eleven, but noted that his agency had a separate oversight program for these multinationals.

Citi was of course at the top of the list. Mr. Conover made the arguments about risks to the larger financial system that would become very familiar to taxpayers in 2008. Since the most recent crisis, regulators have spoken often of the alleged risks of "inter-connectedness" of large financial firms, and Mr. Conover made similar claims about Continental. According to the *Journal*, "Mr. Conover estimated that more than 100 banks with deposits in the troubled Chicago bank would have failed if the government hadn't intervened. He also said that dozens of the bank's corporate cus-tomers also could have collapsed."

And just as in the aftermath of the most recent crisis, executive compensation at a bailed-out bank became a subject of public de-bate. The *Journal* reported:

> Mr. Conover asserted that the former management of Conti-nental "paid a price," an apparent reference to former Chairman Roger Anderson, who resigned under pressure in March.
>
> However, committee Chairman Fernand St. Germain in-terjected, "Let's look at what poor Mr. Anderson is undergo-ing." The Rhode Island Democrat pointed out that Continental granted Mr. Anderson severance pay amounting to nearly $500,000 and agreed to pay for several of his club memberships.[6]

A few days later, on September 25, the *Journal*'s opinion pages ran an editorial titled, "The TBTF and the TSTS." The editorial observed:

> A Swiss banker at a small breakfast gathering in New York was puzzled. What should a Swiss investor do now that U.S. Comp-troller C. Todd Conover has declared he will not let the 11 larg-est U.S. banks fail? "Should I put all my money in those banks?" he asked. "Which bank is number 12, by the way?"
>
> One answer will present itself when we see if the unfavored

banks have to pay higher interest rates to attract deposits. But until then, it's a good question. Eleven American banks are now presumed to be in the TBTF (Too Big to Fail) category, while all the others are TSTS (Too Small to Save). Why did the Comptroller say such a thing?[7]

One could perhaps appreciate Mr. Conover's remarks as truth in advertising. Washington was now making the guarantee for banking giants explicit. Meanwhile, up in New York, the largest of the too-big-to-fail banks was being turned over to a man who had worked at the firm for years but hadn't really been a banker.

John Reed grew up in Argentina and Brazil, where his father was an executive with Armour and Company, the giant meat processor that had been at the center of the financial crisis story reported by the young Frank Vanderlip. Reed earned a joint bachelor's degree in American literature and metallurgy from Washington and Jefferson College and the Massachusetts Institute of Technology, then served in Korea with the US Army Corp of Engineers. Next he joined City in the 1960s, some years before it was renamed Citibank. Then he went back to MIT to pick up a master's degree in management at the Sloan School, where he seems to have impressed at least one member of the faculty. A professor cold-called Walter Wriston and told him that if he had any brains he would hire Reed.

Reed's connections to Argentina, where City did business, and to Armour, a City client, also helped make him an attractive candidate. What's harder to understand is why he was exempted from the bank's regular credit training program for new hires. It might have come in handy in the years ahead. Rather than learning to gather deposits and make loans, Reed went to work on the information systems for the overseas division, which was booming under Wriston's direction.[8]

The new guy quickly got to know Citi's international boss.

Reed's immediate supervisor, James Farley, would usually leave the office at four p.m. and Reed would regularly drop by Wriston's office after five with reports and analysis that Farley would normally have presented. Before long Reed was the one formally reporting to Wriston, and seems to have enjoyed the challenge:

> In analyzing transactions, Wriston invariably used a T-account, a simple chart using debits and credits, to figure out where the money was going. "You couldn't wing something by him," said Reed. "He wasn't going to be embarrassed into thinking he had to pretend to understand something when he didn't." But what struck Reed most about Wriston was his unflinching trust in the smart young crowd he had gathered around him.[9]

As Wriston was working to disrupt and dislodge the longtime bank employees running their overseas fiefdoms, Reed was making himself useful by developing a sophisticated new report for bank management. The Reed analysis showed that many of the old guard who were regarded as big moneymakers for the bank were actually cost centers. One can imagine how well Reed's innovation went over with the people formerly known as profit centers. Actually, one does not need to wonder. Many of the international employees with long tenures at the bank began referring to him as "that little shit."[10]

Pretty soon the ones that still had jobs at the bank would have to refer to him as the boss. Reed started to make his way up the management ranks by taking on ever-larger technological challenges to upgrade Citi's operations. Each project tended to alienate those whose jobs he was disrupting while enhancing his reputation in the eyes of senior management. This disruption was not simply for the sake of enhancing the power of headquarters and greasing the professional ascent of John Reed. The bank's back office was a certified mess. United Parcel Service (UPS) was a longtime Citi customer, but at one point the bank could not even produce a checking account statement for the package-delivery giant. Not unreasonably, UPS threatened to end its banking relationship with Citibank. Luckily for Citi, this was largely an idle threat because other big banks were struggling with similar problems as their businesses had outgrown their ability to competently serve customers. Clients like UPS hung around while Reed and other young technologists started tugging Citi into the information age.[11]

There was an embarrassing recent history in the bank's efforts to process checks. From a manual pigeonhole system similar to what you might see at a post office, the bank spent two years trying to implement a mechanical routine that failed. Next up was an IBM sorter, which relied on a revolving drum: "When, after much testing, the project team finally demonstrated the machine to [Chairman James Stillman] Rockefeller, the drum spit the checks out across the room like hundreds of miniature paper carpets." The chairman, whose bloodlines to the storied builders of the bank are obvious, was not pleased. One manager after another tried and failed to fix the problem. Reed promised a solution. In 1970, he took over the operations department and assumed the title of senior vice president—unheard of at Citi for someone barely thirty years old. The *New York Times* trumpeted Reed as one of the bank's "bright young executives." If he was bright enough to fix the back office, he would be well on his way to the corner office. The newly appointed president, William Spencer, referred to the ongoing challenges to control operations at the bank as getting "some handles on the greased pig."[12]

To follow through on his boast, Reed hired operations experts away from industrial powerhouses like Ford Motor, which also happened to be a Citibank customer. Reed ended up poaching so many employees from Ford that the automaker complained of a brain drain and threatened to end its banking relationship with Citi.

Wherever the new hires came from, it wasn't enough for them to be brainy. Reed expected them to serve the bank at the expense of almost all else. "In Reed's operations group, families were neglected, and divorces and separations were rampant," reports Phillip Zweig. Even with an extreme commitment to solving the problem of check processing, Reed's team had an embarrassing stumble before ultimately succeeding. At one point Citibank failed to meet a deadline to swap checks and fell out of balance with the Federal Reserve by some $5 billion. Some of Citibank's numbers in a report that week from the Fed were listed as "N/A" (not available), which could not have been reassuring to any depositors who happened to notice.[13]

The next big mountain to climb was improving the speed of credit card purchases. Technology was replacing an antiquated process in which retail salesclerks would phone authorization clerks, who would then pore over stacks of computer reports to approve a small purchase. Reed was among those leading the march toward instant approvals for consumers wishing to pay with plastic. And while Citi did not invent the automated teller machine—that honor goes to Chemical Bank—Wriston and Reed as much as anyone made this technology consumer-friendly and ubiquitous. Young customers today may not fully appreciate what this change meant for people who previously had to wait in line during regular hours to receive cash from a human.

Citi, which also pushed the development of online banking for corporate customers, was essentially becoming the research and development shop for an entire industry. The bank rejected efforts by the American Bankers Association, MasterCard, and Visa to set standards in favor of creating its own. Wriston and Reed were also rejecting the old culture that had existed inside Citi. "The new breed of technocrats pitted themselves against the old-line back office managers who had grown up in the world of paper and rubber bands and against genteel corporate bankers from uptown headquarters . . . the redundant employees would have to go . . . Thus, the lifetime employment contract went the way of the green eyeshade, the stiff collar and the hand-cranked calculator."[14]

After his success in upgrading the bank's technology, Reed took over Citi's consumer businesses in 1974. But instead of spending his days consulting experts on credit risk and finance, he seems to have been largely focused on marketing. He brought in specialists from nonfinancial companies like General Mills and Polaroid as he sought to build the Citibank brand.[15] Impressive growth followed.

A decade after becoming Citi's consumer czar, Reed was still only in his early forties when he won the competition to succeed Wriston as CEO. Wriston hit the mandatory retirement age of sixty-five in 1984, and Reed was selected over Thomas Theobald, the executive who had once rubbed the Fed the wrong way by putting the interests of his shareholders first. Of the potential candidates for Citi's top job, Reed was seen as the most entrepreneurial, which is a wonderful quality in industries not backed by taxpayers. Theobald's allies had also pointed out that there was at least one other potential problem with putting John Reed in charge of America's largest bank. "People did object to John on the basis that he has never been a banker and never made a loan," one board member recalled to Phillip Zweig.[16] But the board was willing to overlook it.

Reed for his part seemed by now to understand his limits and rather than embarking on big merger deals he spent much of his first two years as chairman learning about all the business lines he now commanded.[17] Perhaps he should have spent even more time learning about Citi's debts in less-developed countries. He later admitted that before ascending to the top job, "I read about [Third World Debt] in the newspaper, but I didn't pay much attention."

Once in charge, he tried to pay more attention. Reed estimated that during his first six years as chairman he spent half his time on the issue, as government efforts to resolve the debt problem achieved little progress. FDIC chairman William Seidman recalled Reed's effort to address it:

> At one of our breakfasts, early in my term, the subject for discussion was a call we had all received from John Reed . . . He had informed us he was about to create an unprecedented reserve equal to about 30 percent of his bank's loans to Latin America, a reserve to absorb possible losses if the loans were not fully repaid. This meant that the bank was going to show a substantial loss in its earnings that quarter. What it really meant was that the bank was finally acknowledging that it did not expect to collect the entire amount of the loans it had made. Of course, it also was an indication to the debtor countries of Latin America that Citibank was in doubt about its ability to collect on the loans.
>
> Fed Chairman Volcker led off by indicating that he felt Citicorp was being very unwise. He warned that this move would destabilize the delicate international financial situation and make loans harder to collect by advertising to the debtors that the banks expected less than full payment. It would weaken the capital position of all large U.S. banks, since all had Latin American loans; and by marking them closer to their market value, they would cut the value of their assets and their book capital. Volcker had been leading the campaign to keep the debts on the books because he felt that once a public write-down started the debtors would never stop demanding even more of their loans be forgiven. Most of us felt that since there was no way all of the money was going to be repaid, good accounting and honest reporting required banks to start reserving against losses on the loans; and that was just what John Reed was proposing to do.

Volcker suggested that we meet with Reed and persuade him to abandon the idea . . . Nevertheless, as an old auditor and accountant and as a new bank regulator, I had to observe that creating these reserves was long overdue and had long since been accepted in the marketplace. My suggestion was that Reed be accorded a regulatory Medal of Honor for stepping forward and taking his losses. Volcker strongly disagreed and found my observations somewhat out of order from one so new in the business. He seemed to feel that the entire international financial system would be shaken. I timidly whispered that setting aside a reserve was not going to destabilize the marketplace, and that this view had already been conveyed to Reed, along with the thought that taking this courageous action had proven him to be a leader of men.[18]

Reed welcomed the encouragement from Seidman and ignored Volcker's advice. Citi put aside a $3 billion loss provision against Latin American debt in 1987. This essentially wiped out the last four years of earnings under Wriston. The other money center banks followed Citi's lead, sending loss provisions from $5 billion to $14 billion in one year, triggering an unprecedented drop in profitability. Citicorp made it through 1987 relatively unscathed, notwithstanding that fall's stock market crash.[19]

But even after recognizing significant losses, Reed and Citi weren't quite done dealing with the destruction caused by reckless loans to Latin American governments. And the Citibankers were also about to find out how much trouble Middle American mortgage borrowers—and a real estate developer named Donald Trump—could cause.

John Reed, the banker who had never made any loans, was beginning to learn what happens when they aren't repaid. The toughest challenges were still to come, and Washington regulators worked hard to make sure taxpayers never found out about them.

18

Just Another Perfect Storm

n December of 1991, Fred Trump wanted to help his son Donald out of a financial jam. That month, the younger Mr. Trump needed to come up with $18.4 million to pay the interest on bonds issued to fund Trump Castle, one of several casinos he owned in Atlantic City, New Jersey. But if the father made a loan and wanted someday to be repaid, he would have to stand in line behind bondholders and bank lenders who were already owed billions by his son. Also, given the colorful history of casino financing, anyone seeking to lend to such an establishment had to go through a lengthy approval process with the New Jersey Casino Control Commission. Trump Castle needed money right away.

What happened next could almost be a scene in a Steven Soderbergh film. A January 1991 report in the *Wall Street Journal* explained:

Donald Trump can add another individual to his long list of creditors: his father, the quiet real estate mogul Fred Trump. At least that's what New Jersey casino regulators are saying . . . The regulators confirmed that on Dec. 17, an attorney they identified as Howard Snyder, acting on Fred Trump's behalf, purchased more than $3 million in chips from the Trump Castle casino. Mr. Snyder did not gamble with the chips and promptly left the casino under police escort, according to regulators.

That day, Mr. Trump defied the predictions of virtually every casino analyst on Wall Street and paid owners of Trump Castle junk bonds their interest payments. "We don't need an outside infusion," Donald Trump said then.

Casino regulators say they are going to take a close look at the transaction. "It looks like this was a loan, and if it was, then Fred Trump is going to have to qualify as a financial source," said Jack Sweeney, New Jersey Division of Gaming Enforcement executive director. Fred Trump, who is 85 years old, couldn't be reached to comment.

If for any reason the elder Mr. Trump doesn't qualify, his son might have to quickly come up with $3 million in cash. That may be difficult considering that banks have second liens on nearly every one of his assets.

Mr. Sweeney said this was the only known instance of money being transferred from one party to a casino through the purchase of casino chips.

Since Trump Castle was already in default on at least one of its loans, Fred Trump had every reason to avoid standing in line behind all the other nervous creditors. True, the unusual financing did not generate interest payments. But as long as a casino stays open, chips can be redeemed at any time. "It is the ultimate first mortgage," a source told the *Journal*.[1]

Several months after the US economy began sliding into recession, massive cracks were visible in the foundation of the Trump business empire. And by now students of Citi's history can guess which bank had become the most exposed creditor enabling Donald Trump's 1980s borrowing binge.

Why do bad things always happen to Citi? It's not fair to blame a bank for the vicissitudes of the business cycle. But taxpayers and shareholders are bound to lose patience with an institution that takes more risks than its competitors and then blames the economy when it runs into trouble. Nearly a hundred years after National City became the largest bank in the country in part by demonstrating financial strength in times of crisis, Citi in 1990 remained the largest bank but was reliably among the most vulnerable victims—if not one of the causes—of financial turbulence.

CEO John Reed didn't create all of Citi's problems in this period, and he often tried to solve them—when he wasn't allowing his subordinates to create new ones. He had set aside provisions for losses on loans to less-developed countries in 1987, but within a few years he was trying to manage a portfolio of troubled real estate loans that were proudly made in the USA. Donald Trump was just one of the distressed borrowers the bank was trying to help make great again. Thinly capitalized and overexposed to commercial property development, Citi would once again approach failure, though details and documents showing the full extent of its financial troubles have never been disclosed by financial authorities.

Before going further into the details of Citi's lending to borrowers like Mr. Trump, it's instructive to focus on the bank's leadership. Reed's onetime rival Thomas Theobald left Citi in 1987 to take the top job at Continental—the bank that Theobald didn't want to help rescue in 1984. Unlike the man who bested him in the competition to run Citi, Theobald was an experienced evaluator of credit risk. His departure left a hole in Citi's senior management ranks because Reed wasn't the only one who didn't have a traditional banking background. Many of his top lieutenants didn't, either.[2] Reed and his senior team were mainly marketers and operations executives who succeeded in building a large consumer bank, but lacked a thorough understanding of lending and underwriting.

The result was an almost absurd recurring drama in which the man running the largest bank in the country seemed to be receiving on-the-job training in the core business of banking. And after learning how his subordinates had managed to create still another credit mess, Reed would often blame factors beyond the bank's control. It's true that the health of the national economy is a big driver of the results at large national banks, but this is not a secret. During the good times prudent bankers prepare for the downturns by setting aside adequate reserves for losses, maintaining thick capital cushions, and carefully considering whether potential borrowers are likely to repay when times get tough.

Before Citi had the opportunity to operate during the tough times in US banking, it first needed to overcome its problems in Latin American banking. Since Washington considered both the sovereign borrowers south of the border and a number of their US creditors too big to fail, the US government made a series of attempts to help countries like Mexico pay back banks like Citi.

When the debt crisis exploded in the early 1980s, the US government first tried sending aid to the foreign governments that had borrowed too much while also exercising regulatory forbearance at home—allowing banks like Citi to pretend they were healthier than they were. Then in the mid-1980s Washington pursued a plan named for Reagan's second Treasury secretary, James Baker. The idea of the Baker Plan was to exchange new lending to the indebted countries in return for market-oriented reforms such as tax reduction, privatization of state-owned enterprises, reductions in trade barriers, and investment liberalization. Unfortunately, overall debt levels in the indebted countries remained stubbornly high.

For years, Washington seems to have erred in thinking that the problem largely involved a temporary shortage of liquidity. This is why many officials figured that "extending and pretending" with the Latin American loans might allow enough time for both the borrowers and the lenders to recover their financial health. When

Reed decided that Citi would stop pretending in 1987, his bank formally recognized that solvency and long-term payment capacity were in question. The massive debts might never be paid back. Reed caused a broader reckoning at the other banks as they too had to formally recognize the downside.

But the basic problem remained. Enter Nicholas Brady. Appointed secretary of the Treasury in Reagan's final year in office, he would serve throughout the presidency of George H. W. Bush. In March of 1989, he announced still another plan. (Readers may note here one of the benefits of being perceived by politicians and regulators as a too-big-to-fail lender or borrower. If you're big enough and you get into debt trouble, you're not alone. You become Washington's problem, and ultimately the taxpayers' problem.)

The banks wanted to get the illiquid troubled loans off their books and the countries wanted to reduce their debt burdens. So the idea of the Brady plan was to have the banks accept lower repayments in exchange for more liquid, tradable assets. The banks would trade many of their old, dodgy loans for new bonds issued by the foreign governments that had lower interest or principal payments but were backed by US Treasury bonds as collateral. By July, Mexico was the first in line to negotiate. Posing once again as a champion of free markets even as his former bank negotiated yet another Washington deal, Wriston observed: "If the government would get out of the way we could just finish this issue." Consistent with a lobbying push from Citi, the overall plan that emerged from the Treasury called for a 20 percent reduction in debts to the commercial banks.[3]

So began the era of "Brady bonds," issued by developing countries but with Washington's assistance. The Mexico template was replicated by Costa Rica, Venezuela, Uruguay, Argentina, and Brazil through 1992. Most of these deals led to 30 to 35 percent reductions in country debt. Some of these countries, such as Argentina and Mexico, experienced stronger growth as their economies recovered after the so-called lost decade that started in the early 1980s. Others, such as Venezuela, continued to flounder.[4]

Up north in the United States, another economy reliant on petroleum had also been floundering for years. The 1980s slide in oil prices that had ravaged oil-producing countries had also triggered a deep recession in Texas. Eager to forget all the trouble his bank had gotten into in developing countries, Wriston seems to have regarded problems in the US oil patch as a reason to gloat about Citi's performance:

> Americans are still reasonably parochial. They'd rather make a bad loan in Texas, than a good loan in Brazil. My friend Ben Love [former chairman and CEO of Texas Commerce Bancshares, which was acquired by Chemical Banking Corp. in 1987] used to say that Texas Commerce is the soundest, best bank in the world, and you crazy guys in New York are lending money to those folks who speak a funny language. It occurs to me those boys across the street are still around and Texas Commerce isn't. It occurs to me one of those crazy New York banks took it over.[5]

In Texas, nine of the ten largest banks failed or were taken over, and close to six hundred other banks failed during the 1980s and early 1990s. Wriston failed to note that, but for the practice of forbearance applied to those "crazy New York banks," some of them might not have survived the 1980s either.[6] A reasonable question is whether any small bank could have gotten away with as many problems as Citi did without being seized and sold by regulators.

In 1990, the problems in the American economy were not limited to one region. That year, the US slipped into a recession that was relatively mild by most measures—lasting a mere eight months—but included an historic credit contraction. Over the past seven decades of bank lending, there have been only three years during which the US endured a negative rate of growth in loans and leases: 1991, 1992, and 2009.

Real estate lending screeched nearly to a halt after growing at between 12 and 18 percent per year every year from 1984 to 1989. John Reed called it a "regulatory recession," and perhaps he had a point. During the savings-and-loan crisis and related scandals, financial regulators were routinely getting berated at congressional hearings. The Office of the Comptroller of the Currency was accused of waiting too long to intervene at failing banks. The regulators responded with more aggressive oversight of lenders, and the bankers in turn tightened credit.

In early 1990, the Bank of New England, widely considered to be a too-big-to-fail institution, was identified by the Comptroller's office as a five-rated institution, the lowest grade given by regulators. Following a now-familiar scenario, around the time the bank was identified as a problem, the Federal Reserve propped it up with more than $2 billion in lending, while uninsured depositors were fleeing the bank. The FDIC used a newly granted power, bridge bank authority, to take over Bank of New England until it could be marketed and sold to Fleet/Norstar Financial Group.[7]

The recession helped trigger a crash in the real estate market. Citibank seemed to be among the last to know, pushing big loans out the door to real estate developers like Donald Trump well into 1989.[8] That same year, the bank was also the lead lender in providing Mr. Trump with $380 million[9] to buy and operate the Eastern Shuttle and its fleet of old, fuel-guzzling airplanes.

"He got jets worth perhaps $52.5 million, landing rights at three congested airports and a premium-cost airline operating in the Northeast corridor just as a slowdown in the region prompted businesses to cut spending," according to a 1990 story in the *Dallas Morning News*. "The best thing to do may be to just put the keys to all 21 jets in an envelope, mail it to Citibank and say take the whole damn airline," according to a Trump adviser quoted by the paper.[10]

That's more or less what happened. After the 1989 purchase, the renamed "Trump Shuttle" became an immediate and significant drain on the future president's cash flow, and pretty soon Citibank was the lead owner of the airline and a bunch of other stuff that used to be Trump's.

But right up until creditors began to force a dismantling of the empire, Trump maintained his game face. A June 1990 story in the *Wall Street Journal* noted:

> In April, Mr. Trump declared in an interview with this newspaper that he was considering the sale of assets not out of any weakness but because he wanted to become the "king of cash" in order to be able to make new acquisitions. Mr. Trump was so adamant in denying the existence of financial troubles that he threatened to sue this newspaper if it reported that he had cash-flow problems.[11]

By the summer of 1990, Trump was conducting intense negotiations with Citi and other creditors, who had extended him a total of $2 billion in bank debt and more than $1 billion in bond debt. Citi and the other banks gave him another $65 million in emergency financing, but they wanted to see an end to his lavish personal and professional spending. Creditors wanted him to sell his mansions, boats, and personal aircraft, along with a lot of Trump commercial properties. He resisted, and in any case it was a buyer's market, so asset sales were unlikely to yield enough to satisfy the bankers.

For reasons that must have had Citi shareholders gritting their teeth, America's biggest bank became the most reasonable of the Trump creditors. A September report in the *Journal* explained:

Citibank has emerged as a conciliatory force in negotiations with other Trump lenders, largely because it has the most to lose in the event Mr. Trump cedes control of his assets. As part of the bailout, Citibank received second and third mortgages on many Trump assets; should he lose them to other creditors, Citibank's chances of recovering its losses would be greatly diminished. Including the shuttle, Citibank lent Mr. Trump a total of $1.1 billion.[12]

Third mortgages! Some of its original loans to Trump had been unsecured. In its defense, Citi often made efforts to share the risks with other lenders, but in this case the biggest bank also appeared to have been among the least responsible of the Trump creditors. No matter how conciliatory Citi wanted to be in cleaning up the mess, the various Trump enterprises were simply carrying too much debt and the result was a series of bankruptcy filings in the early 1990s. Along with the airline, Citi ended up owning significant stakes in other Trump assets, including a retail chain called Alexander's and the famous Plaza Hotel in Manhattan.

Citi's questionable judgment was not limited to its dealings with Trump. While the real estate mogul was going through his debt workout, his lead creditor increasingly had to answer questions about its own management and risk-taking.

"Honeymoon's Over," read the headline on a page-one *Journal* story in June of 1990. The piece noted the bank had routinely missed earnings targets under Mr. Reed. Shareholders had ample reason to be upset and taxpayers had reason to be concerned. According to the *Journal*:

As troubled loans rise, Citicorp's reserve and capital levels are looking skimpy. In both areas, Citicorp comes in at or near the bottom among big U.S. banks: Its reserves are only 56% of

nonperforming loans, while many big competitors' reserves are
at about 70% or more, and its common-stock equity is below
that of almost all its rivals. By some estimates, Citicorp needs $2
billion in additional capital and reserves.[13]

The bank continued to resist outside calls to operate with more
room for error, trotting out its usual argument that its global, diversified portfolio made it safer than other banks. The paper reported:
"Mr. Reed, who relishes his reputation as a maverick, always has
had a penchant for risk-taking." And even as the economy was
headed south, Citi still didn't see a pressing need to boost its capital
for the rainy days to come. "In April, Mr. Reed's bravado surfaced
again. Citicorp thumbed its nose at critics by announcing a 9.9%
increase in the dividend at the same time its write-offs of bad loans
soared 79% and first-quarter earnings plunged 56%," added the
Journal. Citi's boss acknowledged mistakes but often found fault
outside the bank:

> Mr. Reed complains, however, that something beyond the bank's
> control has repeatedly cropped up and kept it from achieving its
> financial goals. What he calls the "externalities" blighting the
> 1990 outlook are the weakening commercial-real-estate market
> and the disappearance of highly leveraged corporate buy-outs.

In an interview for the *Harvard Business Review* later that year,
Citi's top executive again seemed to be on a journey of personal
discovery into the bank's process of extending credit. He was apparently saddened by what he found, but not sad enough to raise
capital:

> We're being criticized mainly on our real estate assets and on
> the capital front. Both criticisms are valid, and I take them to
> heart. One thing I hate is for people to dismiss criticism. That's

a passport to suicide. At the same time, we cannot overreact. We shouldn't play to the bleachers.

I've gone deeply into the credit portfolio and the credit process, and it's fair to say I've been hurt by it. I haven't told the world that, because who cares? But I'm a little embarrassed professionally—maybe more than a little embarrassed—that I didn't jump on it sooner. We were warned about real estate two years ago, we were warned again a year ago, and we pooh-poohed it. Now I'm damn embarrassed because the critics were right and we were wrong. Sure, the market's changed; we didn't know two years ago what we know today. Values have gone down. But the fact is, they're more right and we're more wrong.

The capital thing is also valid. Visibly, statistically, we look a little naked. Now the statistics may not be worth that much—except everybody looks at them, so you have to pay attention. We've made a calculated decision that this is not the time to raise new equity, which frankly is right for the stockholders.[14]

Citibank was by many measures in the most precarious position of all of the major banks. The level of troubled loans at Citibank that were no longer even accruing interest was nearly equal to its equity capital and its efforts to build loan loss reserves fell far short of its major bank competitors (see Table 14). The slowdown in the economy, combined with the overhang of troubled real estate loans and the provisioning and recognition of losses in the international portfolio left Citi with a wafer-thin layer of capital, and there was no guarantee the economy wouldn't get worse.

In the days of Moses Taylor and the philosophy of ready money, capitalization levels were high. About the time Taylor's tenure as president was coming to an end, National City's capital to asset ratio was in the range of 18 to 19 percent. Reed's bank was nowhere close to that level of safety.

Table 14: Loan Loss Exposure of Large Commercial Banks as of June 30, 1990

	Assets ($s in billions)	Nonaccrual Loans as percentage of equity capital	Loan-Loss Reserves as percentage of equity capital	Unreserved Nonaccrual Loans as percentage of equity capital
Citibank	164.2	98	39	59
Bank of America	90.7	43	55	-12
Chase Manhattan	81.1	85	60	24
Morgan Guaranty Trust	72.0	27	63	-36
Security Pacific National Bank	64.1	36	25	11
Bankers Trust	61.0	63	119	-56
Manufactur- ers Hanover	56.5	82	70	13

Source: *The Future of American Banking* (Columbia University Seminars) (New York: Routledge, 1992), Table 6 in the book.

Note: The figure in the far right column is calculated by subtracting the balance in the fourth column (Loan-Loss Reserves) from the total in the third column (Nonaccrual Loans).

Standards imposed on national banks have changed over time. In Taylor's day, markets provided much of the discipline on lenders. As for the federal standards, they were not based on any ratio, but rather were stated as a static level of $50,000 for banks in cities with fewer than ten thousand persons and $100,000 for banks in cities with more than ten thousand. It was not until the 1930s that ratios such as capital to total deposits and capital to total assets came into use by federal regulators. Early minimum ratios were in the range of 10 percent.

That number came down over the years. With taxpayers bear-

ing more risk over time, equity investors in big banks were required to fund a smaller percentage of the balance sheet. Along the
way, Wriston was particularly successful in persuading regulators
to tolerate more risk. As Citi's chairman he proclaimed: "We determined that our ratio of capital was too high, and we mashed it
down deliberately."

By the end of 1973, with the industry average capital ratio standing at about 6.5 percent, Wriston had Citibank at a little more than
4 percent. He argued that Citibank did not need as much capital as
did small banks, because the little guys were largely undiversified
and allegedly lacked the strong management provided by guys like
him. Citibank also commissioned a book espousing a minimalist
position on bank capital. In the Washington influence game, it was
money well spent. The Comptroller of the Currency in the early
1970s said the book "probably resulted in the agency taking a more
sophisticated look at capital" to consider "more closely what we
were hoping to accomplish with capital and the role debt plays."[15]

By 1990, regulators had enjoyed about all the sophisticated
analysis they could handle and were increasingly worried about
the largest bank in the United States. In November of that year,
top officials at the Federal Reserve called Reed in for a meeting to
discuss Citi's capital. Gerald Corrigan of the New York Fed and
William Taylor, who headed up the division of bank supervision
at the Board of Governors in Washington, warned Reed about the
likely consequences of his bank's exposure to the moribund real
estate market. The pair urged him to consider selling nonstrategic
assets, cutting the dividend, and raising capital, even if it meant
diluting current shareholders.

For the ensuing 2.5 years, all major decisions would need to be
cleared by the Fed and the Comptroller's office. Reed would have
to transition Citi from the Wriston standard to a safer model and
initially this meant raising $4 to $5 billion of new capital[16]:

Over the next two years, we want to become known as a strongly capitalized company. We feel it is important from the stockholder's point of view to strengthen our relative as well as absolute capital positions, and we have developed a plan by which to do so. Given current difficulties, we may not hit every target in this plan exactly on schedule, but we do believe we can put together the necessary steps to achieve our capital goals, including a build-up through retained earnings.[17]

Again from the sidelines Wriston ridiculed the ever-changing capital standards, saying the process "has become a race with no finish line."[18] But the bank now seemed willing to try running it. In February of 1991, Citicorp sold $590 million of preferred stock to Prince Alwaleed bin Talal bin Abdulaziz al Saud, a member of the Saudi royal family. Even before the deal, Alwaleed was the bank's largest shareholder, with a 4.9 percent stake in common stock. In acquiring the new preferred shares, the prince's team negotiated a fat 11 percent dividend with a conversion feature that could bring his stake in Citicorp up to 15 percent. It may be unfair to characterize the deal as a Saudi bailout of America's global bank, but the terms extended to the Saudi royal suggest there were not that many investors standing in line to finance Citi at that particular moment. But the royal money certainly helped attract others. Just a few weeks later, the bank struck another deal, raising $600 million from three dozen institutional investors for a slightly lower dividend of 10.75 percent. Asset sales were completed in rapid succession: municipal bond insurer Ambac; Citibank Italia; and brokerage Lynch, Jones & Ryan along with a stake in Saudi American Bank, among others.[19]

How dire was Citi's need to build up its capital? House Commerce Committee chairman John Dingell, Democrat of Michigan, made headlines at a July 1991 hearing by stating that Citicorp was "technically insolvent" and "struggling to survive." The response from Citi regulators was a swift denial. FDIC chairman William Seidman said, "I don't believe it is insolvent under any standard." But how far was it from the edge of the cliff?

An August 1991 story in the *Journal* reported, "Although still one of the least-capitalized major banks, Citicorp now, at least, has crossed the 4%-of-assets threshold of basic equity capital that regulators insist on by the end of 1992."[20] Reed reported that he was making progress cutting expenses and increasing his capital cushion. As for the bank's recent troubles, he said, "I've spent a lot of time trying to understand what happened."

Whatever he learned, it still didn't persuade him to make big changes, or to significantly shrink the classic too-big-to-fail bank:

> Most banks "under duress," Mr. Reed replies, leave major businesses and markets. "What we're doing is more gutsy." His approach includes avoiding across-the-board personnel cuts, leaving all customer contacts in place and trimming middle- and upper-management positions.[21]

Mr. Reed criticized regulators for pushing the bank to mark loan assets to current value, and lamented the "fundamental repricing of whole classes of assets around the world." Given such external pressures, he also finally seemed to recognize the need to run the business more conservatively, even if he remained reluctant to do so:

> Mr. Reed has discarded Citicorp's traditional view that excess capital is merely excess idle funds. Besides, he adds, "I know when I've been beaten; the markets now want capital."

However, neither Mr. Reed nor Paul Collins, his vice chairman in charge of capital raising and financial controls, were in any rush to sell assets or stock, as analysts were recommending.[22]

In December of that year, the magazine *Institutional Investor* ran a cover story entitled, "The collapse of Citibank's credit culture," featuring an interview with John Reed. The man who had been running the giant bank for seven years still came off as a stranger to its ways:

> I think in a big company you must delegate responsibility. You can't get good people to work for you if you go in and do every-thing for them. It would have been a little hard for me to walk in one day—never having been in the corporate business—and say, "You guys don't know what you're taking about." . . . You pay them a lot of money, and you've got to presume to some degree they know what they're doing.[23]

Reed acknowledged that the bank had been too aggressive in its lending and that he had ignored warning signs, but he also blamed "macro" events in the larger economy, which he obviously viewed as a recurring theme in the recent history of instability at Citi:

> "You know, making a good loan to Chile wasn't the issue," he says. "It was the macro environment that caused all of the highly leveraged foreign countries to get into the moratorium. And so, regardless of how well you assessed the economic policies of Chile or Argentina or whoever, that was irrelevant because it was overwhelmed by the macro." As for real estate, he con-cludes, "we've been in the business for the last twenty years. It's 5 to 6 percent of our business. We never forecast 30 or 35 percent drops in values across the entire stock."[24]

The magazine noted that Reed "downplays the fact that the drop has been caused, in part, by Citi's own massive lending, and he seems not to have accepted the possibility" that lending to poor countries and in US real estate "at this scale was simply misguided." The magazine continued:

> For the chairman of the biggest, baddest bank in America, he seems more like an apprentice than a leader. "I still go through every write-off every month as a learning process, not to try to point fingers at anyone," he says. "But I ask the responsible people to come and sit down and walk through the trail. Then I try to understand. And I'll tell you, you learn a lot." Reed concedes that the process is not easy for him.

As a means to gauge the quality of John Reed's management of Citi during this time, it would be useful to go back and look at the Office of the Comptroller of the Currency's examination reports from 1991 and 1992, as well as for other years during his tenure, to get the examiners' take on his capabilities, as well as the solvency of Citibank. The examination team normally puts particularly juicy details about what it has found in a confidential section that is not shared with the bank. These reports are available going back all the way to the 1860s and 1870s for Moses Taylor, the 1880s for Percy Pyne, the 1890s and 1900s for James Stillman, the 1910s for Frank Vanderlip, the 1920s and early 1930s for Charles Mitchell, and later during the 1930s for James Perkins. But oddly these examination reports cannot be accessed for any period after that due to the Federal Records Act of 1950. Since then, regulators have routinely destroyed the exam reports.

For decades now, the government's standard practice has been to warehouse individual examination reports for banks like Citi for thirty years while refusing to release them, citing exemptions under the Freedom of Information Act (FOIA). After thirty years, the feds then destroy the reports. Based on this schedule, at some point during this year, the federal government will destroy the Citibank examination records from 1988. A few years down the line, the records from the early 1990s downturn will also cease to exist. Counterintuitively, it is much easier for someone researching the history of Citibank to get their hands on an examination report from the 1890s than from the 1990s.[25] It is also certainly easier to repeat history if the lessons of the past are erased.

Fortunately for students of recent financial history, some journalists have occasionally been able to counter the federal effort to destroy historical records in this area. One of the Comptroller's contemporary examination reports was leaked to the *New York Times* in 1992. The report chronicled the troubles of Citicorp Mortgage, which during 1989 was the nation's largest mortgage lender. Its operations went south in the ensuing years and it had negative equity capital of $80 million at the end of 1991. Citicorp then pumped $172 million into its mortgage unit, most of which was consumed by additional losses.

When an institution like Citi has problems on multiple fronts as it did during the early 1990s, a regulator would normally catalog all the bank's weaknesses discovered during the on-site examination and through off-site monitoring in a written agreement. The agreement would be signed by the Office of the Comptroller of the Currency and the bank, with the bank agreeing to improve the areas of weakness outlined in the document. The most common such informal measure is a memorandum of understanding. Citibank was placed under just such an agreement in 1992. But you can't read it.

In response to a recent FOIA request for the memorandum, the Comptroller's office claims that "after a thorough search," staff were "unable to locate the document." The regulator also said that "memorandums of understanding are not disclosed to the public." The Federal Reserve also placed Citicorp under a memorandum and still has a copy of the document, but the Fed refused to provide it upon request, citing an exemption under the FOIA.[26]

Reed was given years to bring Citi into compliance with the

mandates of the Comptroller and the Federal Reserve. Meanwhile, hundreds of smaller institutions were given months. Reed's bank benefited greatly from the breathing room provided by regulators. While he slashed costs, the big consumer bank he had built and his massive credit card operation were generating increasingly large profits. With the economy rebounding under the New Democrat Bill Clinton—and, after 1994, a Republican Congress—the bank posted robust earnings and revenue growth through much of the 1990s. And when Mexico—where Citi had extensive operations—received a US government bailout in 1995, that didn't hurt the bank either.

Things worked out for the Trump family, too. A May 1994 report from the Associated Press had the details:

ATLANTIC CITY, N.J. New Jersey regulators agreed Wednesday to let Donald Trump's father cash in $1.5 million worth of gambling chips, ending a 3 1/2-year saga that began when Fred C. Trump helped bail out one of his son's casinos.

The state Casino Control Commission voted 3–0 to let a representative of the elder Trump redeem the $5,000 chips at a cashier's cage instead of appearing personally.

It was the third such redemption. The other two were each for $1 million.[27]

Four years later, John Reed would enjoy a measure of redemption as well. While his bank had rallied during the period when regulators graciously exercised forbearance, a wave of mergers among his competitors had forced Citi to surrender its crown as America's biggest bank. But he wouldn't have to tolerate also-ran status for long. In 1998, Reed would agree to a merger creating the largest financial services company in the world. Too-big-to-fail banking was about to get much bigger.

19

Creating the Next Crisis

An enduring legend of the 2008 financial panic is that all the trouble began a decade earlier, when Citicorp merged with Travelers to form a $700 billion financial behemoth. A common interpretation holds that this 1998 remarriage of safe Main Street banking and reckless Wall Street gambling spawned economic Armageddon. It's especially easy to believe this tale if one ignores Citi's recent history. It becomes easier still when one observes the Washington lobbying that enabled the creation of this global financial supermarket.

The legend has also been particularly alluring given that it mirrors the Great Depression story of the bank that has been passed down by generations of politicians. More than six decades after Senator Carter Glass blamed Charles Mitchell for the stock-market crash and persuaded congressional colleagues that City Bank had to be separated from Wall Street, Citibank and the Street were reunited. And hell followed with them, according to conventional Beltway lore. But the truth is a bit more complicated, highlighted by an internal FDIC document that has until now remained hidden from the public.

When news broke on April 6, 1998, that John Reed had agreed to merge his Citicorp with Sandy Weill's Travelers Group, the shares of both companies rallied sharply. On that Monday at the New York Stock Exchange, Citicorp shares rose 26 percent, while Travelers shares closed up 18 percent. "In an era of mega-mergers, the blockbuster pact between two of the world's financial powerhouses easily would dwarf all others," reported the *Wall Street Journal*.[1] "The combined Citigroup—using the trademark Travelers red umbrella as its logo—would serve more than 100 million customers in 100 countries world-wide."

America's global bank for consumers and businesses was combining with a Travelers conglomerate that included insurance, mutual funds, and its recently acquired Salomon, Inc. investment bank. A former trading powerhouse, Salomon had almost gone bust in the early 1990s after some of its employees were caught trying to rig the market for US Treasury bonds. Investor Warren Buffett rescued the firm by persuading Treasury to continue doing business with it. Salomon rebounded and, after Travelers bought it, was merged with an older Travelers acquisition—Smith Barney—to form Salomon Smith Barney, a rising force on Wall Street. Now with the new deal it could sell its investment banking services to the blue-chip roster of corporations around the world that were already doing their commercial banking with Citi. The idea was that businesses that had for years gone to Citi to make deposits or to take out loans would now also use the firm to issue bonds or manage an investment portfolio. Attorney Robert Bostrom observed that the merger of Citicorp and Travelers was the "biggest deal of the century."[2]

On that April day in 1998 when Messrs. Reed and Weill announced that all those assets would be joined together in a new empire of money called Citigroup, the *Journal*'s Michael Siconolfi noted that "risks abound" and that such financial supermarkets "have never worked well." Examining the wreckage a decade

later, one could observe that a megabank has never worked so
badly.

But at the time of the merger announcement, the two men who
had agreed to serve as co-CEOs of the new business made a varia-
tion of the old Wriston argument that the gigantic firm was made
safer by its involvement in so many global markets:

> Messrs. Weill and Reed are betting that the broad services of
> their new firm will weather big market swoons. Though the
> Dow industrials eclipsed 9000 Monday for the first time, ex-
> tending the bull market's seven-year run, Mr. Weill said: "Our
> company will be so diversified and in so many different areas
> that we will be able to withstand these storms."[3]

Right away there were storms, all right—in the executive suite
of the new firm. Besides the typical struggles that occur during
corporate mergers when power and money are reallocated, there
was another problem affecting the personnel of the new megabank. Just weeks after the merger closed in October of 1998, Sandy
Weill fired his longtime lieutenant Jamie Dimon, perhaps the
most capable banker of his generation. Having worked together
for nearly twenty years—counting Dimon's work as a summer
intern for Weill's brokerage—the two had engineered a series of
turnarounds at troubled financial firms. But after Dimon chose
not to promote Weill's daughter at the pace that she and her father
believed she deserved, the business relationship went south. She
quit, Weill blamed Dimon for driving her away, and before long
Dimon was also headed for the exit. It's hard to fault anyone for
putting family first, but as a business matter the gargantuan size of
Weill's blunder would become apparent in due course.

Even at the time of Dimon's departure, the market didn't like it.
Citigroup shares dropped nearly 5 percent on the news.[4] Investors
were right to be concerned. Dimon wasn't just one of 160,000 em-

ployees. The new Citigroup, beginning the process of integrating various worldwide businesses, had just gotten rid of the executive most skilled in the operational details of restructuring financial companies.

Roughly a year later, another high-profile personnel move would raise eyebrows for other reasons. Sandy Weill thought he had scored a coup when he hired former Treasury secretary and onetime Goldman Sachs cochairman Robert Rubin. "Snaring Bob was big news. The press had been relentlessly calling into question our merger progress for months, and hiring someone as widely respected as Bob translated into a highly visible public endorsement of our company," recalled Weill in his autobiography.[5]

But the timing and circumstances of Rubin's arrival, not to mention his new job at Citigroup, would feed a perception that allowing Citi's combination of Main Street and Wall Street finance was less about sound policy than effective lobbying. Rubin's hire turned out to be one of the more unseemly transitions in the history of Washington's revolving door, in which senior officials leave government to collect enormous paydays from the industries they once regulated. And in time Rubin would indeed encourage the firm to ramp up its Wall Street trading. But in many ways his hiring represented continuity with what had become a tradition at the firm.

Ninety-eight years after Frank Vanderlip left the Treasury and a few months later started a vaguely defined job at City Bank, Robert Rubin left the Treasury and a few months later started a vaguely defined job at Citigroup. It seems that, over the course of a century in the bank's relationship with Washington, only the names had changed. And whoever was being protected, it sure didn't look like the innocent.

Making the timing particularly awkward was that Citigroup's business model wasn't exactly legal. Regulators and lawmakers, under intense lobbying from the affected industries, had for years been poking holes in the old Glass–Steagall barriers between commercial and investment banking. But enough of the old restrictions remained that a full melding of the new company's various financial businesses would require a change in the law. In September of 1998 the Federal Reserve had approved the Travelers-Citicorp deal because existing law gave bank holding companies a few years to come into compliance. But the new merged company would have to start breaking itself up again if it couldn't get Congress and President Bill Clinton to do a rewrite that allowed financial supermarkets. Ironically—or perhaps not—Citigroup was asking Washington to rewrite the law that Congress had specifically written in response to the bank's earlier troubles.

Clinton signed the rewrite—and enabled the new Citigroup to exist—in November of 1999, just a month after his friend and former Treasury secretary Bob Rubin joined the firm. If the arrangement smelled funny in 1998, it was hardly more aromatic ten years later, when Citi was in crisis. In December of 2008, an editorial in the *Wall Street Journal* reviewed Mr. Rubin's history at the bank:

> On October 18, 1999, Citigroup announced that former Treasury Secretary Robert E. Rubin was joining the firm. But what exactly would Mr. Rubin do at Citigroup? Citi's SEC filing eight days later noted that Mr. Rubin would be joining the bank's board of directors. After that, the message to investors began to get murky. Citi said that Mr. Rubin "will serve as Chairman of the Executive Committee of the Board and will work with Mr. Reed and Mr. Weill, Chairmen and Co-Chief Executive Officers, in a newly constituted three-person office of the Chairman."
>
> Was Mr. Rubin to be primarily a member of the board overseeing management, or a part of the management reporting to the board? Things became even murkier when Messrs. Weill

and Reed described Mr. Rubin's job: "Bob will participate in strategic managerial and operational matters of the Company, but will have no line responsibilities."

As a great man of finance, Mr. Rubin would be paid CEO money—a total of $115 million since 1999, not including stock options—but without having to run a business or be accountable for the results. For years, journalists tried to figure out exactly what Mr. Rubin's job was at Citigroup . . . [6]

The legitimate questions about Mr. Rubin at Citigroup and his senior role in the administration that enabled it have helped feed a perception since the 2008 crisis that its root cause was Bill Clinton's decision to let banks play on Wall Street. But just because policy results from a heavily lobbied Washington deal, that doesn't automatically mean it's the wrong policy. And the narrative of greedy Wall Street traders soiling the pristine business of Main Street bankers cannot withstand a thorough review of Citi's history.

Still, some participants have argued that Wall Street gamblers were responsible for sending Citi to the edge of ruin. John Reed left the bank in 2000 after losing a power struggle with Weill. Years later, when explaining Citi's excessive risk-taking to the government's Financial Crisis Inquiry Commission, he blamed the "dominance of the Salomon Brothers sort of culture"[7] in the years following the big merger.

Sheila Bair ran the FDIC for five years beginning in 2006 and, as we'll see, made significant efforts to prevent taxpayer funds from being used to rescue banking giants like Citi. But in her memoir she seems to have been unaware of the bank's history during previous crises: "In the past, Citi had been led by well-respected industry titans such as John Reed and Walter Wriston." From this premise she made the following conclusion about the bank's problems heading into the crisis of 2008:

[C]iti was no longer a bread and butter commercial bank. It had been hijacked by an investment banking culture that made profits through high-stakes betting on the direction of the markets, in contrast to traditional banking, which focused on making loans to people based on their ability to repay.[8]

This is consistent with Senator Elizabeth Warren's argument that Citi got into trouble because of "speculative trading" on the investment banking side. She says that the "[commercial] banking side needs to stay boring" and has proposed a new Glass-Steagall to split commercial from investment banking:

If people want to take risks, financial institutions want to gamble on derivatives or swaps or on whatever exotic thing that someone has created, this doesn't say they can't do it, it just says that you don't get taxpayer-backed money to do it.[9]

Of course taxpayers don't want the banking system to gamble their money on *anything*. Are traditional loans really safer than other financial instruments? Over the years, journalists covering the creation of Citigroup have sometimes painted the low-key Reed as a stodgy, safe traditional banker in contrast to the dynamic Sandy Weill, a swashbuckling empire builder who made his name in the risky securities markets. Looks can be deceiving.

There's a plausible case that John Reed was the more aggressive risk taker. Reed had been burned in the early 1990s by allowing colleagues he assumed to be experts in corporate lending to take huge risks financing ventures like the Trump Shuttle. But the experience didn't fundamentally change his hands-off approach to subordinates. Weill would later criticize "John's shockingly detached management style."[10] After Weill first approached Reed to suggest the megamerger of their firms in 1998, the Citicorp boss assigned someone else to conduct negotiations while he embarked on a ten-day business trip to Europe and Asia. If negotiating the sale of the business isn't a job for the CEO, what is?

Even after experiencing the Latin American debt debacle, Reed had allowed Citi's commercial bank to make enormous bets on the US real estate market. Having witnessed the crisis years in sovereign borrowing that exposed the flaws in the Wriston model, Reed continued to run the giant bank with a wafer-thin layer of capital. And even after recognizing losses that would have inspired bank regulators to close a smaller institution, he still resisted calls to operate with a safer capital structure. Careful bankers analyzed costs and benefits, risk and reward. Reed, who never much cared for the nuts and bolts of credit risk, was driven by a vision of making his firm "the Coca-Cola of finance."[11]

Weill, on the other hand, had made his fortune and assembled his conglomerate the old-fashioned City Bank way. Like Moses Taylor and James Stillman, Weill thrived in times of crisis. He had mastered the art of picking up troubled firms, turning them around by relentlessly identifying and eliminating unnecessary costs, and then integrating the new outfits into the operations of his existing business. The fact that for decades he had been a healthy buyer during periods of Wall Street stress tells us that he and his colleagues had been disciplined in not taking on too much risk during the boom times and in controlling expenses. Stillman practiced this art during the Gilded Age, and Weill practiced it during the turbulence of the 1970s and 1980s.

In 1970, Weill's upstart firm Cogan, Berlind, Weill & Levitt— dismissed by the Wall Street establishment as "Corned Beef With Lettuce"—bought the much larger stock brokerage Hayden, Stone & Co., with its sixty-two branches nationwide, and adopted its name.[12] As Weill integrated the new acquisition, employees learned that he had mastered the details of the business and was not shy about sharing his analysis. Monica Langley reports:

"That's crappy," he would say about a line item he didn't like. "You stupid son-of-a-bitch," he would bark at someone who screwed up. Sandy's persistent questioning, the degree of detail he sought, the rigor of his reviews, his uncanny ability to sniff out a problem, and his hair trigger temper were like nothing they had ever seen before in a senior brokerage executive. If a manager tried to explain away a number, Sandy would cut him off: "You better check your facts." He could make fast decisions. If he didn't like a proposal, he would shove it back at the author. "No f—ing way, get out of here."[13]

The next few deals put Weill in the top tier of American finance. He first pursued Shearson, Hammill & Company, which after seventy years in business was floundering and vulnerable to a takeover by the smaller Hayden Stone. Weill dictated the terms of the deal, which included cutting half of Shearson's 2,400 employees. Then he bought Loeb, Rhoades & Company, another storied firm that had stumbled after operational problems flowing from a merger. At the time, it was the second-largest brokerage, behind Merrill Lynch. Weill's firm now had the moniker Shearson Loeb Rhoades, closing out the 1970s after picking up another 160 offices and 1,800 employees, doubling its size yet again. Weill sold the company to American Express and became its president, but he resigned in 1985, disappointed he wasn't exercising more authority.[14]

By this time, Weill had developed a close working relationship with Jamie Dimon, who took on the role that his mentor used to play. Weill would plot strategy and identify troubled corporate targets ripe for a turnaround. Dimon would immerse himself in the numbers of each new acquisition and execute the necessary improvements. In 1986, they teamed up on Commercial Credit Company, a medium-sized consumer lender in Baltimore. Employees quickly learned what was expected in a Weill-run business. Shortly after the takeover, a snowstorm hit Maryland. Weill arrived from New York and was appalled to find the building empty: "How can I get here faster than everyone when I'm traveling two hundred miles? If you want snow days, get a job with the government!"[15] Roughly a century before, Stillman had transformed the City Bank staff into world-class competitors with similar demands for punctuality and professional commitment.

A stock-market crash presented more opportunities for Weill, just as the panics of the late 1800s had done for Stillman. Weill's original strategy was to stay close to the consumer finance space where Commercial Credit operated, but that changed after October 1987: "Suddenly, I began to see a wider array of undervalued companies. I didn't surrender the idea of buying consumer finance franchises, but I decided to cast a wider net . . . [B]efore I knew it, I began to see chances for a return to the securities business." Over the course of the next decade, Weill bought a series of underperformers he could count on Dimon to whip into shape. This finally led to the acquisition of Salomon—but not before both men were comfortable that they understood the risks. "Over many years, Salomon had earned a reputation for committing huge amounts of capital on aggressive trades and more recently for pioneering creative uses for newly invented derivatives products, one of the hottest growth areas in the financial services industry." After receiving a detailed debrief from the London-based head of Salomon's proprietary trading unit, Weill's team was comfortable it could manage the risks. Warren Buffett expressed confidence given Weill's history of executing similar deals.[16]

It was a history of rigorous attention to detail. In the 1960s, Mary McDermott began working at the brokerage that would evolve into "Corned Beef With Lettuce." She used to describe for new hires how intently one of the partners followed stock exchange transactions: "Sandy Weill is quiet, stays in his little corner, and looks at the tape all day. You can stand on this desk and take off your clothes, and he won't even notice."[17]

Perhaps John Reed would have noticed. In the 1990s, he divorced his first wife, with whom he had four children, and married a flight attendant from Citi's corporate jet. Weill for his part has been married to the same woman since 1955.

But Weill's business relationships haven't always been built to last. After the merger that created Citigroup, other talented bankers followed Jamie Dimon out the door. Weill explains in his autobiography: "Unfortunately the elation that accompanied the merger didn't last long. I was stunned how quickly squabbles among my executives and unsteady financial markets intruded . . . Our emphasis on speed and secrecy during our merger talks implied we had to defer management assignments until after the deal's announcement. That meant, of course, that we had to determine who'd lead our businesses as quickly as possible once the deal was out in the open. But the complexity of this merger outstripped any we had done before."[18]

Some of those leaving the new Citi had been loyal to Dimon and didn't think he had an obligation to promote the boss's daughter. Salomon Smith Barney's vice chairman, Steve Black, told Weill: "You just blew Jamie's brains out for all the wrong reasons—I can't condone that."

"Then it's time for you to go. I need everybody on the same team," responded Weill.

"Fine, I'm out, I'm done," retorted Black, who ended up taking a senior position at Chase Bank as head of global equities. Others left Citigroup because they were fed up dealing with two dueling CEOs. Heidi Miller, Citigroup's chief financial officer, had a long history with Dimon. She jumped ship and told Robert Rubin, "This is a dysfunctional company." She would return to the financial industry when she reunited with Dimon after he became CEO and chairman of Bank One.[19] The departures of Black and Miller were not isolated incidents. Nearly 80 percent of Citicorp's most senior executives and 60 percent at Travelers had departed in the aftermath of the merger.[20]

No doubt there would have been enormous challenges for Jamie Dimon in helping Weill to manage the new empire called Citigroup and to assimilate all its disparate elements. But it's hard not to imagine how recent financial history might have been different if the two had remained there. By the time the financial storm arrived a decade later, Weill had retired, and Dimon was serving as CEO of JPMorgan Chase & Company, where he sought to maintain a "fortress balance sheet." The concept is not so different from the "ready money" doctrine of Moses Taylor. Both embody the idea that the best deals are done—and the best banks show their mettle—at the trough of the market, not at its peak.

Not unlike National City under James Stillman, Dimon's JPMorgan Chase became so respected that the government would seek *its* help—in rescuing struggling financial firms in 2008. Private market participants showed similar respect in that year of panic. When depositors left troubled institutions, they often headed down the street to Dimon's JPMorgan Chase:

> As we entered the most tumultuous financial markets since the Great Depression, we experienced the opposite of a "run on the bank" as deposits flowed in (in a two-month period, $150 billion flowed in—we barely knew what to do with it).[21]

But back in the early 2000s few people imagined the calamity to come. Regulators in particular spent much of their time pursuing issues that may or may not have benefited consumers but had little to do with ensuring the safety and soundness of giant banks. At Citi, Weill was churning out profits, but his bank was increasingly attracting government investigations—over accusations of unfair consumer lending practices, self-interested stock research, and even allowing money laundering at Citi's private bank for wealthy customers in Japan. This last issue was one of a number that resulted in the Citi unit being completely banned in Japan.

Weill has always maintained that he chose to step down as CEO in 2003, rather than being pushed. But it's also clear that when he chose a successor, it was not strictly about the ability to manage a financial enterprise. Some board members wanted to bring back Jamie Dimon, but Weill missed the chance to reverse his blunder and instead backed his longtime legal expert Chuck Prince. "He enjoyed excellent relationships with our regulators and a keen appreciation for what the new regulatory era entailed. He was also a fast learner," according to Weill.[22]

Was the bright lawyer the right guy to run the country's largest financial firm? He seems to have had his doubts. Weill recalls the moment he suggested the idea to Prince: "The only other time I had seen Chuck's face turn so white followed a ride on a bobsled during one of our winter planning meetings in the Adirondacks. I thought he'd fall out of his chair—he obviously had never dreamed that I might promote him as my successor . . . [h]e looked hesitant."[23] But he ended up taking the job anyway.

It seems that Prince's initial response had been the correct one. According to banking analyst Mike Mayo:

Chuck Prince should never have been in the top spot at Citi in the first place. He had served as general counsel for two decades, aside from short stints in an operating role. This was completely different from most CEOs, who work their way up through the ranks by running successful business lines of increasing size and scope. Prince seemed to get the job primarily because he was a confidant and trusted aide of the former CEO, Sandy Weill, a role in which he had helped the company navigate its many regulatory crises.

But whatever his initial doubts, once in office Prince turned out to be anything but cautious. Though Weill would retain the title of chairman until 2006, it's clear he was no longer calling every shot. Within weeks of Prince becoming CEO, a report in the *Wall Street Journal* noted a significant change in corporate strategy:

Five years after Citigroup Inc. Chairman Sanford I. Weill sharply cut back on risky trading using the firm's own money, the financial-services giant is again looking to expand its in-house trading business . . . Although Citigroup has been generating substantial profits . . . on the strength of its consumer-banking business, it earns far less than its rivals from proprietary trading, which Mr. Weill regarded as too volatile and unpredictable.

Now Charles O. Prince, who took over from Mr. Weill as chief executive officer on Oct. 1, is preparing to change course. The trading initiative follows an internal review of the company's equities business by Mr. Prince; Robert E. Rubin, chairman of its executive committee and former Treasury secretary; and others . . .

Mr. Rubin, a former Goldman Sachs co-chairman before he became Treasury secretary, was the head in the 1980s of Goldman's risk-arbitrage department, where he was accustomed to taking big risks when buying and selling securities. He first asked questions about whether Citigroup had gone too far in shunning trading risk when he arrived at Citigroup in 1999.[24]

The aggressive pursuit of higher profits wasn't limited to proprietary trading in the investment bank. In 2002, Sandy Weill's last full year as CEO, Citigroup had a balance sheet amounting to $1.1 trillion. In five years Prince would double it to $2.2 trillion, and that doesn't even count all the risks that Prince accumulated outside the balance sheet, beyond the view of many investors. By the dawn of the financial crisis, Chuck Prince's Citigroup had more than $1 trillion of off-balance sheet exposures—he was maintaining an opaque second bank as big as the real one he had taken over from Sandy Weill!

Dimon and Weill are the two principal figures in Citi's recent history who proved their ability to manage risks through up and down markets. Both obviously came from the Travelers side of the house, not from John Reed's commercial bank. But Prince had also come from the Travelers side and he failed at risk management. His patron Weill shares part of this failure. So where does that leave the debate about Main Street v. Wall Street?

It certainly seems like an odd coincidence that Chuck Prince, a career lawyer, ended up running the giant bank just a few years after John Reed, the "banker who never made a loan." Imagine for a moment that in 2003 there was no government backstop for Citi and nobody considered it too big to fail. This also requires one to assume that the bank could have survived the Wriston and Reed eras without any government assistance. Is there any plausible scenario—if investors and creditors knew that all of their money really was at risk every day—that they would have tolerated the idea of placing the country's largest and most complicated financial institution in the hands of a man with little experience managing financial institutions? Just to complete the picture, we should note that most of the members of Citi's board in 2003 were from fields *outside* of banking and finance, so the guidance they could offer had its limits.

Prince had the skills to deal with bank regulators, and given the pressure various governments were applying to Weill, perhaps it's understandable that he came to view this as a key criterion in choosing his successor. But why would bank creditors accept this—unless they weren't particularly concerned about the possibility that Citi could fail?

Under Prince the bank didn't just get bigger; it was taking on proportionally more risk. In Weill's last full year as CEO, total shareholder equity was equal to almost 8 percent of total assets— not nearly Moses Taylor levels but well above the Wriston/Reed heyday of thin capital. By 2007 it had fallen below 6 percent—and of course many of the assets were now off–balance sheet. So while Prince's Citigroup appeared to be operating with little room for error, in actuality it was operating with even less. And the assets were getting riskier. For example, at its CitiFinancial unit, the share of subprime loans went from 10 percent of total first mortgages in 2005 to 19 percent in 2007, relying heavily on bulk purchases of loans from correspondent banks. By late 2007, Citigroup acknowledged $55 billion in subprime exposure.[25]

In analyzing the disasters of 2008, many observers have described the dangers of particular types of financial instruments, particularly credit derivatives such as credit-default-swaps, in which sellers offer a form of insurance if a particular bond issuer defaults. Others have emphasized the securities known as collateralized debt obligations (CDOs), which were essentially bonds composed of different slices of other bond issues, often backed by assets such as mortgages. Much of the coverage of the crisis has therefore focused on the swaps and securities traded in the capital markets, and this had led many to the false impression that the problems were all on Wall Street.

The Citi example clearly shows that the troubles were spread across the organization, including the allegedly safer commercial bank. Yes, Citi's CDO desk triggered billions of dollars in losses, and yes, Prince would later tell the federal Financial Crisis Inquiry Commission that neither he nor Rubin knew the details of mortgage-related securities that contributed to the firm's catastrophe.[26]

Furthermore, Citi essentially invented structured investment vehicles in 1988 and was the market leader in managing these vehicles for conducting business off–balance sheet. The result was more debt to fund speculative investments but without the capital regulators and investors demand if it appears on the balance sheet.[27]

But less exotic instruments originating in the commercial bank also helped create the financial dumpster fire at Citi. The bank was a leader in extending credit to heavily indebted firms.[28] Prince was talking about this so-called leveraged lending market before the financial crisis when he described to the *Financial Times* the competitive pressures to keep lending despite the risks. His words would become infamous during the financial panic: "When the music stops, in terms of liquidity, things will be complicated. But as long as the music is playing, you've got to get up and dance. We're still dancing."[29] During later testimony before the Financial Crisis Inquiry Commission, he suggested that if Citi had refused to lend, another bank would have simply taken its place: "It was not credible for one institution to unilaterally back away from this leveraged lending business."[30]

Consumer banking, the business that John Reed spent so much of his early career building, was also taking on more risk. It is difficult to distinguish which of these loans came from the consumer banking components of Reed's Citicorp or the consumer finance components of Weill's financial empire, but the successor organization pursued various forms of high-risk lending, according to regulators.[31]

Also, even in the business of selling CDO securities, it turned out that huge risk-taking occurred in Citi's commercial bank, not just its investment bank. To persuade investors to buy short-term CDO debt, it was often Citibank—the highly regulated taxpayer-insured commercial bank within Citigroup—that offered "liquidity puts" guaranteeing investors they could sell the paper back to Citi if the market for such paper dried up. Over three years from 2003 to 2006, Citi wrote liquidity puts on $25 billion worth of commercial paper issued by CDOs. Citi's internal models estimated that there was only a remote chance that the liquidity puts would ever be triggered, but as it turned out, the entire $25 billion was called upon. In the summer of 2007 lots of risky assets that had been sold to outside investors started flooding back on to Citigroup's balance sheet.

That year brought a series of nasty surprises for Citi shareholders who had not realized just how much risk their company had taken on during the housing boom of the mid-2000s. By November of 2007, the firm's subprime exposure was publicly announced at $55 billion, a full $42 billion more than Citi had told investors just three weeks earlier. The SEC charged Citigroup with misleading investors and the firm ultimately paid a $75 million penalty to settle the charges.[32] In December of 2007, the bank brought another $49 billion of assets on to its balance sheet from structured investment vehicles that shareholders probably hadn't figured they would need to stand behind either.[33]

Citi's periods of instability dating back to the 1820s had always involved a breakdown of bread-and-butter commercial banking activities. Was 2008 any different? In her memoir on the financial crisis FDIC chairman Sheila Bair described the sources of losses, and readers will note that both Main Street and Wall Street are well represented. Citi seems to have erred in almost every way of extending credit, from the most simple to the most complex:

> Citi had not had a profitable quarter since the second quarter of 2007. Its losses were not attributable to uncontrollable "market conditions"; they were attributable to weak management, high levels of leverage, and excessive risk taking. It had major losses driven by their exposures to a virtual hit list of high-risk lending: subprime mortgages, "Alt-A" mortgages, "designer" credit cards, leveraged loans, and poorly underwritten commercial real estate. It had loaded up on exotic CDOs and auction-rate

securities. It was taking losses on credit default swaps entered
into with weak counterparties . . . If you wanted to make a de-
finitive list of all the bad practices that had led to the crisis, all
you had to do was look at Citi's financial strategies.[34]

But which area of the giant firm caused the most trouble?
Regulators couldn't really tell. According to an internal FDIC
memo: "The deficiencies in Board and management oversight are
magnified by the institution's inadequate information technology
infrastructure."[35] Ms. Bair wrote: "[C]itigroup's management information systems were so poor that we really couldn't be certain
which operations were in the bank, and thus subject to the FDIC's
powers and which were outside the bank, and thus beyond our
reach." She later emailed Fed chairman Bernanke: "Can't get the
info we need. The place is in disarray. How can we guarantee
anything if citi can't even identify the assets?" In Ben Bernanke's
separate tome, he complained that "Citi was maddeningly slow in
responding to our requests for information, further reducing our
confidence in the company's management."[36]

An internal 2009 FDIC memo obtained by the authors under
the Freedom of Information Act shows that many of Citi's problems occurred in the regulated commercial bank. Interestingly,
it doesn't even mention credit-default swaps, which inspired so
much commentary during and after the crisis:

> The bank's control structure and risk management practices
> have been criticized at prior examinations as they do not pro-
> vide sufficient information on material exposures and fail to
> serve as an effective check on significant risk-taking. The board
> and senior management's inability to address these shortfalls has
> led to the creation of outsized risk positions, as evidenced by the
> high level of credit concentration risks and market disruption
> effects (i.e., losses).

- Structured Investment Vehicles (SIVs): [Citibank, N.A.] SIVs had total assets of over $100 billion in July 2007. [Citibank, N.A.] has taken write-downs of $3.3 billion on SIVs. In November 2008, [Citibank, N.A.] purchased the remaining $17 billion of mostly illiquid trading account assets in the SIVs.
- Leveraged Finance Commitments: Citigroup's exposure to leveraged finance commitments was $57 billion in September 2007. Citigroup has taken write-downs of $5 billion on these commitments, with [Citibank, N.A.] taking $4 billion of these write-downs.
- Subprime-Related Direct Exposures (Asset-Backed Securities Collateralized Debt Obligations and Lending and Structuring Exposures): Citigroup's exposure to subprime-related direct exposures was $55 billion in September 2007. Citigroup has taken write-downs of $30.8 billion on these exposures with [Citibank, N.A.] taking $19.2 billion of these write-downs.
- Consumer Loans: [similar details to the other categories for balances on consumer loans are redacted].[37]

It's not easy to pinpoint the source of all Citigroup's troubles from the disclosures it filed with the Securities and Exchange Commission. That's because Citi reported many of its losses under a broad category called "Securities and Banking." Still, Citigroup's annual 10-K report for 2008 did provide a revealing chart (see Table 15). By far the greatest damage occurred via direct exposures to subprime assets—nearly two-thirds of the losses during the difficult 2007–2008 period. These losses mainly flowed from credit-related assets that are typical for a commercial bank, with the embedded losses driven by the steep decline in housing prices from 2007 to 2009. This is also the case for so-called Alt-A mortgage securities (pools of high-risk loans, often featuring incomplete documentation of borrowers' assets or income) and commercial real estate exposure. The remaining categories would either be predominantly investment banking activities or hybrids of commercial and investment banking.[38]

Table 15: Breakdown of Losses for 2008 and 2007, Citi Securities and Banking Business

Securities and Banking Business	2008	2007
Subprime-related direct exposures, including CDOs	-$14.3 billion	-$18.3 billion
Monoline insurers credit valuation adjustment (CVA)	-$5.7 billion	-$1.0 billion
Highly leveraged loans and financing commitments	-$4.9 billion	-$1.5 billion
Alt-A mortgage securities	-$3.8 billion	—
Auction rate securities	-$1.7 billion	—
Commercial real estate	-$2.6 billion	—
Structured investment vehicles	-$3.3 billion	—
CVA on Citi liabilities	$4.6 billion	$0.9 billion
TOTAL	**-$31.8 billion**	**-$19.9 billion**

Source: Citigroup's 2008 Annual Report on Form 10-K, 10.

In other segments the commercial bank also hemorrhaged red ink. Massive losses of nearly $27 billion were taken in the consumer sector.[39] Beyond these losses directly identifiable with traditional commercial bank credit, Citibank, the commercial bank subsidiary, was weak enough for the FDIC to consider placing it under its bankruptcy-like receivership process.[40] If the commercial banking activities were so safe, then Citibank would never have been the focus of talk about receivership.

Anyone claiming that the real problem was a "Salomon Brothers sort of culture" across the Citigroup holding company must also reckon with the fact that the merger and the end of Glass-Steagall didn't end bank regulation. By many measures, regulation actually increased. And of course the bank's history before the merger has a lot in common with what followed. As one long-time employee observed: "Citi regularly loses its shirt in real estate every 20 years or so."

20

The Man Who Knew Too Little

The last three months of 2007 marked the first of five straight losing quarters for Citigroup. Over the entire period, the firm would record $28 billion in losses. Looking at all the ways Citi found to lose money—from the simplest commercial bank lending to the most exotic Wall Street derivatives—one might naturally conclude that the problem was the collapse of the housing market, rather than any particular type of financial instrument. This is certainly a reasonable diagnosis for the financial crisis in general. Plenty of firms can make the case that they were caught in a perfect storm of misguided federal credit policy. But the bank at the center of our story and its regulators still have to explain why Citi was in the worst shape of the major banks, and would eventually receive the largest of the bank bailouts. At least one top regulator involved in the banking rescues of 2008 and 2009 even wonders if *any* bailouts would have occurred if Citi had not been so poorly managed.

The housing bubble of the mid-2000s was a bipartisan creation decades in the making. Politicians and regulators for years had been

encouraging more housing risk at the Government-Sponsored Enterprises (GSEs) Fannie Mae and Freddie Mac, created by Washington to facilitate investment in mortgage debt. Washington
also created myriad other programs to encourage borrowing for
homeownership, from Federal Housing Administration loans for
first-time buyers to the mortgage-interest tax deduction. Bank
regulators set capital rules and other regulations that required
banks to follow the judgments of government-anointed credit ratings agencies. When these ratings agencies slapped triple-A grades
on bonds backed by risky mortgages, financial institutions were
rewarded for buying them. The Federal Reserve added more fuel
to the housing bonfire in the early 2000s by keeping interest rates
artificially low, a further subsidy for credit.

Washington's basic deal with big finance was that institutions
would loan lots of money to borrowers that politicians viewed
as deserving and in return the institutions were allowed to run
with high leverage, and enjoy explicit or implicit guarantees that
taxpayers would be there to break their fall if they ever got into
trouble.

On top of all the federal incentives to invest in housing, at the
biggest financial house of all there was a more specific oversight
problem. Citi had helped engineer the hiring of one of its chief
regulators, and he knew even less about managing a financial institution than Chuck Prince did. Much like Prince, who had initially seemed to be in shock at the suggestion that he was qualified
to run Citigroup, Timothy Geithner seems to have thought it was
a joke when he was asked to serve as president of the Federal Reserve Bank of New York:

My first reaction was to laugh, and ask: "How much do you
know about me?" I gently pointed out that it seemed a bit early
in my career for that job.[1]

He had a point. Geithner had spent a few years at the Treasury and at the International Monetary Fund learning how to use taxpayer dollars to save big institutions from the consequences of their mistakes during international financial crises. But no one had ever ascended to the presidency of the New York Fed—the top regulator in the world's financial capital—with such a thin résumé. As Geithner admits in his memoir, he arrived on the job in 2003 with an unconventional background and little ability or inclination to challenge the likes of Fed chairman Alan Greenspan:

> I was only forty-two, and I had never worked in the finance industry.
>
> I felt intimidated by how much I had to learn. The Fed played a central role in responding to financial crises, and although I may have already been "baptized by fire" . . . this job came with a much greater level of responsibility.
>
> And I didn't have much experience with the rest of the Fed's work. I had never supervised or regulated banks or markets.
>
> I hadn't thought much about monetary policy, either; I doubted I could offer much help on that front to Greenspan, who was regarded at the time as a monetary maestro.[2]

Greenspan could have used some help. He was holding real interest rates extremely low and for a time even negative—meaning below the level of inflation. In other words, some savers were paying borrowers for the privilege of lending them money. The maestro was making it not just historically cheap but almost irresistible to borrow. In this way, he managed to conjure a housing boom after the dot-com stock bust of 2000, the carnage of 9/11, and a series of corporate accounting scandals. The economy grew very slowly in 2001 and 2002, but easy money from the Fed helped change that. By the mid-2000s, the housing mania drove US homeownership rates to historic highs. Washington regulators cheered as lenders met increasingly aggressive federal goals for "affordable housing" by extending more and more loans on easier terms, even to "subprime" borrowers with shaky credit who in other eras would not have qualified for loans.

The Federal Reserve's Federal Open Market Committee, which sets interest rates, could have used a dissenting voice. But Mr. Geithner was learning on the job about monetary policy. And as for the other half of his job—overseeing giant bank holding companies like Citigroup that were based in New York—he would likely have found this assignment challenging even if he *had* understood bank regulation.

That's because Citigroup director Robert Rubin was not just Geithner's former boss at the Treasury, but his professional patron as well. Along with Larry Summers, who had also led the Treasury during the Clinton administration, Rubin had advocated on Geithner's behalf for the New York Fed job. Ben Bernanke, who would chair the Fed during the crisis years, writes fondly of Geithner in his memoir but suggests that support from the "heavy hitters" including Rubin and Summers was Geithner's principal qualification at the time of his hiring, since he lacked academic credentials, relevant experience, and a record of achievement.[3]

Geithner would later admit in his own memoir that despite some red flags at the megabank he was supposed to be overseeing, he was reluctant to conclude that his sponsor's bank was a problem. "Bob Rubin's presence at Citi surely tempered my skepticism," writes Geithner. "Even though he had no management responsibility or authority, he sat on the board, and he probably gave Citi an undeserved aura of competence in my mind."[4]

Speaking of a nice paycheck, vaguely defined responsibilities, and a political pedigree, former Clinton official and Rubin protégé Jack Lew would join Citigroup in 2006. He would eventually serve as chief operating officer of a Citi alternative investments unit that imploded during the financial crisis. After that, Messrs. Geithner and Lew would take turns serving as Treasury secretary during the Obama administration. Despite what the Citi org chart had said, Mr. Lew maintained at his Senate confirmation hearing that he knew little about the mortgage meltdowns that occurred on his watch at Citi. This may have been true. A former colleague who worked down the hall from Mr. Lew tells us that Citi employees struggled to figure out what exactly he was doing at the bank.

Is it a mere coincidence that the most politically connected of US banks, which had benefited from federal assistance on numerous occasions in its recent history, would also be the biggest beneficiary of federal help during the financial crisis of 2008?

By now it will likely come as no surprise to readers of our story that before the crisis, the New York Fed boss did not fully appreciate the rising risks at Citigroup. Geithner recalls, "Citi wasn't as well capitalized as we thought—partly because a very small share of its capital was common equity, the strongest bulwark against future losses, partly because we vastly underestimated the riskiness of its AAA-rated mortgage assets."[5] But in his memoir, Geithner does admit that there had been reasons for concern:

> Our supervisors always considered [Citi] a laggard in risk management, unwilling to imagine ugly states of the world, unsure how to evaluate exposures across its far-flung businesses. These weaknesses were troubling, but the firm did not appear nearly as vulnerable as many other institutions, certainly not compared to the investment banks, the GSEs, or other non-banks that didn't have insured deposits and didn't have to hold as much capital.[6]

This statement is particularly troubling because it reveals that even years later Geithner still lacked a basic understanding of capital and financial regulation. In fact, before the crisis, federal regulators had approved for the holding companies of investment banks the same capital standards that applied to bank holding companies like Citi. Both types of firms were encouraged to load up on highly rated mortgage-backed securities while holding very little capital for a rainy day. And of course the lowest capital standards of all occur when regulators like Geithner allow banks like Citi to hide assets. Geithner explains:

> By 2007, Citi's $2 trillion balance sheet was much riskier than it looked. And Citi had stashed another $1.2 trillion in assets off its balance sheet in ways that allowed it to hold virtually no capital against losses in those assets. Citi didn't expect funding for these off-balance-sheet vehicles to dry up, because of the same delusions that made risky securities seem safe to investors and rating agencies. They didn't understand how quickly losses could boomerang back onto its balance sheet, and neither did we.[7]

Geithner is perhaps to be commended for acknowledging how little he knew about finance, monetary policy, and the giant bank he was supposed to be regulating. But it's puzzling why he nevertheless expresses certainty about the consequences of letting Citi fail, right down to predicting the precise level of resulting joblessness. Geithner recalls that the "world was fragile, and they really were so big, that if we didn't want a reprise of the Depression—an obliterated banking sector, 25 percent unemployment, thousands of businesses shuttered—we had to make sure they didn't drag down the system, even if it looked like we were rewarding the reckless."[8]

How would he know what conditions would lead to a replication of the Great Depression? Geithner certainly could and did consult Citi's other regulators, but it's not clear how much help they could offer. While Geithner and his New York Fed staff oversaw the entirety of the Citigroup financial supermarket, the Office of the Comptroller of the Currency was still responsible for Citibank, the federally insured depository inside. This is the same job the regulator has held since the 1860s, though the name and structure of the bank have changed over time.

John Dugan did not become the Comptroller until 2005, so it's hardly fair to blame him for the inflation of the housing bubble, which by then was approaching its height. To his credit, Dugan did immediately begin warning about reckless lending practices in residential and commercial real estate. It's harder to find evidence of concrete action by Dugan to reform Citi or protect taxpayers. Dugan has not written a memoir. He's maintained a relatively low profile like all his predecessors who oversaw Citi during its periods of instability, from the early 1920s (John Skelton Williams) to the early 1930s (John W. Pole) to the early 1980s (C. Todd Conover) to the early 1990s (Robert Clarke). After leaving government in 2010, Dugan returned to his former law firm of Covington & Burling, coincidentally the same firm that represented Charlie Mitchell during his grilling by Ferdinand Pecora.

In 2012 Dugan gave a speech at George Washington University Law School and shared his belief that "the OCC's supervision of Citibank, especially once the crisis began, was successful in achieving the agency's core supervisory goal of avoiding financial panic."[9] Let's review the history:

Scott Waterhouse, a veteran of more than twenty-five years in the Comptroller's office, was the head examiner for Citibank from 2002 through October 2007. He later told the Financial Crisis Inquiry Commission that he had "a team of 40 to 50 examiners there interfacing with the bank."[10] And of course these were not the only regulators keeping an eye on Citigroup, as the New York Fed and various other federal regulators were also overseeing all or parts of the firm. Waterhouse and his team were supposed to be laser-focused on Citibank, the insured depository. Yet Waterhouse testified that he didn't know that the $25 billion in CDO "liquidity puts" that triggered the ousting of Citi CEO Chuck Prince even existed. He seems to have found out about them shortly be-

fore the rest of the world did in late 2007.[11] Speaking of bad news
and the rest of the world, it was in late November of 2007 that
Citi accepted what some consider its first government bailout of
the 2000s crisis. But the rescue didn't come from our government.
Rather, weeks after Citi announced billions of dollars of unexpected subprime-mortgage-related losses, the sovereign wealth
fund of Abu Dhabi came through with $7.5 billion to buy con-
vertible Citi shares paying 11 percent annually.

Back in the US, if extensive regulatory oversight hadn't been
able to prevent a crisis, perhaps Washington connections could
help Citi weather it. After Prince resigned, the retired Sandy Weill
told Geithner he wanted to propose him as the new CEO. For
anyone familiar with Citi's history, it was reminiscent of the time
the bank had hired regulator H. E. Henneman just as it was starting to suffer problems in Cuba and Russia after World War I.
Geithner declined the offer from Weill.[12]

The bank hired hedge-fund operator Vikram Pandit instead.
And if regulators were shocked to learn in November of 2007
about the problems they'd overlooked at Citi, that didn't necessarily mean they wanted to act on them. The Comptroller's office sent
Citi a letter on February 14, 2008, detailing the bank's weaknesses
in corporate governance, risk management, CDO valuation, and
overreliance on credit agency ratings.[13] But it gave no hint that any
enforcement action was imminent.

It wasn't until April 15, 2008, that the New York Fed hand
delivered a letter along with its examination report for year-end
2007 to the Citigroup board of directors. This letter did warn
of impending enforcement action, but otherwise didn't express
much of a sense of urgency for an institution that would be recognized as insolvent within seven months.[14] While the New York
Fed noted some deficiencies at the bank, the regulator gave Citigroup a rating of three on its one-to-five scale.[15] Regulators would
maintain this rating even as the bank received a series of taxpayer

bailouts, in part on the ludicrous theory that government support gave it additional strength. By that logic, every too-big-to-fail bank should enjoy a good rating from regulators because taxpayers always stand ready to help.

When they finally acted, both the New York Fed and the Comptroller's office chose to apply one of the weakest possible enforcement options. Both regulators settled for informal memoranda of understanding (MOU) that were not even legally enforceable. The boards of Citigroup and its Citibank subsidiary made voluntary commitments to try to address problem areas. And to this day the public is not allowed to see them. Although it has been ten years since the institutions were placed under these agreements, the agencies remain unwilling to disclose the details. The authors pursued requests under the Freedom of Information Act (FOIA), but these requests were quickly and unequivocally denied.[16] It's the same story with memoranda for Citigroup and Citibank from the early 1990s. The justification for preventing access to such documents is the need to encourage candid communication between banks and their examiners.[17] Some aspects of the 2008 agreements have been described in other government reports since the crisis, but their full details remain secret.

Bart Dzivi served as special counsel for the Financial Crisis Inquiry Commission, which was responsible under law for investigating the underlying causes of the 2008 panic. He characterizes the approach of relying on a memorandum of understanding for enforcement as part of the New York Fed's "culture of secrecy that pervades their supervision."[18]

While the public can guess, former FDIC chairman Sheila Bair has written that "virtually no meaningful supervisory measures had been taken against the bank" by either regulator. "A smaller bank with those types of problems would have been subject to a supervisory order to take immediate corrective action, and it would have been put on the troubled-bank list." Instead, she adds,

the New York Fed and the Comptroller's office "stood by as that
sick bank continued to pay major dividends and pretended that it
was healthy."[19] Not for the first time in its history, the megabank
and its regulators would work together to ensure that the public
did not learn the extent of Citi's problems.

When Bair describes a "supervisory order," she likely meant a
formal cease and desist order. This involves a formal filing with
a court and can be enforced if the financial institution does not
comply.[20] Why didn't regulators want to impose discipline? After the crisis, the New York Fed would commission a confidential study of bank supervision. A portion was publicly released by
the Financial Crisis Inquiry Commission and provides still more
evidence that the regulatory capture described by Stigler was a
constant problem. The study found that examiners "paid excessive deference to banks and as a result they were less aggressive in
finding issues or in following up on them in a forceful way." One
regulator told the study authors: "Within three weeks on the job,
I saw the capture set in."[21]

Having been largely unaware of the risks accumulating at Citigroup under Chuck Prince, federal regulators might have been especially wary to avoid capture by his successor. But in still another
episode validating Stigler's Nobel prize, government overseers immediately embraced the new management team and opted for perhaps the most gentle treatment available for the bank. Later, staff
of the Financial Crisis Inquiry Commission asked Steve Manzari
of the New York Fed why regulators didn't impose a more severe penalty on Citi in the spring of 2008. Manzari responded
by lauding Citi management for its "very aggressive" effort to fix
the bank's problems. As for the disasters that followed he opined:
"I believe Citi was trapped in what was a pretty vicious financial
system, a systemic event."[22]

The New York Fed study of its oversight failures later found that
"relationship managers [like Manzari] were too deferential to bank

management." Of course the narrative that Citi was "trapped" by circumstances beyond anyone's control also conveniently absolves regulators of responsibility.[23]

Within a few months of allowing Citi to get away without a penalty in 2008, regulators amazingly allowed the sick too-big-to-fail bank to pursue a plan to get even bigger. Since they were hiding Citi's problems from the public, bank executives and their regulators may have thought they could mask them better if Citi merged with another lender. Normally, bank regulators do not allow institutions with serious weaknesses in governance and operations to pursue any type of acquisition. They don't want struggling managements to take on additional complex burdens and possibly create even bigger problems for themselves and the taxpayers who ultimately stand behind the FDIC deposit insurance fund. The policy of limiting mergers among weak institutions is spelled out in the Change in Bank Control Act, and its decision criteria requires consideration of the stability of the institution.[24]

Yet Geithner seems to have spent much of 2008 trying to merge Citi with one financial institution or another. Andrew Ross Sorkin reports that some CEOs became so annoyed at how forcefully Geithner was pressing various proposed corporate marriages that they gave him the nickname "eHarmony."[25]

In September 2008, Washington Mutual was a large and troubled $300 billion institution on the West Coast. It was experiencing a run on its deposits, and its primary supervisor, the Treasury's Office of Thrift Supervision, and the FDIC were both putting pressure on WaMu to raise capital or find a white knight to take it over.[26] Citigroup was assuming WaMu would be taken over by the government and placed into receivership.[27]

Citi made its bid in a September 24, 2008, letter to the FDIC. The letter described a loss sharing proposal, whereby the FDIC would protect Citigroup against some potential losses after a takeover. The government rejected the proposal, took over WaMu—

making it the largest bank failure in US history—and sold its assets to JPMorgan Chase. Jamie Dimon's healthy bank paid $1.9 billion and took on WaMu's loan portfolio, with the resolution imposing no cost on the FDIC or uninsured depositors.[28]

"Some are coming to Washington for help, others are coming to Washington to help," observed Bair.[29] Dimon had become the James Stillman of the 2008 crisis. But what about his former employer Citigroup? Were they looking at potential mergers as opportunities to get camouflaged bailouts from Washington? Before WaMu was resolved, Bair had "questioned whether Citi was financially strong enough to acquire WaMu, but both the Fed and the [Office of the Comptroller of the Currency]—its two primary regulators—said it was strong enough."[30]

Within a few days, Citi was considering acquisition of an even larger target, Wachovia, which was the fourth-largest bank in the United States. Unlike WaMu, which was a savings association under the supervision of the Treasury's Office of Thrift Supervision, Wachovia was a national bank supervised by the Comptroller. As late as the end of June 2008, it was judged to be in the same condition as Citibank, with a rating of three on the one-to-five scale. Wachovia's underlying capital and liquidity components were actually a strong two rating at that time, at least according to its regulators. Also like Citi, Wachovia was placed under a secret memorandum of understanding with the government in August 2008. Within a matter of weeks, Wachovia experienced a run of $30 billion.[31]

Bair says she was kept in the dark about Wachovia's condition and that the Comptroller's office and the Thrift Supervision staff at Treasury "were reluctant to downgrade their larger institutions. Downgrading a bank was, to some extent, an acknowledgement of weakness in the examination program. Ideally, if examiners were on their toes, they would intervene and take measures to stabilize a bank before it ever reached troubled status." She says the

Comptroller's office in particular "was not giving us information that truly reflected the severity of problems at two of its biggest banks, Citi and Wachovia."[32]

Severe as the problems at both banks might have been, Sorkin reports that "Geithner had always liked the idea of merging Citi-group and Wachovia."[33] Geithner for his part writes: "None of us were completely comfortable with it. Citi and Wachovia both had problems, and I knew their merger raised classic two-drunks-in-a-ditch issues."[34] They could drag each other down, and of course it would have made the too-big-to-fail fear even more acute. If the idea of a Citi failure alone panics regulators, how would their blood pressure respond to an even larger institution going down?

Perhaps Geithner realized that not everybody would imme-diately welcome the partnership. Bair says that he "was pushing an FDIC-assisted transaction for Citi to acquire Wachovia" but neither Citi nor Geithner's New York Fed had let the FDIC in on the fact that it would be expected to provide a "ring fence" around troubled assets, essentially insuring the new firm against the cost of some defaults. Bair recalls: "The proposal sounded to me like a 'twofer'—a bailout for Wachovia and a bailout for Citi. I was astounded."[35]

The FDIC board ultimately approved the bailout. Bair put up a fight but, in her words, "acquiesced."[36] The approval was made moot by a voluntary merger of Wachovia with Wells Fargo with-out all of the FDIC assistance sought by Citi.

But before long, Citi would once again be receiving govern-ment assistance—lots of it.

"Save Citigroup at All Costs"

Many Americans may remember the fall of 2008 as a chaotic and frightening series of teetering dominoes—huge financial firms that had bet too much on the housing market. Many Americans may also recall experiencing a tremendous anger as the government rescued one stumbling giant after another. In September, Washington bailed out the government-created mortgage investors Fannie Mae and Freddie Mac. Then the feds rescued the insurance titan AIG, effectively a bailout of all the Wall Street firms to which AIG owed money. Among the great financial houses, only Lehman Brothers was allowed to fail.

But the Lehman moment of market discipline didn't last long. The government then came to the rescue of money market mutual funds and issuers of commercial paper. By early October, President George W. Bush had signed the Emergency Economic Stabilization Act into law, creating the $700 billion Troubled Asset Relief Program. Roughly ten days later, financial regulators began spending this pot of rescue money, announcing direct investments in America's largest banks. But was there one bank in particular that had regulators scared enough to engage in such radical interventions in the economy?

In the fall of 2008, few people in America had access to more information about the health of American financial institutions than FDIC chairman Sheila Bair. Four years later, she looked back on that season of crisis and wrote: "I frequently wonder whether, if Citi had not been in trouble, we would have had those massive bailout programs. So many decisions were made through the prism of that one institution's needs."[1]

Roughly eighty years after Senator Carter Glass blamed City Bank's Charlie Mitchell for the great crash of 1929, another prominent federal official was suggesting the same bank may have been responsible for the historic taxpayer-backed rescues of 2008. But Bair's case was stronger. She was not drawing a grand conclusion about the financial economy, but rather providing an eyewitness account and exploring the discrete question of how she and her fellow regulators came to approve historic interventions.

On Monday, October 13, 2008, Bair, Geithner, Bernanke, and Treasury Secretary Hank Paulson gathered the heads of America's banking giants at the Treasury building in Washington. The regulators told the bankers that their firms were all going to accept government capital investments and also enroll in a temporary FDIC program guaranteeing their debts.

The regulators also told the assembled bankers how much the government would invest in each of their firms: $25 billion each in Citigroup, JPMorgan Chase, and Wells Fargo; $15 billion in Bank of America; $10 billion each in Merrill Lynch, Goldman Sachs, and Morgan Stanley; $3 billion in Bank of New York; and $2 billion in State Street.

The idea was to invest in all the major firms regardless of their health so as not to stigmatize those most in need of capital. But at least one banker, Wells Fargo CEO Richard Kovacevich, didn't want the federal government as a shareholder and said his bank didn't need the money. Under pressure from his regulators, he eventually relented. On the other end of the long table, Citigroup's Vikram Pandit quickly embraced the idea of "cheap capital." Recalls Bair, "Treasury was asking for only a 5% dividend. For Citi, of course, that was cheap; no private investor was likely to invest in Pandit's bank."[2]

When news of these federal capital injections hit the markets, stocks rallied. Along with the money came assurance from regulators that the big banks were all healthy and that the new capital was simply to allow them to lend more to Main Street consumers and businesses in need of credit. But after the initial market euphoria, investors started selling stocks on the theory that the US economy must really be in awful shape if it needed so much help from Washington. This is always the danger when government seeks to restore confidence in markets. How can anyone be confident in a market that requires so much assistance? As in every other sphere of human activity, genuine respect must be earned.

Competitors like Jamie Dimon's JPMorgan Chase enjoyed such respect. But at Citi, it turned out that $25 billion in new taxpayer capital wasn't nearly enough to earn the respect of investors and corporate depositors. On Thursday, October 16, 2008, just three days after Pandit and the other bankers had learned that Uncle Sam was their new shareholder, Citigroup released its quarterly earnings report. It was not pretty.

Revenues had plunged 23 percent. Citi posted a $2.8 billion quarterly loss, its fourth straight. The news was bad on both Main Street and Wall Street. The company announced a $4.4 billion write-down in its "Securities and Banking" segment, and the consumer business around the world was struggling. The *Wall Street Journal* reported: "Citigroup is facing soaring defaults on its giant global portfolios of mortgages and credit-card loans, which dragged its consumer-banking and cards divisions to a combined third-quarter net loss of nearly $2 billion. The trouble isn't confined to the U.S.; Citigroup reported rising defaults in the U.K., Spain, Greece, Mexico, Brazil, Japan and India. Even corporate loans are souring at an increasing clip."[3]

Just days after receiving a huge slug of cheap capital, Citi was in trouble again. By November 19, "its stock price had dropped precipitously. In the view of Secretary Paulson, the company was teetering on the brink of failure. The company's survival was in doubt," according to a 2011 report from the government's inspector general for the Troubled Asset Relief Program.[4]

Preventing such moments from occurring was of course the job of the Federal Reserve and the Office of the Comptroller of the Currency. The Fed—specifically Geithner's Federal Reserve Bank of New York—was supposed to watch over the whole Citigroup enterprise, while Comptroller Dugan's team was supposed to monitor Citibank, the federally insured commercial bank subsidiary inside. But on-site examinations and off-site surveillance by teams of regulators had not succeeded in averting disaster. As for Sheila Bair's FDIC, its main job was regulating smaller institutions, but it also maintains the deposit insurance fund of tens of billions of dollars to address failing institutions of any size. Since even its large checkbook could potentially be overwhelmed by the failure of a giant institution—which would then create the embarrassing need for the FDIC to call on taxpayer assistance—the agency is always wary of being on the hook for the enormous firms where it is not the primary regulator. In banking circles, the old joke is that the agency's initials stand for Forever Demanding Increased Capital. Senior officials at the FDIC have often hoped for a larger capital buffer at banking giants like Citi. Unfortunately, those seeking a safer regulatory system are regularly disappointed.

As FDIC chairman, Bair also found it annoying that her fellow regulators were constantly thinking up ways to use her agency's checkbook or its guarantees to bolster stumbling giants. It's not that she was opposed to government intervention. Bair also favored rescuing people from the consequences of their bad credit decisions. It's just that she preferred rescues of the individuals who borrowed too much rather than the bankers who lent too much.

Also, like every other regulator, she wasn't eager to try to manage the failure of a giant like Citi. The FDIC has never seized such a large institution. And Bair hadn't seized too many smaller ones, either. Appointed FDIC chairman by President George W. Bush in 2006, she had briefly served at the Department of the Treasury as assistant secretary for financial institutions and had earlier been head of government relations at the New York Stock Exchange, a regulator of futures trading and a Senate staffer. Her policy work was concentrated more in securities and commodities than in banking. As for her prior experience with the FDIC, in her memoir Bair explains that she "had worked with the agency during my Treasury days and had also served on an advisory committee it had set up on banking policy," but admits that "I didn't have a lot of personal experience with bank failures."[5]

To her credit, she recognized quickly during the crisis that a federal decision to avoid such a failure by staging a bailout often occurred without substantive deliberation. She writes that the "unfairness" and "the lack of hard analysis showing the necessity of it trouble me to this day. The mere fact that a bunch of large financial institutions is going to lose money does not a systemic event make. And the rationale—to keep them lending—didn't meet expectations."[6]

Citi was losing money, all right, which in most other industries and even for most other banks would mean failure. But Citi plays by a different set of rules. An official at Geithner's New York Fed would later tell the inspector general for the TARP program that the consensus among regulators was that they had to "save Citigroup at all costs" to stabilize the US financial system.[7]

At the time, Citi's Pandit maintained that the bank had enough

capital but was suffering from a tough environment and a perception problem among investors. This argument largely rests on
the fact that at the time the firm was generally sound by the metrics that big banks and regulators had agreed to use in affirming
the health of such institutions. But the crisis proved those metrics
were not reliable measures of financial strength. Big banks and
regulators had essentially agreed that giant firms can safely operate with heavy leverage while betting big on mortgage-backed
securities. Sometimes they can't. It should also be noted that
when regulators conducted a "stress test" on Citi in early 2009,
they concluded the firm needed more than $5 billion in addi-
tional capital, which prompted still another bailout, but let's not
get ahead of ourselves.

However much capital Citi needed, if a bank lacks credibility—
and it's the job of the bank to maintain the trust of market
participants—it cannot survive absent federal assistance. In November of 2008 investors were selling Citigroup stock. It also became increasingly expensive to insure against the risk of a Citi
default by purchasing credit-default swaps. Treasury Secretary
Paulson was concerned that depositors "might start a run on Citigroup," according to the IG's report.[8]

On the morning of Thursday, November 20, 2008, Paulson and
Geithner held a conference call with Bernanke, Bair, and Dugan.
Bernanke told the inspector general they discussed Citigroup's
condition and the too-big-to-fail issue. During the call, Geithner
said, "We've told the world we're not going to let any of our major
institutions fail. We are going to have to make it really clear we're
standing behind Citigroup." According to Chairman Bernanke, it
was "not even a close call to assist them."[9]

At the FDIC, they seem to have been among the last to know
about the severity of the bank's troubles. As late as that Thursday
evening, a report distributed among senior FDIC management
noted challenges, but not a crisis:

Supervisory Perspective: Citigroup and its subsidiary banks have been under enhanced monitoring by FDIC dedicated examiners since the current financial crisis began. Given the recent deterioration in Citigroup's stock price and CDS spreads and the considerable amount of negative inquiries from investors, the region is marshalling additional resources to assist in the risk assessment of the institution, including the use of examination specialists from the Large Bank Section.

Potential Impact on FDIC Insurance and Resolutions Missions: No immediate impact on the Resolution Mission.[10]

A subsequent email circulated that night among senior FDIC managers reported that some wealthy clients had withdrawn funds from Citi and a few hedge funds had reduced their trading with the giant financial house. The Union Bank of Switzerland had also reduced its exposure to the firm, but most big institutions were still willing to trade with Citi, as far as regulators could tell. "However, the considerable amount of inquiries from investors about Citi's viability is a major cause for concern," the FDIC's Mark Richardson wrote.[11]

Overnight, Citigroup's Global Transaction Services unit, which manages cash, facilitates trade, and executes payments for large organizations worldwide, experienced a $14 billion decline in available funds (about 5 percent of the total). On Friday, there were "significant corporate withdrawals (i.e., a run), primarily in the U.S. and secondarily in Europe," according to the inspector general.[12]

That same day, the United Kingdom's Financial Services Authority, which at the time was the regulator of British securities markets, imposed a $6.4 billion cash lockup requirement to protect the interests of Citigroup's brokerage in the UK. It wasn't this regulator's job to keep Citigroup's global financial empire afloat; the agency was charged with ensuring that the brokerage accounts of British customers remained whole. To say the least, the lockup was not a sign of confidence in Citi's viability, and if this regulatory action were repeated elsewhere and applied to other Citi units it would likely take down the entire firm. When a financial company is stumbling toward the edge of a cliff, each regulator tries to secure money for whichever group of consumers they're supposed to be protecting, and this is exactly what was happening at Citi. Back in the US, an FDIC staffer emailed Chairman Bair that foreign governments "are beginning to grab cash/ring fence . . . The FSA is going to look at Citi's UK banks on Monday and may require lockups for them."[13]

The Office of the Comptroller of the Currency and Citigroup guessed that Citibank would be unable to pay obligations or meet expected deposit outflows over the ensuing week. Citigroup's own internal analysis projected that "the firm will be insolvent by Wednesday, November 26."[14] And if there was one group as nervous as the bank's investors and customers it was the bureaucrats who were about to be called upon to manage its failure. As ever, the latest crisis in the banking sector caught many regulators by surprise. FDIC staff did a seat-of-the-pants calculation and estimated the agency's potential exposure to Citibank to be in the range of $60 billion to $120 billion. Even at the low end of that estimated range, losses would "exhaust the $34 billion or so in the [Deposit Insurance Fund]" according to an internal FDIC email on Saturday, November 22.[15]

As time went by, some at the FDIC doubted that the range of exposure was that high given that Citi had largely funded itself with sources other than US-insured deposits. But even at the high end of their initial guess, it would hardly have strained the finances of the federal government to honor its promise to depositors. And of course the government ended up exposing taxpayers to far greater potential losses by extending the safety net to cover people and assets that Washington had *never* promised to insure.

As for the impact on the markets of a Citi failure, the FDIC seems to have accepted Geithner's forecast of catastrophe. Bair later told the IG: "We were told by the New York Fed that problems would occur in the global markets if Citi were to fail. We didn't have our own information to verify this statement, so I didn't want to dispute that with them."[16] Bair initially resisted the idea of a taxpayer rescue but ultimately joined the other financial regulators in the bailout consensus. Writes Bair: "I finally acquiesced. We were all fearful of what would happen to an uncontrolled failure of Citigroup."[17] Treasury, the Fed, and the FDIC announced their new plan to save the firm on November 23, 2008.[18] Treasury would invest another $20 billion in exchange for Citi preferred stock paying an 8 percent dividend. Also, along with the FDIC, Treasury would create a federal safety net under many of Citi's most risky assets.

An internal FDIC document described the arrangement: "To prevent the firm's collapse, Citi management has proposed a guarantee program where more opaque assets are ring-fenced with unexpected losses covered by the U.S. government." The core of this aspect of the bailout was the segregation of a pool of about $300 billion of Citi's most questionable loans and investments. Citigroup would be responsible for the first $37 billion of any losses from this pool, and the government would absorb any additional losses. But because Citi's information systems were so bad, the government couldn't tell exactly what it was insuring. According to an internal FDIC document: "Given the difficulty Citi is having in describing the specific assets within the $300B pool, what is covered by the guarantee will need to be more clearly defined."[19]

However it was defined, the November bailout still wasn't enough to keep Citi standing. By early 2009, the newly installed Treasury Secretary Timothy Geithner was floating a new plan to split the firm into one healthy bank and one sick bank, the latter saddled with the most troubled assets. Recalls Bair:

I was surprised when Tim started reaching out to me directly on the possibility of doing a good-bank/bad-bank structure for Citi. Initially, he raised the idea of the FDIC setting up and funding a bad-bank, without imposing any loss absorption on shareholders and bondholders. I was flabbergasted. Why in the world would the FDIC take all the losses and let Citi's private stakeholders take all of the upside with the good bank? During the second meeting, we discussed a proposal to have [Citi] share-holders help absorb losses . . . That was a nonstarter for Tim. He wanted the FDIC to take a hit . . . It was unbelievable to me how little Treasury was asking of the institution to right itself.[20]

By this point it was getting difficult to keep track of all the ways the federal government was helping the banking giant. We should add that government funding did not begin in the fall of 2008. By the end of 2007, Citigroup already owed $87 billion to the Federal Home Loan Banks, a system of government-sponsored enterprises that provides funding to support housing finance and "community investment."[21] Starting in January 2008, lending from the Federal Reserve began in earnest with $4.5 billion in mid-January rising to $72 billion by the end of the year.[22] The FDIC debt guaran-tee program (TLGP) was tagged onto the other funding sources in mid-October 2008, and Citibank and Citigroup quickly began ramping up their available balances by November.[23] By late Oc-tober, the first $25 billion of TARP funding made its way to Citi, followed by another $20 billion of TARP funding weeks later. Hundreds of billions of asset guarantees also came online after Citi's November rescue.

An internal FDIC document reveals the extent and sources of federal support, which at its peak added up to more than half a trillion dollars (see Table 16). To put this amount in perspective, the market capitalization of Citi at the end of January 2009 was less than $20 billion.[24] So the Fed, the FDIC, the Treasury, and the FHLB—and by extension US taxpayers—had twenty-five times the exposure of the bank's shareholders!

Table 16: Citigroup–US Government Support as of January 31, 2009

Program	Amount ($s in billions)
Fed Commercial Paper Funding Facility (CPFF)	$25.0
Fed Term Auction Facility (TAF)	$25.0
Fed Primary Dealer Credit Facility (PDCF)	$13.0
Fed Term Securities Lending Facility (TSLF)	$40.9
FDIC Guaranteed Term Debt (TLGP)	$13.8
FDIC Guaranteed Commercial Paper (TLGP)	$40.0
Troubled Assets Recover Program (TARP)	$45.0
Federal Home Loan Bank (FHLB)	$79.6
Asset Guarantee Program (Treasury $5 billion; FDIC $10 billion; Fed $220 billion)	$235.0
TOTAL	**$517.3**

Source: FDIC, "[Redacted] Memorandum Rating [Redacted] Comments," undated memo, but likely from February or March 2009, 3. Document 1 obtained as part of *Vern McKinley v. FDIC,* no. 15-cv-1764 (KBJ).[25]

Typically opaque about its operations, the Fed tried to avoid releasing the details of how much it extended to Citi and other institutions throughout the crisis, but Bloomberg and Fox News fought for disclosure in a battle that went all the way to the Supreme Court.[26] The justices declined to reverse the appeals court rulings in favor of the news organizations, and the Fed was compelled to release this data on their lending in March 2011.[27]

It is often said that the Reconstruction Finance Corporation of the 1930s was the inspiration for the 2008 TARP program: direct capital injections by the government to bolster the financial position of banks and restore confidence in a system in crisis.[28] In both cases, Citi was unsurpassed among banks in the amount of government investment. During the Depression, the RFC approved injecting up to $50 million into National City Bank, putting the firm at the top of bank recipients along with Chase and Continental Illinois. During 2008 and 2009 Citi was again at the top of the list of bank recipients of TARP aid.[29] After the bailouts of October and November, Citi would essentially receive still another bailout in 2009 when the government converted its preferred shares to common stock to spare Citi from having to pay a hefty dividend and to improve its capital ratios.

How much did Citi need all the help? Recall that in a letter to National City shareholders during the Depression the new president of the bank, James Perkins, cast the acceptance of RFC funding as a patriotic gesture to renew economic confidence. In announcing the October 2008 capital injections into the major banks, Treasury Secretary Paulson read from the same script:

> These are healthy institutions, and they have taken this step of accepting taxpayer money for the good of the U.S. economy.

Maybe JPMorgan Chase and Wells Fargo were healthy, but Citi? Elizabeth Warren—before she became Senator Warren—chaired a congressional oversight panel that examined TARP spending. At a 2010 hearing she questioned Secretary Paulson's assessment:

> CHAIR WARREN: I'd like to start this morning with Treasury's
> role in overseeing TARP, generally and overseeing Citi,
> in particular. On October 14th, 2008, Secretary Paulson
> announced the creation of the Capital Purchase Program
> and the infusion of cash into nine financial institutions,
> including Citi, and under the program he announced—
> these are the words he used—"These are healthy
> institutions, and they have taken this step of accepting

taxpayer money for the good of the U.S. economy. As these
healthy institutions increase their capital base, they will
be able to increase their funding to U.S. consumers and
businesses." On October 28, under that program, Citi got
$25 billion and was pronounced a "healthy institution."

And yet, on November 23rd, which I think is about
three weeks and four days later, the Secretary of the
Treasury said that Citi was—Citi and Citi alone—was in
such dire straits that it would need an additional $20 billion,
and that was, then, followed by . . . guarantees. What I
want to understand is, how we describe Citi as a "healthy
institution;" what does "healthy" mean now that it didn't
mean on October 14, 2008?

It fell to Herb Allison, then the assistant Treasury secretary for
financial stability, to respond:

MR. ALLISON: Thank you, Chair Warren, for your question.
Again, as you know, the Treasury does not make comments
about the financial health of any particular institutions. In
having the funds repaid—
CHAIR WARREN: I'm sorry, I was quoting the Secretary of
the Treasury on the health of Citi and other financial
institutions
MR. ALLISON: I think at the time that was an extreme situation.
I'm not going to comment or second-guess what the
Secretary of the Treasury at that time had to say.
CHAIR WARREN: So, your position is that we declared it a
healthy institution, and now we take no position on the
financial health of Citi?
MR. ALLISON: It's not our policy to comment on whether any
institution presents a systemic risk or on its particular health.[30]

The half-a-trillion-dollar bailout was a method of bypassing the system of FDIC insurance and resolution of failing institutions. For banks, the framework is relatively simple. Banks pay premiums, the FDIC invests the proceeds, and depositors are compensated for their insured deposits up to a certain amount if the bank fails ($100,000 before the crisis, $250,000 today). With a risk-based system of premiums, banks are punished for taking on higher levels of risk, just as a smoker will likely pay higher premiums for life insurance.[31]

If a bank fails outright, it is placed under receivership and goes out of business. In most cases the assets are sold and the liabilities (including some or all the deposits) are taken on by a third party, usually another bank. Shareholders usually lose everything and depositors above $250,000 and other creditors usually don't get all their money back. Old management of the bank generally gets the boot.

For large or complex banks, a special institution called a "bridge" is created, which, as the name implies, is temporarily controlled by the government to bridge the time while the FDIC evaluates and markets the institution. By 2008, the FDIC had over twenty years of experience with bridge institutions, a reform that arose out of the Continental Illinois bailout and the challenge of resolving the 1980s megabank.[32]

The risk-based premiums and limited coverage, combined with the threat of being shut down, was thought to impose at least some discipline on institutions, even if not as rigorous as pure market discipline. But when the government opted to bail out Citi, uninsured depositors and other creditors were made whole, shareholders maintained at least some value, and the bank continued to operate, even though it should rightly have gone out of business.

Before federal officials threw out the rule book to stage a rescue, Sheila Bair had been willing to at least consider letting Citigroup fail:

As our discussions about how to best stabilize Citi began, I took the position that we should at least consider the feasibility of putting Citibank, Citigroup's insured national bank subsidiary, through our bankruptcy-like receivership process. That would have enabled us to create a good-bank/bad-bank structure, leaving the bad assets in the bad bank, with losses absorbed by its shareholders and unsecured creditors.[33]

The authors wanted to explore this idea further, so more Freedom of Information Act requests were filed and litigation initiated. The FDIC found more than one hundred pages of relevant documents, but fought disclosure for three years.[34] We can only speculate what form the receivership might have taken, but it would probably have involved some type of bridge entity that would have been used to market and sell the various pieces of Citi.

In a typical receivership, the FDIC tries to immediately transfer as much of the assets and liabilities to an interested bank as it can. Whatever assets remain are sold over time so the FDIC, the depositors above the FDIC insurance limit and nondeposit creditors can be repaid. If no banks are interested in the failing bank, the FDIC puts up the funding to cover all the insured depositors and then the FDIC and other creditors get paid back over time as the FDIC sells all of the assets. The FDIC is at risk of losing a large share of the funds it sends out the door. But according to Chairman Bair, in the case of Citibank it turned out that this risk wasn't as large as some might have feared:

[Citi] had a highly unstable funding base; much of its funding came from deposits overseas, which were not covered by strong deposit insurance guarantees similar to those provided by the FDIC. It had very little in the way of domestic deposits that we insured so our direct exposure to it was quite small. Funding its U.S. assets with foreign deposits kept its deposit insurance premiums low.[35]

Is the US government the whole world's insurer against financial loss? Some of Citi's foreign deposits were likely the result of products offered to corporate clients and relatively affluent consumers through Citigold, a banking and wealth management subsidiary that catered to the rich and near-rich.[36] All these depositors were bailed out by US taxpayers.

Because the foreign depositors were at risk and might pull their deposits and cause a run on Citi, this seems to have been treated as another argument in favor of a Washington rescue. Bair recalls:

> To [Paulson and Geithner] pretty much anything that was big and in trouble was systemic and if it was systemic, that meant it was entitled to boatloads of government money and guarantees. The whole tenor of the conversation was that the government owed it to Citi to get it out of trouble. As Hank said in his book, "If they go down, it's our fault."[37]

The argument for intervention should have not only included an explanation of the alleged bad consequences of letting Citi fail, but also an analysis showing that a bridge entity would not have worked. Paulson's argument for intervention was a conclusory statement: "If Citi isn't systemic, I don't know what is."[38] Geithner, the man who has admitted he didn't know the field he was regulating, once again expressed certainty about the impact of allowing a giant business to fail: "The system couldn't have handled the sudden collapse of a $2 trillion institution that provided much of the world's financial plumbing."[39] Fed chairman Bernanke said that "a Citigroup failure had the potential to block access to ATMs and halt the issuing of paychecks by many companies and governments."[40]

But after the crisis passed, when the inspector general reviewed the record he couldn't find much analysis supporting such forecasts of financial Armageddon:

> [T]he conclusion of the various Government actors that Citigroup had to be saved was strikingly ad hoc. While there was consensus that Citigroup was too systemically significant to be allowed to fail, that consensus appeared to be based as much on gut instinct and fear of the unknown as on objective criteria.[41]

Bair certainly wasn't able to pry out of the New York Fed a coherent and detailed explanation of why the financial markets needed a Citi rescue. "To this day, I wonder if we overreacted," she writes.[42] Bernanke, Geithner, and Paulson have maintained that the financial bailouts were necessary and saved the country and the world from catastrophe. But Citi is not a bank that anyone involved in the federal response likes to discuss.

Banking regulators like to talk about problems with "shadow banking," meaning the parts of the financial world that they don't control. Citi, on the other hand, is a 2008 disaster that they have to own. It was America's biggest and most prominent bank, overseen by teams of regulators from multiple federal agencies. Its DC lobbying shop was highly influential, and its top management included people with deep Washington relationships. Just as at the very start of the institution in the early 1800s, Citi in 2008 was arguably America's most political bank.

At one point during the crisis, Bair says she realized that she had underestimated the New York Fed and the Treasury's "determination to make Citi look healthier than it was. They wanted to bolster its ability to compete against the better-managed banks."[43] In his own memoir, Bernanke insists that Citi had to be rescued but acknowledges: "I did agree with Sheila that Citi was being saved from the consequences of its own poor decisions."[44]

Shouldn't somebody have gone through the formality of a substantive explanation for why America couldn't live without a firm
that seemed so deserving of failure? In March of 2011, Citigroup
chairman Dick Parsons painted a dire picture for Bloomberg of
life without a Citi bailout:

"You would go home in a cab, swipe your credit card, and
it wouldn't go through," Parsons says. "You wouldn't be able to
buy a loaf of bread or clear a check. It would be like Egypt. People
would be out in the streets." Parsons had a chummy relationship with the Treasury secretary. "Timmy Geithner would say,
'Call me directly, because this is too important an institution to
go down,'" Parsons says. According to the Treasury secretary's
schedule, available online, Geithner spoke frequently with Parsons
in 2009. The Citigroup chairman also got along well with Dugan,
whom he calls a "good guy."[45]

Mike Mayo, a longtime Wall Street bank analyst who has done
perhaps as much analysis of Citigroup as anyone, asks: "Can that
really be true? Citigroup's continued existence is the only thing
separating the United States and Egypt?"[46] As big as it is, the bank
only holds about 5 percent of US bank deposits.

What is particularly odd is that many of the same regulators who
considered the institution not just important but indispensable to
the economy simultaneously believed that it was not even a well-
run bank. In February of 2009, the *Wall Street Journal* reported:

> Former federal officials have dubbed Citigroup the "Death
> Star," comparing the bank's threat to the financial system with
> the planet-destroying super weapon in the "Star Wars" movies.
> Privately, in the words of one official, they regard the banking
> giant as "unmanageable."[47]

The *Journal* added that some people inside the bank also weren't
exactly impressed:

In a recent meeting with investment bankers, Citigroup's investment-banking chief, John Havens, was pushing his deputies to further streamline operations in order to reduce costs. One executive asked whether the changes needed to be made quickly. The question "is typical Citi," Mr. Havens replied, suggesting that decisions at the company take too long, according to a person at the meeting. "That's why Geithner is so intolerant with us these days," Mr. Havens told the bankers.

Now, gallows humor is setting in. This week, some employees noted that they always thought that working for Citigroup—with its unwieldy bureaucracy and clashing fiefdoms—was like working for the government anyway.[48]

Citi had certainly been working under a lot of government oversight. Bart Dzivi, special counsel to the Financial Crisis Inquiry Commission, studied the regulatory response to Citi's deteriorating condition. Dzivi summarized supervision by the Office of the Comptroller of the Currency as "light touch" and New York Fed oversight as "no touch." He adds that "there were indications in 2004 and 2005 of building problems," but regulators lacked the will to address them.[49]

When the crisis finally struck, hundreds of smaller institutions were shut down.[50] But just as in the 1920s, 1930s, 1980s, and 1990s, the government made sure in 2008 and 2009 that Citi enjoyed the money and/or the regulatory forbearance necessary to survive. Bair advocated giving the same deal to all struggling banks: "I suggested that we at least set up a facility that would be generally available to all banks to purchase their troubled assets and liquidate them over time. I was tired of the attempts to provide special help to Citi." Bair adds that for both the Comptroller's office and the New York Fed, the bank had long been the "premier" institution under their supervision and they didn't dare let Citi fail:

It had a huge international presence, and as such its failure would be not just a domestic, but an international embarrassment for those two regulators. What's more, Tim Geithner's mentor and hero, Bob Rubin, had served as chairman of the organization and . . . had had a big hand in steering it toward the high-risk lending and investment strategies that had led to its downfall.[51]

This determination to protect the bank led to the absurd situation in which the Comptroller's office refused to give Citi a failing grade on the CAMELS system used to evaluate banks. As it was being saved from failure over and over again by the government, the taxpayer assistance became the justification for arguing that the bank was relatively healthy. By this standard, of course, no bank could ever receive poor grades as long as regulators were willing to favor it.[52]

No less absurd was the fact that within five years, the chief operating officer of one of the troubled Citi units that contributed to the firm's struggles would become secretary of the US Treasury. Former Citigroup executive Jack Lew took office in 2013. Coincidentally, he succeeded Timothy Geithner, who had been the chief regulator responsible for overseeing the bank during its years of crisis.

Epilogue

n December of 2009, Citigroup repaid the government $20 billion and tore up the guarantees it had received for its risky assets. "We owe the American taxpayers a debt of gratitude," said CEO Vikram Pandit.

The following year, the Treasury sold the rest of its Citi stake and claimed a profit on the deal, though it had also granted Citi the ability to reduce its tax bills for years to come by deducting much of its crisis-era losses.

As it has done several times in the last one hundred years, the bank followed an era of crisis and government support with a period of retrenchment and caution. In the years following the 2008 crisis, Citigroup took direction from Washington and became a somewhat smaller, less complex, and safer firm. Mr. Pandit eventually gave way as CEO to Michael Corbat, a longtime Citi veteran who is by most accounts a competent executive who understands the business. Reassuringly for taxpayers, he seems more interested in operating a solid firm than in pursuing a grand vision or rapid growth. At least that's how things appear to investors and regulators.

After the recent era of limited ambitions, will Citi eventually ride another boom and bust and ultimately require another federal rescue? And if so, will the next crisis be small enough—and will Washington's finances be strong enough—to manage?

Nobody knows for sure, but taxpayers may get a little nervous when they see announcements like the one Citigroup issued in the summer of 2017. The bank decided it had too much capital and set out a plan to return some of it to shareholders.

It's also worth noting that in October of 2017, Citigroup added a new director to its board: former Comptroller of the Currency John Dugan.

Some things never change.

Acknowledgments

At one point we considered calling this book *House of Pain*. We thought it might describe a bank during moments of crisis but also our households during the research and drafting of this work. We'll be forever grateful for the support of our families while we labored to finish.

We should also thank a few people outside of our households. We received immeasurable help from Tab Lewis and Thomas McAnear, who shared their deep institutional knowledge about the documents available at the National Archives facility in College Park, Maryland. Their assistance was in stark contrast to those at a number of agencies who zealously sought to slam the door on disclosure of federal documents. Thanks to Michael Bekesha at Judicial Watch for helping to open it a crack with his knowledge of the Freedom of Information Act.

Thanks also to Arthur Wilmarth of the George Washington University Law School who shared his research and made himself available to discuss the storied history of 1920s and 1930s universal banking. He also facilitated our access to documents and books available through the George Washington University Library System, and we are grateful to the library for advice and guidance. We also appreciate access provided by the Princeton University Library to the papers of Paul Volcker and by the New York Public

Library to the papers of Moses Taylor. The views presented in this book are those of the authors.

We also thank those authors whose work we relied upon to assemble this history. We benefited greatly from reading various works by Charles Calomiris, George Selgin, and John Taylor and also thank them for their encouragement and kind words.

Monica Langley's *Tearing Down the Walls* is a model of great reporting and great writing. Philip Zweig's *Wriston* is a huge contribution to the history of postwar finance. We also enjoyed Nomi Prins's provocative *All the President's Bankers*. Looking back in history, while we may question decisions made by Frank Vanderlip as a banker, there's no questioning the value of his fascinating autobiography. And we could not have told the story of Moses Taylor without leaning on the efforts of Daniel Hodas.

As for contemporary sources, Sheila Bair's *Bull by the Horns* is both important and compelling. A recent book about a time long ago, *America's First Great Depression* by Alasdair Roberts, was invaluable in understanding the Panic of 1837 and its aftermath.

Chip Dickson generously shared his library and his contacts to assist our understanding of the modern Citigroup. Thanks also to the many Citi alums who shared their insights on background.

Reading both archival and contemporary coverage by the financial reporters at the *Wall Street Journal* was of immense help, and editors like David Reilly also offered further explanation at the coffee machine. Any misunderstandings or errors belong solely to the authors. Over on the editorial page of the *Journal*, we thank Paul Gigot for the opportunities he has afforded us to research and report this story.

We owe a debt of thanks to Judith McCarthy Walsh, Erich Eichman, and Robert Messenger for their invaluable advice on the world of book publishing.

The authors are also deeply grateful to Brian Murray, Hollis Heimbouch, Eric Meyers, Rebecca Raskin, Leslie Cohen, Theresa

Dooley, and the entire team at HarperCollins for their support, their patience, and their good cheer.

Finally, thanks to Rich McKinley, who reprised the role he has played many times, of reading drafts of material too rough to show anyone else and gently offering thoughtful comments. Rest in peace, brother.

Notes

INTRODUCTION

1. Monica Langley and David Enrich, "USA Inc.: Citigroup Chafes Under U.S. Overseers," *Wall Street Journal*, Feb. 25, 2009.

I: A BANK FOR THE TREASURY SECRETARY

1. Some consider the Bank of North America, which was the first bank chartered in the US, to also be the first central bank in the US. For further information, see Lawrence Lewis Jr., *A History of the Bank of North America: The First Bank Chartered in the United States* (Philadelphia: J. B. Lippincott & Company, 1882), https://archive.org/stream/cu31924032535753#page/n49/mode/2up.

2. The Avalon Project, "Jefferson's Opinion on the Constitutionality of a National Bank: 1791." http://avalon.law.yale.edu/18th_century/bank-tj.asp citing Ford, Paul Leicester, *The Federalist: A Commentary on the Constitution of the United States* by Alexander Hamilton, James Madison, and John Jay edited with notes, illustrative documents, and a copious index by Paul Leicester Ford (New York: Henry Holt and Company, 1898).

3. Walter Dellinger and H. Jefferson Powell, "The Constitutionality of the Bank Bill: The Attorney General's First Constitutional Law Opinions," *Duke Law Journal* 44 (1994): 127 [Hereinafter "Constitutionality of the Bank Bill"].

4. John Thom Holdsworth and Davis R. Dewey for the National Monetary Commission, "The First and Second Banks of the United States," 61st Congress, 2nd Session, 29, 36–40 [Hereinafter National Monetary Commission Report].

5. Federal Reserve Bank of Philadelphia, "The First Bank of the United States: A Chapter in the History of Central Banking" (2009), 2–3 [Hereinafter "First Bank of the United States"], http://philadelphiafed.org

/publications/economic-education/first-bank.pdf. "Chapter X: An Act to incorporate the subscribers to the Bank of the United States," 1st Congress, 3rd Session, February 25, 1791, https://fraser.stlouisfed.org/docs/histori cal/congressional/first-bank-united-states.pdf. The three state-chartered banks at the time were the Bank of North America, the Bank of New York, and the Bank of Massachusetts.

6. Forrest McDonald, *Alexander Hamilton: A Biography* (New York: W. W. Norton & Company, 1979), 193.

7. Thomas K. McCraw, *The Founders and Finance* (Cambridge, MA: Harvard University Press, 2012), 113 [Hereinafter referenced as McCraw].

8. Ibid.

9. Ibid.

10. "The Constitutionality of the Bank Bill," 131.

11. Statute III, Chapter X, Preamble, "An Act to incorporate the subscribers to the Bank of the United States," February 25, 1791 (". . . will tend to give facility to the obtaining of loans, for the use of the government, in sudden emergencies"); Richard H. Timberlake, *The Origins of Central Banking in the United States* (Cambridge, MA: Harvard University Press, 1978), 8–14 [hereinafter, *Origins of Central Banking*]; Richard H. Timberlake, *Monetary Policy in the United States* (Chicago: University of Chicago Press, 1978), 4.

12. McCraw, 111.

13. Ibid., 121.

14. National Monetary Commission Report, 36–40. One indicator of the size of the New York branch of the Bank of the United States is the capital level at the parent and branches: Philadelphia, $4.7 million; New York, $1.8 million; Boston, $0.7 million; Baltimore, $0.6 million; and Charleston, $0.6 million.

15. "First Bank of the United States," 4, 9.

16. James O. Wettereau, "The Branches of the First Bank of the United States," *Journal of Economic History* 2 (December 1942): 99.

2: WHEN FAILURE WAS ALLOWED
(BECAUSE GOVERNMENT WASN'T BIG ENOUGH TO HELP)

1. J. C. A. Stagg, *The War of 1812: Conflict for a Continent* (Cambridge, UK: Cambridge University Press, 2012), 53 [Hereinafter Stagg].

2. Citigroup, *Celebrating the Past, Defining the Future* (Citigroup Inc., 2011), 24 [Hereinafter *Celebrating the Past*].

3. National City Bank of New York, *A Short History of the National City Bank of New York Together with a Description of the Building* (New York: National City Bank, 1915), 15; Harold van B. Cleveland and Thomas F. Huertas, *Citibank 1812–1970* (Cambridge, MA: Harvard University Press, 1985), 8 [Hereinafter *Citibank 1812–1970*].

4. *Citibank 1812–1970*, 5–6; James O. Wettereau, "The Branches of the First Bank of the United States," *Journal of Economic History* 2 (December 1942): 66.

5. Eric C. Breitenstein and John M. McGee, "Brick-and-Mortar Banking Remains Prevalent in an Increasingly Virtual World," *FDIC Quarterly* 9, no. 1, 44, https://www.fdic.gov/bank/analytical/quarterly/2015-vol9-1/fdic-4q2014-v9n1-brickandmortar.pdf.

6. Stagg, 54.

7. Ibid., 55.

8. Donald R. Hickey, *The War of 1812: A Forgotten Conflict* (Champaign, IL: University of Illinois Press, 1989), 171.

9. Stagg, 18–21.

10. Ibid., 53–54.

11. Ibid., 58.

12. Ibid., 56.

13. Ibid., 57.

14. McCraw, 302.

15. Ibid.

16. Ibid.

17. TreasuryDirect, "Historical Debt Outstanding, Annual 1790–1849," https://www.treasurydirect.gov/govt/reports/pd/histdebt/histdebt_histo1.htm.

18. *Citibank 1812–1970*, 10.

19. *Celebrating the Past*, 31.

20. Ibid., 31.

21. Office of the Comptroller of the Currency, Examiners Report of Condition, April 12, 1872, Charles A. Meigs, Examiner, 1-2.

22. *Celebrating the Past*, 26.

23. Ibid., 26.

24. *Citibank 1812–1970*, 10.

25. History of the Federal Reserve, "Chapter 1: Early Experiments in Central Banking," Federal Reserve Bank of Boston (1999): 9, https://www.bostonfed.org/about/pubs/historical-beginnings/chapter1.pdf.

26. The authors were not able to uncover any documentation of any loans or discounts extended to City Bank at the National Archives and Records Administration (NARA) or the Library of Congress (LOC). NARA has documents housed in Record Group 53, which are from the New York branch of the Second Bank of the United States. However, they are limited to ledger books whereby stockholders of the bank acknowledged receipt of dividends. The LOC has records for the Second Bank of the United States, but they are only for the Baltimore branch, not the New York branch.

27. *Celebrating the Past*, 26.

28. Robert E. Wright, Richard Sylla, and Charles M. Royce, *Genealogy of*

American Finance (New York: Columbia Business School Publishing, 2015), 101; *Citibank 1812–1970*, 11, 13.

3: CITY OF INSTABILITY

1. *Citibank 1812–1970*, 12–14, 319.
2. Ibid., 14.
3. Alasdair Roberts, *America's First Great Depression: Economic Crisis and Political Disorder after the Panic of 1837* (Ithaca, NY: Cornell University Press, 2012) [Hereinafter Roberts].
4. Milton Friedman and Anna Jacobson Schwartz, *A Monetary History of the United States, 1867–1960* (Princeton, NJ: Princeton University Press, 1963), 299 [Hereinafter *A Monetary History of the United States*].
5. Roberts, 14.
6. Daniel Walker Howe, *What Hath God Wrought: The Transformation of America, 1815–1848* (Oxford, UK: Oxford University Press, 2007), 505 [Hereinafter Howe].
7. Daniel Shuchman, "When America Paid Its Debts," *Wall Street Journal*, January 22, 2015.
8. Arthur J. Rolnick, Bruce D. Smith, and Warren E. Weber, "The Suffolk Bank and the Panic of 1837," *Federal Reserve Bank of Minneapolis Quarterly Review*, April 1, 2000 [Hereinafter Rolnick, Smith, and Weber].
9. Roberts, 28.
10. Ibid.
11. Ibid.
12. Ibid.
13. Ibid., 29.
14. Fergus Bordewich, "When Labor Was Capital," *Wall Street Journal*, September 6, 2014.
15. Roberts, 32.
16. Ibid., 32.
17. Howe, 503.
18. Roberts, 31.
19. Ibid., 36–42.
20. Rolnick, Smith, and Weber, 4.
21. W. H. Erle, "Let U.S. be a Debtor but Not a Deadbeat," *Wall Street Journal*, February 27, 1984.
22. *Citibank 1812–1970*, 15.

4: ASTOR TO THE RESCUE

1. *Celebrating the Past*, 32.
2. Cynthia Crossen, "Monopoly Personified," *Wall Street Journal*, March 2,

2001. https://www.wsj.com/articles/SB983491754756358141 [Hereinafter Crossen].

3. Ibid.

4. Kenneth H. Williams, "John Jacob Astor," American National Biography, http://www.anb.org/view/10.1093/anb/9780198606697.001.0001/anb-9780198606697-e-1000054; Axel Madsen, *John Jacob Astor: America's First Multimillionaire* (Hoboken, NJ: John Wiley & Sons, 2001); Alexander Emmerich, *John Jacob Astor and the First American Fortune* (Jefferson, NC: McFarland, 2013); Justin Kaplan, *When the Astors Owned New York* (New York: Penguin Books, 2007); *Citibank 1812–1970*, 15–17.

5. John Steele Gordon, "Don't Bet Against New York," *Wall Street Journal*, September 19, 2009.

6. Daniel Hodas, *The Business Career of Moses Taylor: Merchant, Finance Capitalist, and Industrialist* (Ishi Press International, 2010), 6 [Hereinafter Hodas].

7. Ibid., 3–6.

8. Federal Reserve Bank of Minneapolis CPI Calculator, https://www.minneapolisfed.org/community/teaching-aids/cpi-calculator-information/consumer-price-index-1800

9. Hodas, 10.

10. Ibid., 10.

11. Ibid., 3.

12. Ibid., 4.

13. Ibid., 5.

14. Ibid.

15. Ibid., 40.

16. Papers of Moses Taylor, New York Public Library, Box 209: Taylor personal correspondence, 1837–1849 [Hereinafter Papers of Moses Taylor].

17. Hodas, 5.

18. *Celebrating the Past*, 36.

19. Hodas, 6, 10, 29–30.

20. Ibid., 25.

21. Papers of Moses Taylor, New York Public Library.

22. *Celebrating the Past*, 38.

23. Hodas, 63–74.

24. *Citibank 1812–1970*, 15–23; Hodas, 54–55.

25. John Steele Gordon, "Don't Bet Against New York," *Wall Street Journal*, September 19, 2009.

26. Office of the Comptroller of the Currency, Examiners Report of Condition, April 12, 1872, Charles A. Meigs, Examiner, 3.

27. Hodas, 32.

28. James Grant, *Money of the Mind* [Hereinafter *Money of the Mind*]. (New York: Farrar, Straus & Giroux, 1992), 62. Grant details some of the history

of the conservative lending approach of National City Bank in a chapter appropriately titled "The Timid Bank"; *Citibank 1812–1970,* 25, 28.

29. Hodas, 61.

5: TAYLOR'S BANK IN AN AGE OF PANICS

1. John Steele Gordon, "Don't Bet Against New York," *Wall Street Journal,* September 19, 2009.
2. Hodas, 178–79.
3. Ibid., 180.
4. Office of the Comptroller of the Currency, "A Short History," Revised November 2011, 4, https://www.occ.treas.gov/about/what-we-do/history /OCC%20history%20final.pdf.
5. George Selgin, "New York's Bank: The National Monetary Commission and the Founding of the Fed," Cato Institute Policy Analysis No. 793, June 21, 2016, 4 [Hereinafter Selgin, National Monetary Commision].
6. Federal Reserve Bank of Minneapolis CPI Calulator, https://www .minneapolisfed.org/community/teaching-aids/cpi-calculator-informa tion/consumer-price-index-1800.
7. Charles W. Calomiris, "Thinking Historically about Banking Crises and Bailouts," *Atlanta Fed,* May 12, 2015; John R. Walter, "Depression-Era Bank Failures: The Great Contagion or the Great Shakeout," *Federal Bank of Richmond Economic Quarterly* 91, no. 1 (Winter 2005): 44.
8. Gary Richardson and Tim Sablik, "Banking Panics of the Gilded Age, 1863–1913," Federal Reserve Bank of Richmond: Federal Reserve History, http://www.federalreservehistory.org/Events/DetailView/98.
9. *Money of the Mind,* 62.
10. Office of the Comptroller of the Currency, Examiners Report of Condition, April 12, 1876, Charles A. Meigs, Examiner.
11. *Citibank 1812–1970,* 24–25; Jesse Stiller, "OCC Bank Examination: A Historical Overview," Essays in the History of the National Banking System, August 1995, 1, 4–5.
12. Office of the Comptroller of the Currency, Examiners Report of Condition, April 8, 1868, Charles Callender, Examiner.
13. "Miscellaneous," *New York Herald,* January 14, 1868, 4.
14. "The City Bank Defalcation," *Daily Alta California,* June 7, 1868.
15. OCC examination, April 8, 1868.
16. Office of the Comptroller of the Currency, Examiners Report of Condition, April 12, 1872, Charles A. Meigs, Examiner.
17. *Citibank 1812–1970,* 25, 28–30, 51.
18. John Moody and George Kibbe Turner, "Masters of Capital in America, Wall Street, The City Bank: The Federation of the Great Merchants," 74 [Hereinafter "Masters of Capital"].

19. Office of the Comptroller of the Currency, Examiners Report of Condition, July 1, 1874, Charles A. Meigs, Examiner.

20. Office of the Comptroller of the Currency, Examiners Report of Condition, February 2, 1887, V. P. Snyder, Examiner.

21. *Citibank 1812–1970*, 29.

22. Ibid., 25.

23. Hodas, 272.

24. Ibid., 273.

25. Ibid., 60–61.

26. Ibid., 198.

27. Papers of Moses Taylor, New York Public Library, Box 209: Letters from Taylor, 1847–1879.

28. Ibid.

29. https://www.minneapolisfed.org/community/teaching-aids/cpi-calcu lator-information/consumer-price-index-1800.

30. *Celebrating the Past*, 38.

31. Office of the Comptroller of the Currency, Examiners Report of Condition, January 16, 1882, Charles A. Meigs, Examiner.

32. *Money of the Mind*, 63–64. The quote is drawn from an OCC examiners report, February 24, 1891, A. B. Hepburn, Examiner.

6: THE ROCKEFELLER BANK

1. Ron Chernow, *Titan: The Life of John D. Rockefeller, Sr.* (New York: Vintage, 1998), 375–76.

2. "Masters of Capital," 76.

3. *Citibank 1812–1970*, 35.

4. Ibid., 30. United States Trust Company and Bowery Savings Bank both held assets of over $50 million at the time.

5. Ibid., 32, 306; John K. Winkler, *The First Billion: The Stillmans and National City Bank* (New York: Vanguard Press, 1934), 69 [Hereinafter *The First Billion*]. These sources give conflicting numbers for officers and employees ("two officers, the president and the cashier, and a handful of employees when Stillman took over" [*Citibank 1812–1970*] as compared to "the four officers and 70 employees" [*The First Billion*].)

6. "Masters of Capital," 77.

7. *The First Billion*, 67.

8. Ibid., 69–70.

9. "Masters of Capital," 86.

10. *The First Billion*, 71.

11. Frank A. Vanderlip and Boyden Sparks, *From Farm Boy to Financier* (New York: D. Appleton & Company, 1935), 93 [Hereinafter *From Farm Boy to Financier*].

12. Chernow, 376.

13. "Masters of Capital," 78.

14. Edwin Lefevre, "Captains of Industry: James Stillman," *The Cosmopolitan*, 333–36. This magazine is a predecessor of *Cosmopolitan* magazine, but it was more family-oriented than the modern-day version.

15. *From Farm Boy to Financier*, 111.

16. Lindley H. Clark Jr., "Growing Up: A Maturing Nation Flexes Its Economic Muscles," *Wall Street Journal*, June 23, 1989.

17. Charles R. Geisst, *Wall Street: A History* (Oxford, UK: Oxford University Press, 1997), 109.

18. Benn Steil and Manuel Hinds, *Money, Markets, and Sovereignty* (New Haven, CT: Yale University Press, 2009), 168.

19. "The Silver Act's Cloudy Lining, 1890," *Wall Street Journal*, January 12, 1989.

20. Geisst, 111; "Stocks Derail, and a Panic Ensues, 1893," *Wall Street Journal*, January 18, 1989.

21. *The First Billion*, 74.

22. Ibid., 76.

23. Ibid., 78–79.

24. *Citibank 1812–1970*, 25, 51, 320. The data regarding the extent of the surge varies depending upon the source. The most reliable appears to be call report data reported to the OCC, which shows the following levels of deposits: 1892: $19.7 million; 1893: $25 million; 1894: $43 million. Other sources quote an increase from $12 million in 1891 to $30 million in 1893. *The First Billion*, 73, and another source notes that deposits during 1893 "more than doubled"; Anna Robeson Brown Burr, *The Portrait of a Banker: James Stillman, 1850–1918* (New York: Arno Press, 1975), 87 [Hereinafter Burr].

25. *Citibank 1812–1970*, 36–37, 40–41; *The First Billion*, 96. Total participations throughout the 1890s in the reorganization were as follows: Kuhn, Loeb ($6.54 million), James Stillman ($5.82 million), E. H. Harriman ($3.63 million; Harriman managed Union Pacific), National City Bank ($1.79 million). Some of these transactions raise the possibility of a conflict of interest for Stillman in his individual role and as president of NCB; "Masters of Capital," 82.

26. United States Treasury, "Transactions with Certain National Banks," Letter from the Secretary of the Treasury, In Response to Resolution of the Senate of January 4, 1900, US Senate 56th Congress, 1st Session, Document no. 71, 1, 7, 13.

27. *Citibank 1812–1970*, 48.

28. Burr, 138–139; *Citibank 1812–1970*, 48; *The First Billion*, 109.

29. *Citibank 1812–1970*, 44. A contemporary quote commenting on the merger appears to contradict the possibility of failure, while recognizing its financial difficulties. From Frederick D. Tappen, President of Gallatin National

Bank: "A very good business arrangement. Most excellent. The Third National is solvent, of course, but will go into liquidation. It passes away because it was not a money maker, as bank men put it"; "National Banks Merge: The Third Goes Out of Existence, Its Business Being Taken by the City," *New York Times*, May 21, 1897 [Hereinafter "National Banks Merge"].

30. "National Banks Merge"; "Two Banks Consolidated: National City to Absorb the Third Nationals' Business," *New York Tribune*, May 21, 1897. This article details the balance sheets of both banks and shows that NCB had $48 million and TNB had $14 million in assets as of the date of the merger.

7: A POLITICAL "BIG SHOT"

1. *From Farm Boy to Financier*, 94–95.
2. Ibid., 95
3. Ibid., 96.
4. Ibid., 97.
5. "Jack Lew's Golden Parachute," *Wall Street Journal*, February 25, 2013.
6. *From Farm Boy to Financier*, 20.
7. Ibid., 21–22.
8. Ibid., 27.
9. Ibid., 28.
10. Ibid., 46.
11. Ibid., 52–53.
12. Ibid., 54.
13. Ibid., 45.
14. Ibid., 54.
15. Ibid., 56–57.
16. Ibid., 59.
17. Ibid., 62.
18. Ibid.
19. Ibid., 62–63.
20. Ibid., 63.
21. Ibid., 98.
22. Ibid.
23. Ibid., 102, 103, 107, 116.
24. Ibid., 111.
25. Burr, 212.
26. Burr, 220.
27. Jon Moen and Ellis Tallman, "Close But Not a Central Bank: The New York Clearing House and Issues of Clearing House Loan Certificates," Federal Reserve Bank of Cleveland, Working Paper no. 13–08, 1–2, 4.

28. Burr, 212, 217–22.

29. Ibid., 225.

30. Lester V. Chandler, *Benjamin Strong: Central Banker* (Washington, DC: The Brookings Institution, 1958), 28 [Hereinafter Chandler]; Robert F. Brunner and Sean D. Carr, *The Panic of 1907: Lessons Learned from the Market's Perfect Storm* (Hoboken, NJ: John Wiley and Sons, 2007), 74–76, 84, 91, 93 [Hereinafter *The Panic of 1907*]; Nomi Prins, *All the Presidents' Bankers* (New York: Nation Books, 2014), 10 [Hereinafter Prins]; Richard T. McCulley, *Banks and Politics during the Progressive Era* (Abingdon, UK: Routledge, 1992), 147.

31. Letter from Benjamin Strong to Thomas W. Lamont, 1924, as cited in Chandler, 29.

32. Charles W. Calomiris and Gary Gorton, *U.S. Bank Deregulation in Historical Perspective* (Cambridge, UK: Cambridge University Press, 2000), 150; Elmus Wicker, *Banking Panics of the Gilded Age* (Cambridge, UK: Cambridge University Press, 2000), 87.

8: A CITY BANKER HELPS CREATE THE FED

1. *From Farm Boy to Financier*, 110–11.

2. Ibid., 211.

3. Report of the National Monetary Commission, January 8, 1912, 4.

4. *From Farm Boy to Financier*, 212.

5. James Neal Primm, *A Foregone Conclusion: The Founding of the Federal Reserve Bank of St. Louis* (St. Louis, KY: Federal Reserve Bank of St. Louis, 1989), 15, https://www.stlouisfed.org/~/media/Files/PDFs/A-Foregone-Conclusion.pdf.

6. *From Farm Boy to Financier*, 210.

7. Roger Lowenstein, *America's Bank* (New York: Penguin Books, 2015), 108.

8. *From Farm Boy to Financier*, 213–214.

9. Ibid., 214.

10. Ibid., 215–218. The title of president is in modern times bestowed on this office, which used to be governor.

11. Ibid., 210.

12. Suggested Plan for Monetary Legislation, Submitted by Honorable Nelson W. Aldrich before the National Monetary Commission, 61st Congress, 3rd Session, document 784, January 16, 1911.

13. Bruce W. Hetherington, "Bank Entry and the Low Issue of National Bank Notes: A Re-Examination," *The Journal of Economic History* 50, no. 3 (September 1990): 670, http://www.jstor.org/stable/2122824.

14. Michael D. Bordo and David C. Wheelock, "The Promise and Performance of the Federal Reserve as Lender of Last Resort 1914–1933," in *The Origins, History, and Future of the Federal Reserve*, ed. Michael D. Bordo and

William Roberds (Cambridge, UK: Cambridge University Press, 2013), 61–62 [Hereinafter "Promise and Performance"]; Charles W. Calomiris and Stephen H. Haber, *Fragile by Design: The Political Origins of Banking Crises and Scarce Credit* (Princeton, NJ: Princeton University Press, 2014), 154, 181–85.

15. Selgin, National Monetary Commission, 5.
16. Ibid., 5.
17. "Promise and Performance," 65.
18. Selgin, National Monetary Commission, 18–19.
19. Robert Mayer, "The Origins of the American Banking Empire in Latin America: Frank A. Vanderlip and the National City Bank," *Journal of Inter-American Studies and World Affairs* 15, no. 1 (Feb. 1973): 60, 63 [Hereinafter "American Banking Empire"], 60, 73 (note 4).
20. "American Banking Empire," 63.
21. Use of Ailes was described by Vanderlip in his autobiography as acting as a "resident agent in Washington. In that way any National Bank in the country having some matter that required representation before the comptroller of the currency could, through us, be represented by Mr. Ailes"; *From Farm Boy to Financier*, 117. Another description of the representation referred to Vanderlip instructing his "Washington lobby, led by Milton Ailes of the Riggs National Bank to begin negotiations designed to remove the legal restrictions [on foreign branches]"; "American Banking Empire," 63.
22. William Howard Taft, State of the Union, December 6, 1910. ("AMERICAN BRANCH BANKS ABROAD: I cannot leave this subject without emphasizing the necessity of such legislation as will make possible and convenient the establishment of American banks and branches of American banks in foreign countries. Only by such means can our foreign trade be favorably financed, necessary credits be arranged, and proper avail be made of commercial opportunities in foreign countries, and most especially in Latin America.") http://www.let.rug.nl/usa/presidents/william-howard-taft/state-of-the-union-1910.php.
23. Aldrich Bill, 17.
24. 51ˢᵗ Congress Rec 434 (December 8, 1913). Section 25 in part states that "[a]ny national banking association possessing a capital and surplus of $1,000,000 or more may file application with the Federal Reserve Board, upon such conditions and under such regulations as may be prescribed by said board, for the purpose of securing authority to establish branches in foreign countries or dependencies of the United States for the furtherance of the foreign commerce of the United States, and to act, if required to do so, as fiscal agents of the United States."
25. Ibid.
26. *From Farm Boy to Financier*, 213–214.

27. Ibid., 218.
28. Paul M. Warburg, "The Discount System in Europe," National Monetary Commission, 61st Congress, 2nd Session, Senate Document no. 402, 1910. Warburg ultimately became vice governor of the Federal Reserve Board.
29. Aldrich Bill, 14. ("The Reserve Association may rediscount notes and bills of exchange arising out of commercial transactions, for and with the indorsement of any bank having a deposit with it . . .")
30. For a summary of legislated changes to the Federal Reserve Act, see "Promise and Performance," 91.

9: "OUR FRIENDLY MONSTER" GOES GLOBAL

1. *From Farm Boy to Financier,* 260.
2. "Resolution Plan for Citigroup Inc. and Citibank, N.A., Section 1: Public Section," June 29, 2012, 3. https://www.federalreserve.gov/bankinforeg /resolution-plans/citigroup-1g-20120702.pdf.
3. "American Banking Empire," 63–66.
4. *From Farm Boy to Financier,* 276.
5. *Citibank 1812–1970,* 72.
6. Federal Reserve, Third Annual Report: Covering Operations for the Year 1916, Exhibit K, Foreign Branches Authorized, 147, https://fraser.stlouis fed.org/docs/publications/arfr/1910s/arfr_1916.pdf. *Citibank 1812–1970,* 78; "American Banking Empire," 66–67.
7. *Citibank 1812–1970,* 78–79, 324; "American Banking Empire," 70.
8. J. T. W. Hubbard, *For Each, the Strength of All: A History of Banking in the State of New York* (New York: NYU University Press, 1995), 63–66.
9. *The Panic of 1907,* 197; *Citibank 1812–1970,* 99–101; "American Banking Empire," 71.
10. *From Farm Boy to Financier,* 260.
11. "American Banking Empire," 67–69.
12. *From Farm Boy to Financier,* 285.
13. Ibid., 286.
14. Ibid., 263–266.
15. Ibid., 300.
16. *The Panic of 1907,* 197; *Citibank 1812–1970,* 99–101. The historical book commissioned by Citibank notes with regard to the meeting: "It involved in all probability the question of responsibility for the Russian fiasco"; *From Farm Boy to Financier,* 272–280, in a chapter titled "Trouble with a Rockefeller."
17. Section 21, Federal Reserve Act ("The Comptroller of the Currency, with the approval of the Secretary of the Treasury, shall appoint examiners, who shall examine every member bank at least twice in each calendar year and oftener if considered necessary"), Section 5240 US. Revised Statutes, as amended 1913.

18. Office of the Comptroller of the Currency, Examiners Report of Condition, June 26–29, 1919, H. E. Henneman, Examiner.

19. Ibid.

20. Peter James Hudson, "The National City Bank of New York and Haiti, 1909–1922, *Radical History Review* 115 (Winter 2013): 91, 101.

21. Office of the Comptroller of the Currency, Examiners Report of Condition, June 26–29, 1919, H. E. Henneman, Examiner.

22. Michel Tereshchenko, *The First Oligarch*, intended by Glagoslav Publications as an English translation of the younger Tereshchenko's book in Ukrainian, *Перший олігарх: Михайло Іванович Терещенко*. It was ultimately never published in English. This detail was provided by Max Mendor of Glagoslav Publications.

23. These were the only examinations available as part of the OCC collection at the National Archives, so it is assumed there were no other OCC examinations during 1919.

24. Office of the Comptroller of the Currency, Examiners Report of Condition, February 13, 1920, to March 24, 1920, E-2, Sherrill Smith, Examiner.

25. Ibid.

26. Hubbard, *The Strength of All*, 181.

27. "Economic and Financial Conditions in Cuba, *Federal Reserve Bulletin* (November 1920): 1162–63; *Citibank 1812–1970*, 105–7.

28. James Grant, *The Forgotten Depression, 1921: The Crash That Cured Itself* (New York: Simon and Schuster, 2014) [Hereinafter *The Forgotten Depression*]. Although an agreed-upon definition of recession has been established and implemented by the National Bureau of Economic Research, there is less agreement on what constitutes an economic depression. Unofficially, the most common definition of an economic depression is that it is simply a very long or very deep recession.

29. The National Bureau of Economic Research, "US Business Cycle Expansions and Contractions," http://nber.org/cycles/cyclesmain.html.

30. *The Forgotten Depression*, 67–68.

31. Office of the Comptroller of the Currency, Stenographic Transcript, Meeting with National City Bank, February 22, 1921, 1–2.

32. *Citibank 1812–1970*, 105–7.

10: "SUNSHINE CHARLIE" DOUBLES DOWN ON SUGAR

1. *Citibank 1812–1970*, 103–4.

2. Associated Press, "Baby Guy Held Son of Banker," *Sacramento Union*, September 30, 1922, https://cdnc.ucr.edu/cgi-bin/cdnc?a=d&d=SU19220930.2.2.

3. "C. E. Mitchell's First Job Was for $10 a Week," *Wall Street Journal*, March 5, 1923 [Hereinafter C. E. Mitchell's First Job . . .].

4. Committee on the History of the Federal Reserve System, "Charles Edwin Mitchell: Biographical Note," November 4, 1955.

5. "C. E. Mitchell's First Job Was for $10 a Week."

6. Ibid.

7. *Citibank 1812–1970*, 107, 321.

8. Office of the Comptroller of the Currency, Examiners Report of Condition, June 24, 1921, to September 2, 1921, D (confidential section), Sherrill Smith, Examiner.

9. "C. E. Mitchell's First Job Was for $10 a Week."

10. Testimony of Gordon Rentschler, Lobby Investigation: Hearings Before a Subcommittee of the Committee on the Judiciary, United States Senate, November 19, 1929, to January 17, 1930, 1317–27 [hereinafter, Rentschler Lobbying Testimony]; *Citibank 1812–1970*, 108–9, 372; Irving Kaufman, *Blue Skies*, January 6, 1927, https://www.youtube.com/watch?v=V7cPcE a4e8I. For an interview with Charles Mitchell's children, who discuss *Blue Skies* in the context of their father, see WGBH and PBS, "The Crash of 1929," American Experience, http://documentazione.altervista.org/The _Crash_of_1929.html [Hereinafter Mitchell Family Interview]. ("Rita Mitchell Cushman: That was the whole tenor of the day. I mean, people believed that everything was going to be great always. There was a feeling of optimism in the air that you cannot even describe today.")

11. *Citibank 1812–1970*, 108–9; Hubbard, 185; "Stock Exchange Practices: Hearings Before a Subcommittee of the Committee on Banking and Currency, United States Senate on S. Res. 84 and S. Res. 239," 72nd Congress, 1933, 1793 [hereinafter, Senate Hearing on Stock Exchange Practices]; Rentschler Lobbying Testimony, 1325–26.

12. Rentschler Lobbying Testimony, 1325.

13. *Citibank 1812–1970*, 109.

14. Examinations through this period included: June 24, 1921, to September 2, 1921 (Sherrill Smith, Examiner); July 21, 1922, to November 10, 1922 (D. C. Borden, Lead Examiner); June 15, 1923, to August 9, 1923 (D. C. Borden, Lead Examiner); April 25, 1924, to June 2, 1924 (Owen T. Reeves Jr., Lead Examiner); November 14, 1924, to December 30, 1924 (Ernest H. Watson, Lead Examiner); June 15, 1925, to July 3, 1925 (Roy H. Griffin, Lead Examiner); November 27, 1925, to January 9, 1926 (Roy H. Griffin, Lead Examiner); April 30, 1926, to June 5, 1926 (T. R. Dwyer, Lead Examiner); October 22, 1926, to November 27, 1926 (T. R. Dwyer, Lead Examiner).

15. National City Bank, *Annual Report 1927* (New York: National City Bank, 1928) as cited in *Citibank 1812–1970*, 372.

16. Senate Hearing on Stock Exchange Practices, 1788–97; *Citibank 1812–1970*, 110, 185.

17. Office of the Comptroller of the Currency, Examiners Report of Condition, April 22, 1927–June 1, 1927, 6-A-1, T. R. Dwyer, Examiner.

18. *Citibank 1812–1970*, 112.

19. "Curtailment of Branch System," *Federal Reserve Bulletin*, November 1921, 1267.

20. *Citibank 1812–1970*, 121, 324.

21. Ibid., 120–21; Arthur H. Ham, *The Campaign Against the Loan Shark* (New York: Russell Sage Foundation, 1912).

22. The $75,000 salary is listed as part of the examination conducted from June to August 1923; April to June 1924; November to December 1924; November 1925 to January 1926; April 1926 to June 1926; October 1926 to November 1926; April 1927 to June 1927; October 1927 to November 1927; March 1928 to Not Available; October 1928 to Not Available; March 1929 to April 1929; October 1929 to November 1929; *From Farm Boy to Financier*, 263 ("I occupied one of the most conspicuous banking positions in the world and my salary was $100,000 a year"); Harmwell Wells, "No Man Can Be Worth $1,000,000 a Year: The Fight Over Executive Compensation in 1930s America," *University of Richmond Law Review* 44, 689, 714–715.

23. Office of the Comptroller of the Currency, Examiners Report of Condition, November 27, 1925–January 9, 1926, B1, Roy H. Griffin, Examiner. At that time, the confidential section of an OCC examination was on yellow paper to highlight the nature of this section of the report.

24. Examinations in 1926, 1927, and 1928 did not mention the management fund.

25. *Citibank 1812–1970*, 372, note 71.

26. Office of the Comptroller of the Currency, Examiners Report of Condition, March 8, 1929–April 10, 1929, Memo-1, P. J. Lorang, Examiner.

11: MITCHELL AND THE MANIA

1. Office of the Comptroller of the Currency, Examiners Report of Condition, November 14, 1924–December 30, 1924, B. Ernest H. Watson was the examiner in charge who likely wrote this passage.

2. Office of the Comptroller of the Currency, Examiners Report of Condition, October 22, 1926–November 27, 1926, B-1. T. R. Dwyer was the examiner in charge who likely wrote this passage.

3. Office of the Comptroller of the Currency, Examiners Report of Condition, March 30, 1928, B-1. T. R. Dwyer was the examiner in charge who likely wrote this passage.

4. "C. E. Mitchell's First Job Was for $10 a Week."

5. Office of the Comptroller of the Currency, Examiners Report of Condition, March 8, 1929–April 10, 1929, B. P. J. Lorang was the examiner in charge who likely wrote this passage.

6. Thomas F. Huertas and Joan L. Silverman, "Charles E. Mitchell: Scapegoat of the Crash?" *Business History Review* 60, no. 1 (Spring 1986): 87 [Hereinafter *Charles E. Mitchell: Scapegoat of the Crash?*].

7. FRED Economic Research, "Dow Jones Industrial Stock Price Index for United States, Updated August 15, 2012, https://fred.stlouisfed.org/series /M1109BUSM293NNBR.

8. *Citibank 1812–1970*, 63.

9. Ibid., 62–64, 84–85.

10. Senate Hearing on Stock Exchange Practices, 2030, 2040, 2042; Arthur E. Wilmarth Jr., "Prelude to Glass-Steagall: Abusive Securities Practices by National City Bank and Chase National Bank During the Roaring Twenties," 1292–93 [Hereinafter "Abusive Securities Practices"].

11. U.S. Department of the Treasury on the State of the Finances, Annual Report: 1910, 6–7; *Citibank 1812–1970*, 63, 66.

12. *NYT*, August 25, 1911; *Citibank 1812–1970*, 66, 67; "Abusive Securities Practices," 1293.

13. "Abusive Securities Practices," 1294; *Citibank 1812–1970*, 86.

14. *From Farm Boy to Financier*, 287.

15. *Citibank 1812–1970*, 87; "Abusive Securities Practices," 1296.

16. Ibid., 136.

17. Ibid., 114, 136.

18. Ibid., 130–31, 381 (note 52). The short-term Treasury bill was introduced in 1929. The New York Clearing House set a ceiling of 2.5 percent on corporate and interbank demand deposits. Federal Reserve, "The Discount Rate Controversy Between the Federal Reserve Board and the Federal Reserve Bank of New York," Document X-6737, November 1, 1930 [Hereinafter "Discount Rate Controversy"]. Discount rates increased from 3.5 percent in 1927 up to 5 percent by July 1928, where they stayed until an increase to 6 percent in August 1929. After they reached this peak they were steadily reduced beginning in November 1929 through 1930 when they stood at 2.5 percent.

19. Senate Hearing on Stock Exchange Practices, 1879. In response to a question of whether National City Company borrowed money from National City Bank, Gordon Rentschler cited the legal lending limit of "10 percent of our capital and surplus" and that it was "about $20,000,000."

20. Office of the Comptroller of the Currency, Examiners Report of Condition, June 24, 1921–September 2, 1921, 3-c and November 12, 1920–January 7, 1921, 7-d; Office of the Comptroller of the Currency, Examiners Report of Condition, April 25, 1924–June 2, 1924, 6-A-1; Office of the Comptroller of the Currency, Examiners Report of Condition, November 14, 1924–December 30, 1924, 6-A.

21. Charles D. Ellis, *The Partnership: The Making of Goldman Sachs* (New York: Penguin Press, 2008), 5–6, 14–15.

22. William D. Cohan, *Money and Power: How Goldman Sachs Came to Rule the World* (New York: Anchor, 2012), 63.

23. *Citibank 1812–1970*, 321, 390 (note 44). Estimate was developed by taking

the change in the equity account plus dividends paid minus increases in capitalization from new stock issues between the OCC examinations of November 1925 and September 1929. The estimate of profits during this time is necessary because NCB refused to provide the OCC with more detailed financials for NCC, which included income statements, as discussed in the next chapter.

24. *The Hellhound of Wall Street* (New York: Penguin Press, 2010) 82 [Hereinafter *The Hellhound of Wall Street*].
25. Mitchell Family Interview.
26. "Charles E. Mitchell: Scapegoat of the Crash?" 85–86.
27. Prins, 79.
28. "Taxation Is Oppressive: Head of National City Bank of New York Sees Nothing but Disaster in Government Attempt to Run Business," *Herald Democrat*, September 26, 1923.
29. Letter from Charles Mitchell to the Comptroller of the Currency, January 18, 1928. Reportedly, the delays were due to a heavy workload and the lack of availability of a high-qualified typist to take on the task.
30. Allan H. Meltzer, *A History of the Federal Reserve, Volume I: 1913–1951* (Chicago: University of Chicago Press, 2003), 75–76 [Hereinafter Meltzer]. Peter Conti-Brown, *Power and Independence of the Federal Reserve* (Princeton, NJ: Princeton University Press, 2016), 23–24.
31. Federal Reserve Act of 1913, Section 4.
32. Benjamin Strong to Owen D. Young, August 18, 1928, as quoted in *Citibank 1812–1970*, 382 (note 56).
33. Federal Reserve Bank of New York, Fourteenth Annual Report, Year Ended December 31, 1928, 26.
34. Federal Reserve Bank of New York, Annual Reports, Years Ended December 31, 1928; December 31, 1929; December 31, 1930; and December 31, 1931.
35. Milton Friedman and Anna Jacobson Schwartz, *A Monetary History of the United States, 1867–1960* (Princeton, NJ: Princeton University Press, 1963), 256–57.
36. "Discount Rate Controversy," 5.
37. Federal Reserve Board, Letter to Gates W. McGarrah, chairman of the Federal Reserve Bank of New York, February 2, 1929.
38. "Discount Rate Controversy," 5; *A Monetary History of the United States*, 257.
39. Ibid. Friedman and Schwartz expressed skepticism that this approach would actually work as it was laid out by Harrison. Federal Reserve Board, Press Statement, February 7, 1929.
40. *A Monetary History of the United States*, 258–59, drawn from the diary of Charles S. Hamlin, who was the first governor of the Federal Reserve Board from 1914 to 1916 and then remained on the board from 1916 to 1936, http://www.federalreservehistory.org/People/DetailView/17.

41. *A Monetary History of the United States*, 259.

42. "Discount Rate Controversy," 5. The dates of those meetings were March 3, March 21, March 28, April 4, April 18, April 25, May 9, May 16, and May 23.

43. John Kenneth Galbraith, *The Great Crash 1929*, (Boston, MA: Houghton Mifflin Harcourt, 1954), 42 [Hereinafter Galbraith].

44. "Discount Rate Controversy," 2, 8; Prins, 110.

45. C. S. Hamlin, "Banking Conditions at Time of Statement, March 26, 1929," Document X-6873, April 27, 1931, 1–2 [Hereinafter "Banking Conditions"]; Galbraith, 41.

46. "Banking Conditions," 2, quoting from an interview in the *New York Times* of March 29, 1929.

47. "Banking Conditions," 2, quoting from an interview of March 26, 1929, that appeared in the March 27, 1929, edition of the *New York Herald Tribune*.

48. Meltzer, 247, note 181.

49. "Banking Conditions," 2, quoting the *New York Times*, March 29, 1929.

50. *Citibank 1812–1970*, 132–33; *New York Times*, March 29, 1929, and March 30, 1929.

51. Galbraith, 42, 99.

12: DID CITY BANK CAUSE THE CRASH?

1. Geisst, 202.

2. Federal Reserve Bank of St. Louis, https://fred.stlouisfed.org/series /M0892AUSM156SNBR.

3. Lucette Lagnado, "Memories of the Depression Still Sear," *Wall Street Journal*, November 15, 2008.

4. Letter from Owen Reeves, chief examiner, to J. W. Pole, Comptroller of the Currency, December 4, 1929 ("Examiner Lorang started the examination of the NCB in New York on Friday afternoon, October 4th . . . we had 92 men available to cover this examination which included 14 Federal Reserve Bank men.") References to "men" highlight the dearth of female examiners at this time. Adelia M. Stewart became the first commissioned examiner for the OCC in 1921, but it was rare to have an examination team, no matter how large, with a female examiner. See Office of the Comptroller of the Currency, "Office of the Comptroller: A Short History," 16, https://www.occ.treas.gov/about/what-we-do/history/OCC %20history%20final.pdf.

5. Office of the Comptroller of the Currency, Examiners Report of Condition, October 4, 1929, to November 30, 1929, B-2 (confidential section) [Hereinafter October 4, 1929, Examination Report].

6. October 4, 1929, Examination Report, B-2.

7. Letter from Owen Reeves, chief examiner, to J. W. Pole, Comptroller of the Currency, December 4, 1929.

8. Office of the Comptroller of the Currency, Examiners Report of Condition, September 12, 1930, to December 5, 1930, 11-A-2, 11-D, B-2-b (confidential section).

9. Office of the Comptroller of the Currency, Examiners Report of Condition, October 9, 1931, to January 13, 1932, B-4, Otis W. Beaton, Examiner.

10. Office of the Comptroller of the Currency, Examiners Report of Condition, September 30, 1932, to November 26, 1932, B, Otis W. Beaton, Examiner.

11. National Bureau of Economic Research, "US Business Cycle Expansions and Contractions," http://www.nber.org/cycles/cyclesmain.html.

12. *NYT*, October 25, 1929, as quoted in Federal Reserve Archive, "C. E. Mitchell," Memo from C.S. Hamlin, The Papers of Charles Hamlin, Document X-6873, April 27, 1931.

13. *NYT*, November 29, 1929; *The Hellhound of Wall Street*, 85.

14. U.S. Congress, Senate Subcommittee of the Committee on Manufacture, Hearings on the Establishment of a National Economic Council, 71st Congress, 1st Session, 1931, 525–26, as cited in *Citibank 1812–1970*, 174, 175.

15. *A Monetary History of the United States*, 298, quote from https://fee.org /articles/money-in-the-1920s-and-1930s/.

16. Amity Shlaes, *The Forgotten Man: A New History of the Great Depression*, (New York: Harper Perennial, 2007), 39 [hereinafter, *The Forgotten Man*].

17. Timothy Cogley, "Monetary Policy and the Great Crash of 1929: A Bursting Bubble or Collapsing Fundamentals," *Economic Letter*, 1999-10 (March 26, 1999), http://www.frbsf.org/economic-research/publications /economic-letter/1999/march/monetary-policy-and-the-great-crash-of -1929-a-bursting-bubble-or-collapsing-fundamentals/

18. *Citibank 1812–1970*, 159–60.

19. Ibid.

20. *The Forgotten Man*, 42; Joseph L. Lucia, "The Failure of the Bank of United States: A Reappraisal," *Explorations in Economic History* 22, issue 4 (October 1985), 409, 412–414.

21. For a good example of how this was reflected on the books of NCB, see National City Bank, Condensed Statement of Condition, December 31, 1923, 4–5, http://www.columbia.edu/cu/lweb/digital/collections/cul /texts/ldpd_6282727_000/ldpd_6282727_000.pdf. Of NCB's total assets of $920 million, it reflected an $8.5 million "Ownership of International Banking Corporation," but no equivalent ownership interest in National City Company. In the report's Remarks of the President, it explains: "The National City Company has enjoyed a profitable year. It has paid dividends, reaching the shareholders of the Bank, equivalent to 4 per cent

on the Bank shares, and has added to its capital surplus account, which account is in excess of the amount of its $10,000,000 of capital stock."

22. Office of the Comptroller of the Currency, Examiners Report of Condition, March 8, 1929, to April 10, 1929, 1; *Citibank 1812–1970*, 133, 321. The year-end reported capital to asset ratio increased from 10.1 percent to 11.4 percent from 1928 to 1929.

23. Federal Deposit Insurance Corporation, Quarterly Banking Profile, as of December 31, 2016, issued February 28, 2017.

24. Office of the Comptroller of the Currency, Examiners Report of Condition, April 22, 1932, to June 30, 1932, 11-E-2.

25. June 1, 1934, examination, 11-D-1. Chilean government balance of $14 million with only $1.4 million classified as slow; Chilean State Railroad balance of $1 million with $0.4 million classified as slow.

26. Office of the Comptroller of the Currency, Examiners Report of Condition, September 30, 1932, to November 26, 1932, 6-A-9, 7–21–7–23, B-3. Similar classifications are reflected in the April 1932 OCC examination. For further detail on the Chilean sovereign debt crisis of 1931 and the other Latin American sovereign defaults during this period, see Graciela Laura Kaminsky and Pablo Vega-Garcia, "Varieties of Sovereign Crises: Latin America: 1820-1931," April 2014, 10, 23, http://economics.ucdavis .edu/events/departmentseminars/papers/Kaminsky513.pdf.

27. Office of the Comptroller of the Currency, Examiners Report of Condition, October 9, 1931, to January 13, 1932, 11-D.

28. Federal Reserve Bank of New York, "Banking and Credit Abroad," Monthly Review of Credit and Business Conditions, October 1, 1931, 75–76. The use of the word "*Stillhaltung*" is unclear, as the best translation would be "*Stillhalteabkommen.*"

29. Letter from O. W. Beaton, National Bank Examiner, to Comptroller of the Currency, July 1, 1931.

30. Ibid.

31. Office of the Comptroller of the Currency, Examiners Report of Condition, October 9, 1931, to January 13, 1932, B-6 (confidential section).

32. Office of the Comptroller of the Currency, Examiners Report of Condition, September 30, 1932, to November 26, 1932, B-3 (confidential section).

33. *A Monetary History of the United States*, 299.

34. "Bank Bills Pushed in Both Chambers," *New York Times*, May 20, 1933. Richard E. Farley, *Wall Street Wars* (New York: Regan Arts, 2015), 81.

35. Ferdinand Pecora, *Wall Street Under Oath* (New York: Graymalkin Media, 2014), 71.

36. *The Hellhound of Wall Street*, 132, 147.

37. Ibid., 88–89, 93–94, 97, 103. Photo of Charles Mitchell and his wife taken by Acme Newspictures, Inc., February 11, 1933.

38. *The Hellhound of Wall Street*, 135–36.

39. Vern McKinley, *Financing Failure* (Oakland, CA: The Independent Institute, 2011), 45–47; *A Monetary History*, 314, 324–26 [Hereinafter *Financing Failure*].

40. FRED Economic Data, "Dow Jones Industrials Stock Price Index for U.S.," https://fred.stlouisfed.org/series/M1109BUSM293NNBR.

41. "Stock Exchange Practices," Hearing on S. Res. 84 and S. Res. 239 Before a Subcommittee of the S. Comm. On Banking and Currency, 72d Cong. 2040 (1933) 1811–14 [Hereinafter Pecora Hearing Transcript].

42. *New York Times*, February 22, 1933; *Washington Post*, February 22, 1933; *Wall Street Journal*, February 22, 1933; *The Hellhound of Wall Street*, 155, 156.

43. Report of the Committee on Banking and Currency, "Stock Exchange Practices," June 6, 1934, Report no. 1455, 73rd Congress, 2nd Session, 322 ("Charles E. Mitchell, chairman of the National City Bank, sold to his wife in 1929, 18,300 shares of National City Bank stock at a loss of $2,872,305.50."). *NYT*, February 25, 1933, as cited in *The Hellhound of Wall Street*, 192–93; 297–98.

44. Robert Daines and Charles M. Jones, "Truth or Consequences: Mandatory Disclosure and the Impact of the 1934 Act," Stanford University Working Paper, May 2012, https://www.law.stanford.edu/publications/truth-or-consequences-mandatory-disclosure-and-the-impact-of-the-1934-act.

45. Pecora Hearing Transcript, 1819–20.

46. Pecora Hearing Transcript, 1769–86.

47. Estimates calculated using the Bureau of Labor Statistics, CPI Inflation Calculator, https://www.bls.gov/data/inflation_calculator.htm.

48. *Citibank 1812–1970*, 186.

49. National City Bank, Monthly Economic Letter, March 1933, 33. Hamlin diary as quoted in *Citibank 1812–1970*, 186–87.

50. *The Hellhound of Wall Street*, 225–26.

51. Franklin D. Roosevelt, Inaugural Address, March 4, 1933, http://www.presidency.ucsb.edu/ws/?pid=14473.

52. Raymond Moley, *After Seven Years* (Harper and Brothers Publishers: New York and London, 1939), 337.

53. *Gallin v. National City Bank of New York*, 152 Misc. 679 (N.Y. Misc. 1934). Opinion of Judge Dore. Other key defendants included Hugh Baker, Gordon Rentschler, Colonel Deeds, Percy R. Pyne III, Percy Rockefeller, James Stillman, and James H. Perkins.

54. *Gallin v. National City Bank of New York*, 155 Misc. 880 (N.Y. Misc. 1935). Opinion of Referee Frank C. Laughlin.

55. Michael Perino, "The Hellhound of Wall Street," PointofLaw.com (blog), May 3, 2011, http://www.pointoflaw.com/archives/2011/05/the-hellhound-o.php.

56. National City Bank of New York, Statement of Condition, December 31,

1915, 3; *Citibank 1812–1970*, 89–90, 155, 187, 191–92; Prins, 119, 122, citing letter to James Perkins, March 9, 1933, FDR Library.

57. *Financing Failure*, 48–55.

58. Jesse Jones, *Fifty Billion Dollars: My Thirteen Years with the RTC (1932–1945)* (New York: Macmillan, 1951), 35 [Hereinafter Jones].

59. Minutes, Reconstruction Finance Corporation, December 1–4, 1933, Volume XXIII, Part 1, 1–586, 579. Common stock represents a portion of the equity of the bank. Office of the Comptroller of the Currency, Examiners Report of Condition, June 1, 1934, to July 27, 1934, confidential section, B-2-a, C-1; James S. Olson, *Saving Capitalism: The Reconstruction Finance Corporation and the New Deal, 1933–1940* (Princeton, NJ: Princeton University Press, 1988), 80, from a letter from Jones to Roosevelt dated December 4, 1933.

60. James H. Perkins, letter to the shareholders, December 5, 1933. http:// bklyn.newspapers.com/image/59975204/ [Hereinafter James H. Perkins letter].

61. As quoted in the James H. Perkins letter.

62. Robert Lynn Fuller, *Phantom of Fear: The Banking Panic of 1933* (Jefferson, NC: McFarland & Company, 2012), 225; Barrie Wigmore, *The Crash and Its Aftermath: A History of the Securities Market in the United States* (Westport, CT: Greenwood Press, 1985), 354–61.

63. Minutes, Reconstruction Finance Corporation, March 26–28, 1934, Volume XXVI, Part 8, 4999–5697, 5682. The amount of NCB preferred stock cancelled for RFC purchase was $907,000, and stock canceled for Chase $3,777,840 and for Continental $333.33. Jones, 47.

64. James Grant, "Out for Blood," *Wall Street Journal*, October 14, 2010.

65. Public Law 73–66, 48 Stat. 162. Sec. 20. "After one year from the date of the enactment of this Act, no member bank shall be affiliated in any manner described in section 2 (b) hereof with any corporation, association, business trust, or other similar organization engaged principally in the issue, flotation, underwriting, public sale, or distribution at wholesale or retail or through syndicate participation of stocks, bonds, debentures, notes, or other securities," https://fraser.stlouisfed.org/scribd/?title_id=991&file path=/files/docs/historical/congressional/1933_bankingact_publiclaw66 .pdf.

66. *Citibank 1812–1970*, 197–98.

67. Letter from James Perkins to Comptroller of the Currency, May 23, 1934.

13: BANK FOR THE UNITED STATES

1. Office of the Comptroller of the Currency, Examiners Report of Condition, June 1, 1934, to July 27, 1934, B-2-a, B-2-b, and B-2-c (confidential section) [Hereinafter June 1, 1934, examination report].

2. *Citibank 1812–1970,* 210–11, citing OCC examination reports during this period.

3. Office of the Comptroller of the Currency, Examiners Report of Condition, October 25, 1935, to December 14, 1935, B-2 (confidential section).

4. Office of the Comptroller of the Currency, Examiners Report of Condition, October 23, 1936, B-3-a (confidential section).

5. Office of the Comptroller of the Currency, Examiners Report of Condition, April 23, 1937, to June 30, 1937, B-3-b (confidential section).

6. June 1, 1934, examination report, B-2-a and B-2-c (confidential section).

7. *Citibank 1812–1970,* , 205, 324.

8. *Citibank 1812–1970,* 224.

9. Phillip L. Zweig, *Wriston: Walter Wriston, Citibank and the Rise and Fall of American Financial Supremacy* (New York: Crown, 1995) [Hereinafter *Wriston*], 45–46.

10. National City Bank, Annual Report, 1933, as quoted in *Citibank 1812–1970,* 205.

11. Office of the Comptroller of the Currency, Examiners Report of Condition, May 24, 1935, to July 11, 1935, A-2-A, B-3 (confidential section). Salaries as of the May 1935 examination: Perkins $45,000; Rentschler $75,000; and Simonson $65,000 noted on A-2-A (confidential section). Salaries as of the October 1935 examination: Perkins $100,000; Rentschler $100,000; and Simonson $75,000 noted on A-2-A (confidential section). There is no mention of any type of compensation by means of a management fund as there was during the Mitchell days.

12. James H. Perkins, "The Economic Situation: Extract from the Report to Shareholders," January 11, 1938, FDR Library, as quoted in Prins, 151.

13. Perkins Obituary, *New York Times,* July 13, 1940.

14. *Wriston,* 46.

15. *Geisst,* 266.

16. Ibid., 267.

17. *Wriston,* 46.

18. *Citibank 1812–1970,* 214.

19. *Celebrating the Past,* 115.

20. Ibid., 112.

21. *Citibank 1812–1970,* 216–17.

22. Ibid., 217–18.

23. Ibid., 218.

24. Ibid., 217.

14: WALTER WRISTON AND THE CULTURE OF RISK

1. *Wriston,* 16–21.

2. Ibid., 12–17.

3. Ibid., 15.

4. Ibid., 19.

5. Ibid.

6. Ibid., 19–29.

7. Ibid., 50.

8. Ibid.

9. Ibid., 56.

10. Ibid., 62–66.

11. Ibid., 66.

12. Ibid., 55, 57–58, 61–64, 72, 82–83; *Citibank 1812–1970*, 231, 238–41, 322.

13. Ibid., 86.

14. Ibid., 85–86, 92–93, 101, 104, 107.

15. Ibid., 94.

16. Ibid., 115.

17. George S. Moore, "International Banking Tomorrow," Address to the Bankers Association for Foreign Trade," Hot Springs, VA, May 17, 1978, as quoted in *Citibank 1812–1970*, 259. Moore became president of FNCB in 1959. The reference is made to Citibank given the date of the address in 1978 was after the name change. *Wriston*, 84.

18. *Citibank 1812–1970*, 260; *Wriston*, 129, 133–37.

19. Walter B. Wriston, "Address to Overseas Division Dinner," New York, 1963, as quoted in *Citibank 1812–1970*, 261, 433.

20. *Wriston*, 239, 448.

21. "Economic Strategy for the Reagan Administration," A Report to President-Elect Ronald Reagan from His Coordinating Committee on Economic Policy, November 16, 1980.

22. *Wriston*, 711, 785.

23. See Martin H. Wolfson, *Financial Crises: Understanding the Postwar Experience* (London: M. E. Sharpe, 1986). It describes the following as crises during this period based on the definition contained therein: the credit crunch of 1966, Penn Central, Franklin National Bank, and the Silver Crisis of 1980, among others. Focus here will be on Penn Central and later Franklin National Bank because of the role First National City Bank played in each.

24. U.S. Securities and Exchange Commission, "The Financial Collapse of the Penn Central Company," Staff Report of the Securities and Exchange Commission to the Special Subcommittee on Investigation, August 1972, IX, 11 [Hereinafter SEC Staff Report on Collapse of the Penn Central Company]; *Wriston*, 313–14.

25. SEC Staff Report on Collapse of the Penn Central Company, 95, 97; *Wriston*, 314–15.

26. SEC Staff Report on Collapse of the Penn Central Company, 103, 104.

27. *Wriston*, 316–17.

28. SEC Staff Report on Collapse of the Penn Central Company, 104.

29. *Wriston*, 316–18; *TIME*, Cover, January 26, 1968, http://content.time.com /time/covers/0,16641,19680126,00.html.

30. Charles W. Calomiris, "Is the Discount Window Necessary? A Penn Central Perspective," *The Federal Reserve Bank of St. Louis Review* 76, no. 3, May/June 1994, 31, 37 [Hereinafter Calomiris]. See "US Business Cycle Expansions and Contractions," which shows that the recession lasted from December 1969 to November 1970. Historical data is conflicting on the precise level of Penn Central's commercial paper. *Wriston*, 318, notes that: "When it collapsed, Penn Central had more than $100 million in commercial paper coming due over the next several months."

31. Calomiris, 45.

32. Thomas Timlen, "Commercial Paper—Penn Central and Others," in *Financial Crises: Institutions and Markets in a Fragile Environment*, ed. Edward I. Altman and Arnold W. Sametz (Hoboken, NJ: John Wiley & Sons, 1977), 223.

33. H. Erich Heinemann, "City Bank Assays Its 1970 Results," *New York Times*, June 21, 1971, as cited in *Wriston*, 333. *Citibank 1812–1970*, 322. Reported capital declined slightly for 1970, in part due to the recognized loss for Penn Central.

15: NOT THAT BIG, BUT TOO BIG TO FAIL?

1. *Wriston*, 133, 139, 449. Joan E. Spero, *The Failure of the Franklin National Bank: Challenge to the International Banking System* (New York: Columbia University Press, 1980), 46 [Hereinafter Spero].

2. Spero, 11, 26, 29–30; *United States v. Michele Sindona*, 636 F.2d 792 (1980), https://scholar.google.com/scholar_case?case=884156288990522748 0&q =united+states+v. l sindona&hl=cn&as_sdt=6,47&as_vis=1.

3. "Oversight Hearings into the Effectiveness of Federal Bank Regulation, Hearings Before a Subcommittee of the Committee on Government Operations," House of Representatives, 94th Congress, 2nd Session, February 10, May 25–26, and June 1, 1976, 89, Tables 2 and 3, and 228 [Hereinafter Franklin Hearings].

4. Federal Reserve Bank of New York, "Annual Report—1974," 23. "Letter from the Federal Reserve dated October 7, 1974," as quoted in Franklin Hearings, 200.

5. Inquiry into Continental Illinois Corp. and Continental Illinois National Bank, Hearings Before the Subcommittee on Financial Institutions Supervision, Regulation and Insurance of the Committee on Banking, Finance and Urban Affairs, House of Representatives, 98th Congress, 2nd Session, September 18 and 19, 1984, and October 4, 1984, Report 98–111, Testimony of William Isaac, October 4, 1984, 467. Also see Christine M.

Bradley, "A Historical Perspective on Deposit Insurance Coverage," *FDIC Banking Review* 13, no. 2 (2000), 16, note 159 ("By the end of July, FNB had lost 71 percent of its domestic and foreign money-market resources").

6. Anna J. Schwartz, "The Misuse of the Fed's Discount Window," Federal Reserve Bank of St. Louis Review (September/October 1992), 64, https://research.stlouisfed.org/publications/review/1992/09/01/the-misuse-of-the-feds-discount-window/.

7. *Wriston*, 450–52, 466.

8. Spero, 137–42; *Wriston*, 466, 469; General Accounting Office (GAO), "Financial Crisis Management: Four Financial Crises in the 1980s," GAO/GGD-97-96, May 1997, 16. US House, "Adequacy of the Office of the Comptroller of the Currency's Supervision of Franklin National Bank," 1, as quoted in *The Failure of the Franklin National Bank*, 208. The form of transaction in the resolution of Franklin was a purchase and assumption.

9. Timothy Curry et al., "The LDC Debt Crisis," *History of the Eighties: Lessons for the Future, Volume I: An Examination of the Banking Crises of the 1980s and Early 1990s,* Federal Deposit Insurance Corporation, 1997, 195–97 [Hereinafter FDIC LDC Debt Crisis].

10. *Citibank 1812–1970*, 224–25, 324–25, 434. National City had sixty-one overseas branches in 1955; Chase Manhattan had nineteen; First National Bank of Boston had fourteen; and Bank of America had nine. Comptroller of the Currency Annual Report, 1955, 154, https://fraser.stlouisfed.org/files/docs/publications/comp/1950s/1955/compcurr_1955.pdf.

11. Ben Weberman, "Foreign Deposits Top Domestic at Citibank, Morgan Guaranty, *American Banker*, August 7, 1973. *Wriston*, 162–63, 386–87, 408, 410, 420.

12. Arthur F. Burns, "The Need for Order in International Finance," Annual Dinner of the Columbia University Graduate School of Business, April 12, 1977, https://www.richmondfed.org/publications/research/economic_review/1977/pdf/er630403.pdf.

13. General Accounting Office, "Bank Examination for Country Risk and International Lending," GAO/ID-82-52, September 2, 1982, I, http://www.gao.gov/assets/140/138583.pdf [Hereinafter Bank Examination Analysis]. General Accounting Office, "International Banking: Supervision of Overseas Lending Is Inadequate," GAO/NSIAD-88-87, May 1988, 14. FDIC LDC Debt Crisis, 203. *Wriston*, 579.

14. 12 U.S.C. 84, Lending Limits. FDIC LDC Debt Crisis, 203–4.

15. Bank Examination Analysis, iv, 5, 20–23. Bank exposures were itemized and specially commented if exposures exceed 10 percent of capital in weak countries and 15 percent of capital in moderately strong countries.

16. William Greider, *Secrets of the Temple* (New York: Simon and Schuster, 1989), 438.

17. Ann Crittenden, "The President's Choice for the Fed," *New York Times,*

January 1, 1978, http://www.nytimes.com/1978/01/01/archives/the-pres
idents-choice-the-presidents-choice-for-the-fed-the-search.html, as quoted
in William L. Silber, *Volcker: The Triumph of Persistence* (New York: Blooms-
bury Press, 2012), 136–37, 141 [Hereinafter Silber]. *Wriston*, 635, 638.
18. Silber, 1–2, 121, 125–26.
19. Robert D. Hershey Jr., "In Remembrance of Real Money," *New York
Times*, December 10, 1985, http://www.nytimes.com/1985/12/10/us/in
-remembrance-of-real-money.html. Volcker's response: "A complete flop
is a little harsh, but it hurts all the more because Bill Martin is a personal
hero of mine. I clearly had more work to do on supervision—but also on
monetary policy." Silber, 227. Volcker biographer William L. Silber also
notes that "[t]his comment by Martin came after the failure of Continental
Illinois . . . and was not in response to Mexico per se." Silber, 400.
20. *Wriston*, 578–80.

16: WHEN COUNTRIES FAIL

1. *Wriston*, 675–76, 705, 719, 726, 730, 762.
2. Pointing out the fallout from Volcker's efforts is not intended as an argument against taking those steps. Seidman, 38–39. FDIC LDC Debt Crisis,
205–6. *Wriston*, 638–39.
3. Silber, 225–27.
4. "Poor Nations' Huge Debt Creates Fear of Default by Big Lenders," *Wall
Street Journal*, January 28, 1981.
5. Ibid.
6. Silber, 219.
7. "Bank Claims on Selected Countries," data as of December 31, 1981, Paul
A. Volcker Papers, Princeton University. Mexico led the list of claims with
$21.4 billion; Brazil followed with $16.3 billion; Venezuela $10.5 billion;
South Korea $8.9 billion; and Argentina with $8.1 billion. "Bank Claims
on Selected Countries," data as of December 31, 1980, Paul A. Volcker Papers, Princeton University. Brazil led the list of claims with $16.2 billion;
Mexico followed with $15.9 billion; Venezuela with $9.1 billion; Argentina with $7.9 billion; and South Korea with $7.1 billion.
8. Memo from Division of International Finance to Board of Governors,
"Financial Troublespots in the International Economy," May 7, 1982.
9. Joseph A. Whitt Jr., "The Mexican Peso Crisis," *Federal Reserve Bank of Atlanta Economic Review* (January/February 1996), 1. Rabobank, "The Mexican 1982 Debt Crisis" (September 19, 2013). FDIC LDC Debt Crisis, 202.
Silber, 221, 398. *Wriston*, 744, 747, 750. Paul Volcker and Toyoo Gyohten,
*Changing Fortunes: The World's Money and the Threat to American Leader-
ship* (New York: Times Books, 1992), 199. Robert A. Bennett, "Citicorp
Rating Cut by Moody's," *New York Times*, January 27, 1982, http://www

.nytimes.com/1982/01/27/business/citicorp-rating-cut-by-moody-s.html ?pagewanted=print.

10. *Wriston*, 756–57.

11. Ibid., 757–59, 769.

12. Meeting of the Federal Open Market Committee, October 5, 1982, transcript, 19.

13. Silber, 223.

14. "Bank Claims on Selected Countries," data as of December 31, 1981, Paul A. Volcker Papers, Princeton University.

15. Based on the available data from different sources in Tables 11 and 12, the exposure for Citibank to Mexico was approximately 48 percent, to Brazil 32 percent. Exposure to Argentina was 24 percent; see Federal Reserve, "Exposure by Large BHCs to Mexico and Argentina In Terms of Capital," data as of December 31, 1981. *Wriston*, 771, 781, 789.

16. Reports of the exposure of Citibank to Brazil vary, with some estimates of exposure as high as $4.6 billion and as a percentage of capital as high as 83 percent. However, these estimates are not considered reliable as they give no source for their cited exposures. See R. C. Longworth, "Brazil Broke, U.S. Banks Holding Bag," *Chicago Tribune*, August 14, 1983, 1, 14.

17. International Debt: Hearings Before the Subcommittee on International Finance and Monetary Policy of the Committee on Banking, Housing and Urban Affairs, United State Senate, 98th Congress, 1st Session, February 17, 1983, 237–38 [Hereinafter International Debt Hearing].

18. International Debt Hearing, 239.

19. International Debt Hearing, 247–48.

20. L. William Seidman, *Full Faith and Credit: The Great S&L Debacle and Other Washington Sagas* (Washington, DC: Beard Books, 1993) [Hereinafter Seidman].

21. Robert Eisenbeis and Paul M. Horvitz, "The Role of Forbearance and Its Costs in Handling Troubled and Failed Depository Institutions," *Reforming Financial Institutions in the United States*, ed. George Kaufman (1993), 49–52 [Hereinafter "Role of Forbearance"].

22. "Role of Forbearance," 60.

23. Walter Wriston, "Was I Exacting? Sure. Was I Occasionally Sarcastic? Of Course," *Institutional Investor* (June 1987): 17, 20.

17: THE BANKER WHO "NEVER MADE A LOAN"

1. FDIC, "Continental Illinois and Too Big to Fail," Chapter 7, *An Examination of the Banking Crises of the 1980s and Early 1990s* (Washington, DC: FDIC, 1997) 237, 239. https://www.fdic.gov/bank/historical/history /235_258.pdf

2. Ibid, 239, 240.

3. *Wriston*, 818.
4. Silber, 245; *Wriston*, 817–18, 857; Richard B. Miller, *Citicorp: The Story of a Bank in Crisis* (New York: McGraw-Hill, 1993), 47 [Hereinafter Miller].
5. Charles W. Schumer, "Banks Aren't for Gambling," *New York Times*, June 7, 1984, 10A.
6. Tim Carrington, "U.S. Won't Let 11 Biggest Banks in Nation Fail: Testimony by Comptroller at House Hearing is First Policy Acknowledgement," *Wall Street Journal*, September 20, 1984.
7. Editorial Board, "The TBTF and TSTS," *Wall Street Journal*, September 25, 1984.
8. "John Reed Nominated to Chair MIT Corporation," *MIT News*, April 12, 2010; *Wriston*, 183–84.
9. *Wriston*, 188.
10. *Wriston*, 185–89.
11. Ibid., 274.
12. "City Bank Picks New Leadership Team," *New York Times*, March 18, 1970, http://www.nytimes.com/1970/03/18/archives/city-bank-picks-new-leadership-team-wriston-to-become-the-chairman.html; *Wriston*, 275–77.
13. *Wriston*, 278–82.
14. Ibid., 285, 292–95, 300–1.
15. Ibid., 532, 535–39, 549, 556.
16. Ibid., 654, 656–57, 792–93.
17. Miller, 176–77. Stephen A. Rhoades, "Bank Mergers and Industrywide Structure: 1980–1994," Board of Governors Staff Studies (January 1996) 20–21; *Wriston*, 846, 847.
18. Seidman, 125–26.
19. Mary M. McLaughlin and Martin H. Wolfson, "The Profitability of Insured Commercial Banks in 1987," *Federal Reserve Bulletin* (July 1987): 403–7, https://fraser.stlouisfed.org/files/docs/publications/FRB/1980s/frb_071988.pdf; *Wriston*, 847, 852, 859.

18: JUST ANOTHER PERFECT STORM

1. Neil Barsky, "Donald Trump Gets $3 Million in Chips Off the Old Block," *Wall Street Journal*, January 21, 1991.
2. Laurie Cohen and Bill Barnhart, "A Sense of Urgency in Continental Job," *Chicago Tribune*, August 2, 1987, http://articles.chicagotribune.com/1987-08-02/business/8702260412_1_edward-harshfield-citicorp-thomas-theobald; *Wriston*, 857; *Financing Failure*, 90.
3. Ian Vasquez, "The Brady Plan and Market-Based Solutions to Debt Crises," *Cato Journal* 16, no. 2 (Fall 1996): 233–39 [hereinafter, Vasquez]. Trade Association for the Emerging Markets, "The Brady Plan," https://www.emta.org/template.aspx?id=35&terms=brady+plan; *Wriston*, 860–61.

4. James E. Lebherz, "Brady Bonds Score Successes," *Washington Post*, May 24, 1992; *Vasquez*, 235–36, 241; *Wriston*, 861.

5. *Wriston*, 859.

6. *Financing Failure*, 73.

7. "US Business Cycle Expansions and Contractions." FDIC Loans and Leases, Table CB11, https://www5.fdic.gov/hsob/HSOBRpt.asp?state=1&rptType=1&Rpt_Num=11; *Wriston*, 868; "The Failure of the Bank of New England Corporation and Its Affiliate Banks, Hearings Before the Committee on Banking, Finance and Urban Affairs," 102nd Congress, serial no. 102–49, June 13, 1991; Stacy L. Shreft and Raymond E. Owens, "Survey Evidence of Tighter Credit Conditions: What Does It Mean? Working Paper 91–05, Federal Reserve Bank of Richmond, May 15, 1991; Vern McKinley, "Run, Run, Run: Was the Financial Crisis Panic Over Institution Runs Justified?" Cato Institute Policy Analysis 747, April 10, 2014, 7–9, [hereinafter, "Run, Run, Run"] https://www.cato.org/publications/policy-analysis/run-run-run-was-financial-crisis-panic-over-institution-runs-justified.

8. *Wriston*, 869–70.

9. "Trump Shuttle May Go on Sale Again, Lenders Say," *Wall Street Journal*, September 27, 1990.

10. "Trump getting beaten at his own game: Shuttle deal shows how far deal-maker has plummeted," *Dallas Morning News*, August 26, 1990.

11. "Shaky Empire: Trump's Bankers Join to Seek Restructuring of Developer's Assets," *Wall Street Journal*, June 4, 1990.

12. "Trump Bankers Expected to Seek Shuttle Pay Cuts," *Wall Street Journal*, September 26, 1990.

13. "Honeymoon's Over: Citicorp's Chief Comes Under Fire as Earnings Remain Disappointing," *Wall Street Journal*, June 21, 1990.

14. Noel Tichy and Ram Charan, "Citicorp Faces the World: An Interview with John Reed," *Harvard Business Review*, November–December 1990, https://hbr.org/1990/11/citicorp-faces-the-world-an-interview-with-john-reed, as quoted in James Grant, *Money of the Mind*, 430.

15. *Citibank 1812–1970*, 320; Sandra L. Ryon, "History of Bank Capital Adequacy Analysis," FDIC Working Paper No. 69–4, Section 6, Paragraph 3, National Bank Act of 1863, 2–9, https://fraser.stlouisfed.org/scribd/?title_id=1111&filepath=/files/docs/historical/congressional/national-bank-act-1863.pdf; *The Banker's Magazine* (Fall 1974), as quoted in Miller, 91; *Wriston*, 353–56.

16. Citicorp, Annual Report 1991 as quoted in Miller, 16, 18; Brett D. Fromson and Jerry Knight, "The Saving of Citibank," *Washington Post*, May 16, 1993 [Hereinafter "Saving of Citibank"].

17. Miller, 16. The quote is from a January 1991 meeting with stock analysts.

18. *Wriston*, 879.

19. Miller, 19–22, 25–26; Kathleen Day and Robert J. McCartney, "Saudi Invests $590 Million in Citicorp," *Washington Post,* February 22, 1991.

20. "Fred R. Bleakley," Weakened Giant: As Big Rivals Surge, Citicorp's John Reed Is at a Crossroads," *Wall Street Journal,* August 16, 1991.

21. Ibid.

22. Ibid.

23. John W. Milligan "The collapse of Citibank's credit culture," *Institutional Investor,* December 1, 1991.

24. Ibid.

25. The OCC examinations from 1868 to 1939 are available at the National Archives and Records Administration in College Park, Maryland. Information on the OCC record retention schedule was detailed in a letter from Frank D. Vance Jr., the manager of the disclosure services and Freedom of Information Act Office of the OCC, March 29, 2017.

26. Michael Quint, "Citicorp Criticized on Mortgages That Expose It to Too Much Risk," *New York Times,* September 3, 1992; *Wriston,* 874. Detail on the inability to locate a copy of the MOU was set forth in a letter from Frank D. Vance Jr., the manager of the disclosure services and Freedom of Information Act Office of the OCC, August 31, 2017. The letter regarding the Federal Reserve MOU is from Margaret McCloskey Shanks, deputy secretary of the board, September 1, 2017.

27. "Trump's Dad Gets OK to Cash in Chips," *Associated Press,* May 19, 1994.

19: CREATING THE NEXT CRISIS

1. Michael Siconolfi, "Citicorp Merger with Travelers Signals New Era," *Wall Street Journal,* April 7, 1998.

2. Ibid.

3. Ibid.

4. Monica Langley, *Tearing Down the Walls* (New York: Wall Street Journal Books, 2003), 321 [Hereinafter Langley].

5. Sandy Weill and Judah S. Kraushaar, *The Real Deal* (New York: Warner Business Books, 2006), 360–63 [Hereinafter *The Real Deal*].

6. Review and Outlook, "No Line Responsibilities," *Wall Street Journal,* December 3, 2008.

7. Financial Crisis Inquiry Commission, "Interview of John Reed," March 24, 2010, 30–31.

8. Sheila Bair, *Bull by the Horns: Fighting to Save Main Street from Wall Street and Wall Street from Itself* (New York: Free Press, 2012), 122 [Hereinafter *Bull by the Horns*].

9. "Senator Elizabeth Warren—Reinstating Glass-Steagall—CNBC," YouTube video, @0:40, posted by "Marie Marr," July 12, 2013, http://www.youtube.com/watch?v=M6rnsLNvXzM; "Sen. Elizabeth Warren Pitches

21st Century Glass-Steagall Bill," Fox News website, @2:08 and @4:42, July 12, 2013, http://video.foxbusiness.com/v/2542020700001/?#sp=show -clips.

10. *The Real Deal*, 383.

11. Langley, 324–25.

12. Langley, 37–39.

13. Langley, 44.

14. Langley, 47–48; *The Real Deal*, 137–57, 508.

15. *The Real Deal*, 194.

16. Jonathan Fuerbringer, "A Wall Street Behemoth: A Big Investor; Using Fancy Footwork, Buffett Makes a Go of It," *New York Times*, September 25, 1997. ("Over several decades Sandy has demonstrated genius in creating huge value for his shareholders by skillfully blending and managing acquisitions in the financial services industry.") http://www.nytimes .com/1997/09/25/business/wall-street-behemoth-big-investor-using -fancy-footwork-buffett-makes-go-it.html; *Langley*, 266–67, 269–70; *The Real Deal*, 201, 288–89.

17. Langley, 25.

18. *The Real Deal*, 323.

19. Langley, 322, 351.

20. Ibid., 349–54.

21. Matt Phillips, "The Fed Was Not Impressed with Jamie Dimon's Fortress Balance Sheet," *Quartz,* April 9, 2014; Edward Teach, "A Fortress Balance Sheet," CFO.com, June 18, 2009; JPMorgan Chase, "Letter to Shareholders," Annual Report, 2009, 28.

22. *The Real Deal*, 455; Langley, 412.

23. *The Real Deal*, 458–59.

24. "Heard on the Street: Citigroup to Expand Its Trading," *Wall Street Journal*, November 19, 2003.

25. Kathleen C. Engel and Patricia A. McCoy, *The Subprime Virus: Reckless Credit, Regulatory Failures and Next Steps* (New York: Oxford University Press, 2011), 203; Jonathan Stempel, "Citigroup Names Stuckey Subprime Portfolio Chief," *Reuters,* November 7, 2007; Bradley Keoun, "Citigroup's Stuckey to Retire After Whittling Assets," Bloomberg, April 30, 2010.

26. Testimony of Charles Prince, Former Chairman and CEO of Citigroup, Inc., Before the Financial Crisis Inquiry Commission, April 8, 2010; Bradley Keoun, "Citi's Prince Says No One Saw CDO Losses Coming," Bloomberg, April 8, 2010.

27. FCIC Report, 252–53, 427; Ben S. Bernanke, *The Courage to Act: A Memoir of a Crisis and Its Aftermath* (New York: WW Norton and Company, 2015), 177 [Hereinafter Bernanke]; Shannon D. Harrington and Elizabeth Hester, "Citigroup Rescues SIVs with $58 billion Debt Bailout," *Bloomberg*, December 14, 2007 [Hereinafter "Citigroup Rescues SIVs"]; Arthur E.

Wilmarth Jr., "Citigroup: A Case Study in Managerial and Regulatory Failures," *Indiana Law Review*, 100–1 [Hereinafter "Citigroup: A Case Study"].

28. Bernanke, 249; FCIC Report, 174; "Citigroup: A Case Study," 105–6.

29. Michiyo Nakamoto, "Citigroup Chief Stays Bullish on Buy-Outs," *Financial Times*, July 9, 2007.

30. Testimony before the FCIC, Hearing on Subprime Lending and Securitization and Government-Sponsored Enterprises (GSEs), Day 2, Session 1: Citigroup Senior Management, April 8, 2010, transcript, 49–50.

31. *Bull by the Horns*, 121. One example given by Bair is designer credit cards ("[Citi] had major losses driven by their exposures to a virtual hit list of high-risk lending: subprime mortgages, 'Alt-A' mortgages, 'designer' credit cards, leveraged loans, and poorly underwritten commercial real estate.")

32. Memo for Interview with Janice Warne, February 2, 2010, 14. FCIC Report, 138–39, 196; Citigroup Q2 2007 Earnings Call, July 20, 2007, https://seekingalpha.com/article/41799-citigroup-q2–2007-earnings -call-transcript; U.S. Securities and Exchange Commission, "SEC Charges Citigroup Inc. in Connection with Misleading Disclosures Regarding Its Exposure to Sub-Prime Assets," *Securities and Exchange Commission v. Citigroup Inc.*, Civil Action no. 1:10-CV-01277 (ESH) (D.D.C. July 29, 2010), https://www.sec.gov/litigation/litreleases/2010/lr21605.htm.

33. "Citigroup Rescues SIVs"; Robin Sidel, David Reilly, and David Enrich, "Citigroup Alters Course, Bails Out Affiliated Funds," *Wall Street Journal*, December 14, 2007; FCIC Report, 252–53; "Citigroup: A Case Study," 101; Bernanke, 177.

34. *Bull by the Horns*, 121.

35. FDIC, Obtained from Vision, "[Redacted] Memorandum and Rating [Redacted]," May 26, 2009, 2. Document 12 obtained as part of *Vern McKinley v. FDIC*, no. 15 cv-1764 (KBJ). See opinion of District Judge Brown-Jackson of the DC District Court, https://scholar.google.com /scholar_case?case=17504452081421242979&q=mckinley+v+federal +deposit+insurance+corporation&hl=en&as_sdt=6,47.

36. *Bull by the Horns*, 124; Bernanke, 370.

37. FDIC, Obtained from Vision, "[Redacted] Memorandum and Rating [Redacted]," 1–2. Documents 1 (after January 31, 2009) and 12 (May 26, 2009), obtained as part of *Vern McKinley v. FDIC*, no. 15-cv-1764 (KBJ). After the original Freedom of Information Act request, the FDIC refused to provide any documents. After litigation and the opinion issued by Judge Brown-Jackson, the FDIC released redacted documents.

38. Citigroup's 2008 Annual Report on Form 10-K, 10, 69. ("The valuation as of December 31, 2008, assumes a cumulative decline in U.S. housing prices from peak to trough of 33%. This rate assumes declines of 16% and

13% in 2008 and 2009, respectively, the remainder of the 33% decline having already occurred before the end of 2007.") ("The Company, through
its business activities and as a capital markets participant, incurs exposures
that are directly or indirectly tied to the global commercial real estate
market.")

39. These included a $6.3 billion increase in credit reserves during 2007 in
Global Consumer ($5.0 billion in the US and $1.3 billion in International); a $10.8 billion increase in credit reserves during 2008 in Consumer
($8.2 billion in North America and $2.6 billion outside North America);
and a $9.6 billion Goodwill impairment charge in North America Con-
sumer Banking, Latin America Consumer Banking, and EMEA Consumer Banking. 2007 Citi 10-K, 7; 2008 Citi 10-K, 6, 11.

40. *Bull by the Horns*, 123. ("As our discussions about how best to stabilize Citi
began, I took the position that we should at least consider the feasibility
of putting Citibank, Citigroup's insured national bank subsidiary, through
our bankruptcy-like receivership process.")

20: THE MAN WHO KNEW TOO LITTLE

1. Timothy F. Geithner, *Stress Test: Reflections on Financial Crises*, (New York:
Crown Publishers, 2014), 75 [Hereinafter *Stress Test*].

2. Ibid., 32, 76–77.

3. Bernanke, 78.

4. *Stress Test*, 135.

5. Ibid., 90, 135.

6. Ibid., 135.

7. Ibid., 136.

8. Ibid., 5. This reference was to both Citi and Bank of America.

9. John C. Dugan, "Three Years Later: Reflections on the Financial Crisis
and the OCC," Remarks before the George Washington University Law
School Center for Law, Economics and Finance, Fourth Annual Regulatory Reform Symposium, 12.

10. FCIC Interview with Scott Waterhouse @1:24:20.

11. FCIC Interview with Scott Waterhouse @1:09:00.

12. Stress Test, 137.

13. Comptroller of the Currency, Letter to the Chief Executive Officer
Vikram Pandit, February 14, 2008, http://fcic-static.law.stanford.edu/cdn
_media/fcic-docs/2008–02–14_OCC_Letter_from_John_C_Lyons_to
_Vikram_Pandit_Serious_Problems_at_Citibank.pdf.

14. "Assessment of Citigroup's Asset Valuation," November 23, 2008, Evaluation jointly conducted by FDIC, FRBNY & OCC, 1. Document 14
obtained as part of *Vern McKinley v. FDIC*, no. 15-cv-1764 (KBJ).

15. Memo to the FDIC Board of Directors from James R. Wigand and Her-

bert J. Held, Subject Citibank, National Association, et al., November 23, 2008, 6.

16. Federal Deposit Insurance Corporation, "Other Supervisory Activities," https://www.fdic.gov/news/news/financial/2006/7cep_other.pdf. Letter from Frank D. Vance Jr., Manager: Disclosure Services and Freedom of Information Act Officer, Office of the Comptroller of the Currency, June 23, 2015. ("Your request for the MOU is denied. The authority for withholding this information is 5 U.S.C. 552(b)(8) and 12 C.F.R. 4.12(b)(8), contained in or related to examination, operating, or condition reports prepared by, on behalf of, or for the use of an agency responsible for the regulation or supervision of financial institutions.") Letter from Margaret McCloskey Shanks, Deputy Secretary of the Board, June 30, 2015. (Language similar to the June 23, 2015, letter cited above was repeated with the following additional fact: "Accordingly, approximately 11 pages of information will be withheld from you in full.") The MOU was the instrument of choice applied when Citi stumbled with their real estate portfolio in the early 1990s.

17. Keeping documents like this secret is referred to as the "bank examination privilege." As summarized in a recent federal district court case in New York: "[T]he bank examination privilege is a qualified privilege that protects communications between banks and their examiners in order to preserve absolute candor essential to the effective supervision of banks. It arises out of the practical need for openness and honesty between bank examiners and the banks they regulate, and is intended to protect the integrity of the regulatory process by privileging such communications . . . The privilege may be defeated 'where necessary to promote the paramount interest of the Government in having justice done between litigants . . . or to shed light on alleged government malfeasance, . . . or in other circumstances when the public's interest in effective government would be furthered by disclosure'" *Wultz v. Bank of China Ltd.*, 2013 WL 1453258 (S.D. N.Y. April 9, 2013).

18. Interview and follow-up with Dzivi in January and February 2018.

19. *Bull by the Horns*, 121.

20. The power to invoke a cease and desist order is contained in 12 U.S.C. 1818(b).

21. David Beim and Christopher McCurdy for the Federal Reserve Bank of New York, "Report on Systemic Risk and Bank Supervision," Discussion Draft, August 18, 2009, 8–9, https://fcic-static.law.stanford.edu/cdn_media/fcic-docs/2009–08–05%20FRBNY%20Report%200n%20Systemic%20Risk%20and%20Supervision%20Draft.pdf [hereinafter, New York Fed 2009 Study]; Thomas H. Stanton, *Why Some Firms Thrive While Others Fail: Governance and Management Lessons from the Financial Crisis* (Oxford, UK: Oxford University Press, 2012), 160–62.

22. FCIC Interview with Dianne Dobbeck and Steve Manzari led by Bart Dzivi, part 2, @38:45, https://fcic-static.law.stanford.edu/cdn_media/fcic -audio/2010-04-26%20FCIC%20staff%20audiotape%20of%20interview %20with%20Dianne%20Dobbeck%20and%20Steve%20Manzari,%20Fed eral%20Reserve%20Bank%20of%20New%20York%20(Part%202).mp3.

23. New York Fed 2009 Study, 19.

24. For example, Office of the Comptroller of the Currency, "Change in Bank Control," Comptroller's Licensing Manual, January 2007. ("Either the financial condition of any acquiring party or the future prospects of the bank is such as might jeopardize the stability of the bank or preju- dice the interest of its depositors.") The manual has been updated by the OCC as of September 2017.

25. Andrew Ross Sorkin, *Too Big to Fail: The Inside Story of How Wall Street and Washington Fought to Save the Financial System—and Themselves* (New York: Viking, 2009), 456, 480; *Stress Test*, 205.

26. Kirsten Grind, *The Lost Bank: The Story of Washington Mutual—The Biggest Bank Failure in American History* (New York: Simon and Schuster, 2013), 3, 271.

27. Ibid., 282–83, 289–90.

28. Memo to the FDIC Board of Directors from James R. Wigand and Her- bert J. Held, "Washington Mutual Bank," September 24, 2008; FDIC Failed Bank Information, "Information for Washington Mutual Bank," https://www.fdic.gov/bank/individual/failed/wamu.html.

29. Robin Sidel, David Enrich, and Dan Fitzpatrick, "WaMu Is Seized, Sold Off to J.P. Morgan, in Largest Failure in U.S. Banking History," *Wall Street Journal*, September 26, 2008.

30. *Bull by the Horns*, 90.

31. "Run, Run, Run," 15.

32. *Bull by the Horns*, 79.

33. *Too Big to Fail*, 496.

34. *Stress Test*, 219. Although the imagery may be clear, the origin of this term is not entirely clear. It may be a form of the phrase "ditch drunk," which is defined as "when you are so [totally] wasted that you aimlessly [wander] around outside and [wake up] the next morning in a ditch." Urban Dictio- nary, http://www.urbandictionary.com/define.php?term=Ditch+Drunk.

35. *Bull by the Horns*, 96–97.

36. FDIC Wachovia Transcript, September 29, 2008, 21.

21: "SAVE CITIGROUP AT ALL COSTS"

1. *Bull by the Horns*, 124–25.

2. Ibid., 5.

3. "Citigroup Posts a Big Loss as Banks' Woes Are Exposed," *Wall Street Journal*, October 17, 2008.

4. Special Inspector General for the Troubled Asset Relief Program, "Extraordinary Financial Assistance Provided to Citigroup, Inc." SIGTARP Report 11-002, January 13, 2011, 3 [Hereinafter SIGTARP Citigroup Report].

5. *Bull by the Horns*, 12–13, 87. Some of the chairmen in recent decades had banking agency experience. Bill Taylor, appointed by Bush 41 in the midst of the real estate problems of the early 1990s, started his career as a bank examiner in Chicago in the early 1960s. He also spent time as a commercial and mortgage banker. By the early 1990s he was the lead Washington-based supervisor at the Fed who gave John Reed a good talking to in order to put Citi back on track as Reed rescued its real estate portfolio and bolstered its capital; Jerry Knight, "William Taylor Likely FDIC Chief," *Washington Post*, May 4, 1990; Stephen Labaton, "William Taylor of FDIC Dead at 53," *New York Times*, August 21, 1992; Ricky Tigert had prior experience as associate general counsel at the board of governors of the Federal Reserve and as a partner in the banking practice at the law firm of Gibson, Dunn & Crutcher. FDIC; "List of Chairmen of the FDIC," https://www.fdic.gov/about/history/chairmen.html.

6. *Bull by the Horns*, 120.

7. SIGTARP Citigroup Report, 13.

8. SIGTARP Citigroup Report, 10.

9. SIGTARP Citigroup Report, 13.

10. Email from John H. Corston to Jason C. Cave, Sandra L. Thompson, Christopher J. Spoth, Diane Ellis, and Arthur J. Murton, "Fw: CONFIDENTIAL—Citigroup—Deterioration of Stock Price and CDS Spreads," 18:48:38, Thursday, November 20, 2008.

11. Email from John H. Corston to Jason C. Cave, Sandra L. Thompson, Christopher J. Spoth, Diane Ellis, and Arthur J. Murton, "Fw: CONFIDENTIAL—Citigroup—Deterioration of Stock Price and CDS Spreads," 19:09, Thursday, November 20, 2008; email from Mark D. Richardson to John H. Corston, Jason C. Cave, Sandra L. Thompson, Christopher J. Spoth, Diane Ellis, and Arthur J. Murton, 19:38:02, Thursday, November 20, 2008.

12. SIGTARP Citigroup Report, 10–11; "Run, Run, Run," 20–21.

13. Email from Christopher J. Spoth to Sheila Bair, no subject line, 23:32:46, Friday, November 21, 2008.

14. "Assessment of Citigroup's Asset Valuation," November 23, 2008, evaluation jointly conducted by FDIC, FRBNY & OCC, 1. Document 14 obtained as part of *Vern McKinley v. FDIC*, no. 15-cv-1764 (KBJ) [Hereinafter "Citigroup's Asset Valuation"]. See opinion of District Judge Brown-Jackson of the DC District Court, https://scholar.google.com/scholar_case?case=17504452081421242979&q=mckinley+v+federal+deposit+insurance+corporation&hl=en&as_sdt=6,47. The SIGTARP report, in fact, defines the term "solvency" in the glossary of one of its

attached appendices, but strangely enough never uses the term "solvency" elsewhere in the report and never launches into a discussion of whether or not Citigroup or Citibank were in fact insolvent. SIGTARP Citigroup report, 55.

15. Email from John V. Thomas to Michael Krimminger, Jason Cave, Sandra L. Thompson, Christopher J. Spoth, John M. Lane, James Wigand, Mitchell Glassman, Richard Osterman, Richard T. Aboussie, Marilyn Anderson, and Arthur J. Murton, "Proposed Conduit," 9:57, Saturday, November 22, 2008.

16. SIGTARP Citigroup Report, 14.

17. *Bull by the Horns*, 125.

18. "Joint Statement of Treasury, the Federal Reserve and the FDIC on Citigroup," November 23, 2008, https://www.treasury.gov/press-center/press-releases/Pages/hp1287.aspx.

19. "Citigroup's Asset Valuation," Document 14, 1; SIGTARP Citigroup Report, 19.

20. *Bull by the Horns*, 165–67.

21. Citigroup, Annual Report 2008, 169. Federal Home Loan Banks, "Member-Owned Cooperatives," http://www.fhlbanks.com/#what.

22. Spreadsheet from the Federal Reserve, pursuant to *Bloomberg LP v. Board of Governors of the Federal Reserve System.* District Court Southern District of New York: 649 F.Supp.2d 262 (2009). United States Court of Appeals 2nd Circuit: 601. F.3d 143 (2010).

23. FDIC, "Temporary Liquidity Guarantee Program," https://www.fdic.gov/regulations/resources/tlgp/.

24. Citigroup Market Cap History, *Macrotrends*, http://www.macrotrends.net/stocks/charts/C/market-cap/citigroup-inc-market-cap-history. Spreadsheet from the Federal Reserve, pursuant to the Bloomberg case.

25. The available government sources show some discrepancies regarding the outstanding balances. Although the FDIC document shows the TSLF outstanding balance as $40 billion as of January 31, 2009, the spreadsheet provided by the Fed as part of the Bloomberg lawsuit shows a balance of $34 billion.

26. *Bloomberg*: District Court Southern District of New York: 649 F.Supp.2d 262 (2009); United States Court of Appeals 2nd Circuit: 601 F.3d 143 (2010). *Fox News*: District Court Southern District of New York: 639 F. Supp.2d 384 (2009); United States Court of Appeals 2nd Circuit: 601 F.3d 158 (2010). For a video of arguments in these cases at the Appeals Court level, see C-SPAN, "Freedom of Information Cases," January 11, 2010, total run time is 1:50:06. https://www.c-span.org/video/?291182–1/freedom-information-cases.

27. Craig Torres, "Fed Releases Discount-Window Loan Records Under Court Order," *Bloomberg Businessweek*, March 31, 2011; Bob Ivry and Craig

Torres, "Fed's Court-Ordered Disclosure Shows Americans' 'Right to Know,'" *Bloomberg Businessweek*, March 22, 2011.

28. Alex J. Pollock, "TARP on a Businesslike Basis," *AEI*, November 19, 2009, http://www.aei.org/publication/tarp-on-a-businesslike-basis/.

29. A nonbank, AIG, drew $68 billion. ProPublica, Bailout Tracker, https://projects.propublica.org/bailout/.

30. "Citigroup and the Troubled Asset Relief Program," Hearing Before the Congressional Oversight Panel," One Hundred Eleventh Congress, Second Session, March 4, 2010, S. Hearing 111–472, https://www.gpo.gov/fdsys/pkg/CHRG-111shrg56805/html/CHRG-111shrg56805.htm.

31. FDIC, "Risk-Based Assessment System," https://www.fdic.gov/deposit/insurance/risk/.

32. FDIC, "Resolutions Handbook," https://www.fdic.gov/bank/historical/reshandbook/resolutions-handbook.pdf#nameddest=Ch4, December 23, 2014, 18–19; FDIC, "Continental Illinois and Too Big to Fail," Chapter 7, in *An Examination of the Banking Crises of the 1980s and Early 1990s: Volume I*, 254, https://www.fdic.gov/bank/historical/history/235_258.pdf.

33. *Bull by the Horns*, 123; Senator Warren in her book on the crisis echoed Bair's arguments about considering receivership. Elizabeth Warren, *A Fighting Chance* (New York: Metropolitan Books, 2014), 110 and related endnote on 300.

34. *Vern McKinley v. FDIC*, no. 15-cv-1764 (KBJ), https://scholar.google.com/scholar_case?case=17504452081421242979&q=%22vern+mckinley%22&hl=en&as_sdt=3,47.

35. *Bull by the Horns*, 98.

36. Citigold, https://online.citi.com/US/JRS/pands/detail.do?ID=Citigold Overview&JFP_TOKEN=DVVoXUZZ; Felix Salmon, "Citi's Achilles Heel: Foreign Depositors," *Seeking Alpha*, November 14, 2008, https://seekingalpha.com/article/106089-citis-achilles-heel-foreign-depositors; During 2016, CitiGold members must maintain at least $200,000 in total account balances; "Citi to Reserve CitiGold for the Rich Starting November," https://www.doctorofcredit.com/citi-reserve-citigold-rich-starting-november/. Notwithstanding the implicit coverage of these high wealth depositors, Citigold's promotional materials now sternly warn: "Foreign deposit accounts are: not FDIC insured, not guaranteed by the bank, not accessible through a Citibank branch in the US, subject to cross border and currency exchange risks, and may have a lesser preference in case of a liquidation event."

37. *Bull by the Horns*, 123–24.

38. Henry M. Paulson Jr., *On the Brink: Inside the Race to Step the Collapse of the Global Financial System* (New York: Business Plus, 2010), 411–12.

39. *Stress Test*, 252–53. It does not appear that Geithner is even familiar with a bridge institution, as the concept is not even referenced in his memoir.

40. SIGTARP Citigroup Report, 14.

41. SIGTARP Citigroup Report, 42.

42. *Bull by the Horns*, 119.

43. *Bull by the Horns*, 206.

44. Bernanke, 369–70.

45. Devin Leonard, "Dick Parsons, Captain Emergency," *Bloomberg*, March 24, 2011.

46. Mike Mayo, *Exile on Wall Street: One Analyst's Fight to Save the Big Banks from Themselves* (Hoboken, NJ: John Wiley and Sons, 2012).

47. Monica Langley and David Enrich, "USA Inc.: Citigroup Chafes Under U.S. Overseers," *Wall Street Journal*, February 25, 2009.

48. Ibid.

49. Interview and follow-up with Dzivi in January and February 2018.

50. United States Government Accountability Office, "Bank Regulation: Modified Prompt Corrective Action Framework Would Improve Effectiveness," GAO-11–612, 22. ("In addition, some officials and an industry group said that large banks with capital deficiencies are more likely to receive financial assistance or time to recapitalize than are smaller banks . . . For example, some large institutions did not fail but received other assistance authorized under systemic risk determinations related to (1) the banking system as a whole through the Temporary Liquidity Guarantee Facility; (2) Citigroup and its insured institution subsidiaries.")

51. *Bull by the Horns*, 124–25.

52. FDIC board meeting transcript, November 23, 2008, 20–21.

Index

Page numbers of Tables and Figures appear in italics.

Citi and City are used to refer to Citibank, Citigroup, National City Bank, and City Bank.

About the Authors

JAMES FREEMAN is assistant editor of the *Wall Street Journal's* editorial page. He previously served as investor advocate at the US Securities and Exchange Commission.

VERN MCKINLEY, a visiting scholar at George Washington University Law School, is a consultant and attorney who specializes in diagnosing financial instability in banking systems.